Collected Memoirs

Michael Gottlieb

Collected Memoirs

Michael Gottlieb

chax

2024

ISBN: 978-1-946104-49-6

Library of Congress Control Number: 2023947474

Chax Press
6181 East 4th Street
Tucson Arizona 85711-1613
USA

chaxpress@chax.org

Chax Press books are supported in part by individual donors and by sales of books. Please visit *https://chax.org/membership-support/* if you would like to contribute to our mission to make an impact on the literature and culture of our time.

We thank our current assistants, Ben Leitner and Erika Cruz, for their work on Chax book projects. Our Art Director, Cynthia Miller, contributes to all books Chax publishes.

for Isabel and Lucas

CONTENTS

Introduction

Steven Fraccaro

With this volume we have three distinct memoirs: "The Colorama," "The Empire City," and "The Life We Have Chosen." Each spans approximately two decades, from the 1950s through 2011. The first two have previously been published in somewhat different form. "The Life We Have Chosen" appears for the first time.

Michael Gottlieb was born in 1951. To separate individuals by generation ("Boomer" vs "Generation X" vs "millennial") is to ignore the differences in circumstance and characteristics that distinguish people born more or less at the same time from each other. A poet born in any decade will have a very different life and outlook from someone with an MBA, and will have more in common with a poet born in a different era. This is obvious, but is all too often forgotten. There is also the distinction between a memoir and an autobiography, though the exact nature of the difference is hard to pin down. Memoirs are perhaps more impressionistic, whereas an autobiography aims for a sort of temporal completeness, "this happened in 1963, then this happened in 1965, then this happened." Michael Gottlieb has written something different, and absolutely compelling.

I first met Michael in the late 1970s, along with various other members of the New York Language group. But it wasn't until the early 2000s that I got to know him better through Alan Davies, whom I had stayed in touch with over the years. A few years later, I was fascinated and amused when "Empire City" came out as part of *Memoir and Essay*. Michael's recollections of that time and milieu struck me as on the money. He very definitely *chose* to be a poet. His parents did not break out the champagne when he announced his career path. Becoming a poet is not usually thought of as something a responsible adult would do. Getting a job and raising a family is. But being a poet entails a certain responsibility to craft. Not the same type of responsibility as raising a child, but responsibility nevertheless. Gottlieb writes of his failures as well as of his successes, and he stares truth in the face. This requires courage. But I don't want to give the reader the wrong idea. Much of the writing here is very, very funny. Comical, yes, but it shows how he was shaped as a writer, and in certain places these memoirs refer directly to the poetry he wrote. Together with his *Selected Poems*

(2021) and *Collected Essays (2023)*, both also published by Chax Press, in a uniform edition, these memoirs provide a comprehensive view of one writer's life and work.

The title of "The Colorama" refers to the huge color photograph that used to hang at the eastern end of the main interior of Grand Central Terminal. It inevitably displayed a scene of idyllic suburban life, perhaps with the intent of showing to weary commuters, generally male at the time, what was waiting for them at home. It is this world, that of a middle-class Westchester suburb, that Gottlieb plunges us into, a childhood in Hartsdale, NY in the 1950s. It is worth noting that this middle-class existence was not easily won. Gottlieb's parents, themselves the offspring of immigrants, made the ascent from the Lower East Side to Harlem (yes Harlem), the Bronx, and finally Westchester. Which wasn't easy on his father, whom late in "The Colorama" is described:

> ...he was lame, and his back was curved. One leg was longer than another, all a product of a poverty-stricken, disease-ridden youth. There had been TB, and polio too. A spell, two, at least two, on what was then called Welfare Island, now Roosevelt Island, in the state hospitals. And yet he had survived, married a beauty, the love of his life, raised a family, thrived...

We get only a brief glimpse of this, but it explains much about his parents' character and behavior. That said, the love of his mother and father comes through, as puzzling as some of their behavior appears to the young Michael, whose point of view is relatively solitary. His brothers were ten and twelve years older than he was, forming a mythical presence, largely unseen. What we have is a series of snapshots, not necessarily in chronological order, an emotional record of childhood and adolescent struggles and triumphs, a way of apprehending the world, an attempt to survive the insults of one's schoolmates and the irrational demands of adults. He has an extreme eye for detail, including the toys, clothing, and cars, particularly the cars, of the Fifties and Sixties. Memorable scenes predominate, but several that stick in my mind are the adventures and fights with neighborhood kids, his discovery of reading through the Random House Landmark series at the Scarsdale public library, his first romantic encounters, and how he discovers a copy of *Evergreen Review*, with writing by Samuel Beckett, Terry Southern, and Allen Ginsberg in a box in his parents' basement, books left behind by his brothers. The story of how he thwarts his own promising teenage romance by accidentally calling a girl's house at 6:45 in the morning is priceless. Then, a few years later, the encounter with SDS, student rebellion, and an enraged taxi driver who attempts to mow down Michael and his friends on Broadway, across from the Columbia campus. The year is 1968.

With "Empire City," we're taken necessarily into the 1970s, and we encounter the three themes that form the core of these memoirs: the nature of language, New York as a living and dying entity, and the life of the poet. For Michael, discovering the Gotham Book Mart and reading Clark Coolidge are revelations. The formation of the New York Language poetry scene follows, a core group that included James Sherry, Alan Davies, Bruce Andrews, Charles Bernstein, Ray DiPalma, Nick Piombino, and later Diane Ward. From this group came *Roof* magazine, edited by James Sherry (which Michael helped edit for much of its run), and L=A=N=G=U=A=G=E, edited by Charles Bernstein and Bruce Andrews. They were also in contact with the San Francisco Language poets Ron Silliman, Lyn Hejinian, Bob Perelman, and Barrett Watten, among others. Then came Gottlieb's first published book, *Local Color/Eidetic Deniers,* and his own small press, Casement Books. Although the three memoirs are divided from each other chronologically, within each one, time dilates and events are not necessarily related in sequential order. This wouldn't be the case in a standard biography or autobiography. Perhaps someday someone will write an exhaustive history of Language poetry, including both West Coast and East Coast groupings, explain who was influenced by whom, as well as who fought with whom. "Empire City" does something else, it gives us a specific insider's view. And it gives us downtown New York in all its weird 1970s glory, not something that every account of the era gets right.

As for striking anecdotes, it would be hard to beat Hannah Weiner's very physical reaction to a woman Michael brought along to a poetry gathering, a glamorous nonpoet. Let's just say there was a certain amount of low-level violence involved. I laughed out loud when I first read it. Aside from the anecdotes and the self-analysis, there's brilliant writing in "Empire," including the analysis of John V. Lindsey's well-worn shoes as a form of New York social history and the description of how skyscrapers create their own weather patterns.

When we reach the final memoir, "The Life We Have Chosen," Michael and his wife Robin have left the city. It's worth noting that some of his most memorable poetry was written once he's left New York. I'm thinking of "The Great Pavement," "The Ulterior Parkways," "River Road," "Gorgeous Plunge," "The Dust," and "The Voices," all of which are well represented in the *Selected Poems*.

It is in "The Life We Have Chosen" that Gottlieb's major themes coalesce—New York over six decades, the tropes and intricacies of language, and what it means to be a poet. A major question is, how can poets earn a living, a point he discusses at length in his *Collected Essays*. In spite of all the gut-wrenching self-doubt and periods of unemployment, Michael manages to land on his feet. He has certainly had a startling range of jobs over the years. These have included cashier at a camera store, as an aide in reading program, dealer in African art, factotum at Warner Brothers, private investigator for a detective agency, founder of a start up, and finally, executive at a major software company. Bt the time he and Robin move to rural Connecticut in 1991 he has started a business, initially staffed by himself and then a few family members, and eventually an increasing number of employees. The idea he came up with was to provide a specific type of analysis, evaluating customer service. There was a growing demand for this throughout the 1990s, the service was hugely successful, then expanded too rapidly, and was subsequently faced with well-armed competition. The business then crashed and burned, as did so many such companies in the early 2000s. Yet all through this time, Michael was writing—poetry, memoirs, and a novel. When he returns to live in New York in 2005, it is to a radically altered city. No longer the decaying metropolis of the 1970s, wealth is everywhere. Not only does he espy an uncommon number of BMWs and Bentleys, but the investment bankers who own them have the effrontery to leave them parked on the street overnight. In the past, these ritualized objects of conspicuous consumption wouldn't have made it through many nights without being either stolen or vandalized. Michael finds this ironic, but also sobering. It isn't his city anymore, but he doesn't want to surrender it just yet. Beyond this, there are the issues inherent in raising children, growing older, facing life-threatening illness—first his daughter's, then his own—and ultimately surviving. He doesn't simply relate these events, he examines and weighs them, from multiple angles.

What are we doing then, when we delve into the past, our own or someone else's? Are we engaging in (auto)biography, archeology, history, a form of fiction, or nonfiction? Isn't examining the past a poetry of a sorts? Not merely nostalgia, but something else, something less easy to pin down. No doubt we delve into the past to make sense of our lives, perhaps even to justify them, but that's only part of the story. With these three memoirs, we read a life. Not at all a bad one, one well worth living, and well worth reading about.

THE COLORAMA

1950s - 1960s

1. At Grand Central

Grand Central Station. What, as children, we always called it.

Grand Central *Terminal.* The proper name. Some loss in assonance, as well as the defining, slamming, clanging, closing of it. Like the tall echoing gates rattling shut. Like the ghostly whirring of the giant arrival and destination boards high above as they remade themselves every few minutes. The spinning plaques blurring into cascades descending down the wall, eradicating all mention of the trains that had already arrived, that had departed, that were now gone, one and all. Terminal, *terminus.* The end, and of course, the beginning: the line, all of the lines, right here — they started here, and from here raced up out of the City past us, our little suburb, steaming, streaming, pelting across the country, the whole continent, we told ourselves, the world and all we knew of it.

First, I must tell you a little bit about my father and how he made his living — for that, I have come to understand, may be the key to it all. My father, you see, was in the camera business. He worked for the same company most of his life, his working life. It was a big company. It owned photo finishing labs. It was almost as big a processor as Kodak itself. The company also imported and distributed cameras from Japan and Germany. They were responsible for bringing in some of the first Japanese cameras. And it operated chains of camera stores.

And they had flagship stores. Not until I started reading Horatio Hornblower did that phrase meant anything to me. Both of its flagship stores were in New York. Willoughby's was one, the other was Peerless. The World's Biggest Camera Stores, it said right there on the shopping bags.

And that name: Peerless. It was so optimistic. All those hopeful, boosterish corporate monikers from back then: Ideal, Supreme, Summit, Paramount, Matchless, Peerless. And Acme too. How easy it would have been for the cut ups in the cartoon unit at Warner's to have picked Peerless instead of Acme. But back then it didn't seem in the least insipid or ingenuous.

Peerless was located on Lexington Avenue. Opposite, on the south side of 43rd Street, sat the Chrysler Building. Across the street, on the west side of Lexington was Grand Central.

When I was a little boy, in the mid 1950s, my father was the comptroller at Peerless and going to New York back then meant taking the train down to Grand Central. Through the suburbs, down to the treeless Bronx, sinking into the cut, and then across the river, skimming above Harlem. Through the dark tunnel, clacking over the switches to the gate, the train stopping, all the passengers solemnly rising. Then holding my mother's hand as we ventured from the dimness, along the close, ozone filled platforms out into the awesome, airy, echoing expanse of Grand Central.

When I was growing up, I had the impression that there was a connection, nay, an identity between where I lived and something larger: where we lived, the way we lived, all of that was the way it was because *everywhere* was that way.

We were entirely typical. We were like everyone else. Everywhere was like here.

The proof was all around.

I remember, one autumn, it occurred to me that the road on the way to Sunday school must have been photographed, just days before, blown up by Eastman Kodak and spread over half the eastern wall of Grand Central Station. That was Mamaroneck Avenue up there. I knew it was.

The Colorama, like a huge Kodachrome slide, bigger than a movie palace's screen, spread out above us, seemingly taking up the entire eastern wall of Grand Central's vast concourse. An entire city block-long, glowing up there, pulsing with the life I thought, I knew, I was certain — was ours. I would stand there beneath it, transfixed. It didn't matter if I had seen it before — they only changed it a few times a year — I couldn't tear my eyes away. My mother would have to pull me along, across the echoing space, then through one of the passageways beneath it, under the Graybar Building, out to the blaring, tawdry bustle of Lexington Avenue and across it into Peerless's safe, welcoming aisles.

Then there were the books. From time to time my father would bring home grand looking children's books, filled with four-color plates. There was the book about the kids in a suburban neighborhood. Now it seems suburban, now middle class, then it was just a lawn with a stone wall by a bend in the road, just like that one in Scarsdale. The house, the corner, the trees, everything. And there was the book about the farm. The farm had a vegetable stand. And I was sure it was the same vegetable stand that the school bus passed going up Hartsdale Avenue every afternoon.

The proof was everywhere all around.

He would also occasionally bring home expensive, framed, dye transfer prints: scenes of skaters on a pond, edged by a picturesque stone dam, a cozy colonial in the background, chimney smoking — just like the pond, remarkably like that pond, we would pass in our car, that pond in Edgemont, on the way to my aunt and uncle's place.

There was nothing particularly auspicious about it. It just seemed natural to me. In my five-year-old, six-year-old, seven-year old sense of the world. It suggested perfect order.

I am sure it was because Peerless was Eastman Kodak's largest retail account. It was the world's largest camera store. That's why my father kept coming home with the little gifts, the presents. It was the Colorama, though — those were images I always carried around with me. That Kodachrome warmth that made everything so cozy, of a piece. Girls in their sweaters. The station wagons waiting for the train. The teenagers raking the leaves. Years later, going through my father's things, I came across some old Kodak guides: "How to Take Good Flash Photos," "Using Filters." Though those illustrations were black and white the feeling, the sensations, that world — it was all the same, even without the color.

It was a world that is gone now, utterly gone. Perhaps it never really existed, and my childish identification was nothing more than wish fulfillment. But back then I knew, I was certain: when it came to that world up there in the Colorama, there was, somehow, an identity between it and me. We were connected. And it was because me, my family, all of us, we were typical, perfectly typical. And that, at least, was a comforting thought.

2.   *In the Carriage*

But, earlier than that…

Is it just another photograph that I remember? Am I the only one who thinks it truly happened? That this is really a memory, not a — a what? A wish, a willed creation?

I am in my carriage, dark blue like everyone else's, hooded, solid white tires on dark wire wheels. And a long curving chrome ornament, turning into a serif at either end, one on each side. A decoration of the sort you see these days only on hearses, on their window pillars.

Rocking over the sill, then past the edge of our walk, the curb, back and forth, now easy, now brisk on the great chrome springs. My mother is taking me out. White blanket, white satin hem, white woolen bonnet scratching beneath my chin.

We roll beyond the pebbly driveway, out onto sloping Healy Avenue, near where Townsend Avenue meets it in a wide corner.

There are no leaves on the trees. Gray sky. Black telephone wires. It's cold.

I am bundled up. More than bundled up, I am bundled — I am a bundle. I was born in June so now I must be been about six months old, or a year and a half, or perhaps two and a half — but by two and a half, surely, I was out of the carriage. Wasn't I?

And suddenly we are surrounded by kids — my brothers, they were ten and twelve now, and the Fenny kids from down the street and some girls. Faces, fingers, grimaces and leers. Dirty chins and smeared mouths. Mugging and cooing. They peer in at me, laughing, jostling. My mother's voice, from behind me, from above, speaking to them. There are words in the air. What kind of words?

Then, just as suddenly, one and all, all of them are gone. The creak of the carriage wheels.

The wide, sweeping corner, bare again. The careless ruled lines of the telephone wires. Years later, I asked my mother, "Don't you remember this?"

"You can't remember anything from back then," she scoffed, "It's impossible."

Surely, she was right. But I've always had this problem: I can't forget.

3.   *The Invention of Pizza*

It was a percolator. Old even then. Chipped black Bakelite handles. That matte brushed aluminum that was popular in the Thirties, when my parents married.

The jammed bin beneath our oven that rattled raucously when you pulled it open; full of pots and pans fashioned from the same stuff. I have a few in our cupboard still. WEAR-EVER, it reads on the bottom. *ALUMINUM* incised in letters as bold as the brand. Surely it must have been a selling point. The Twentieth Century Limited. Howard Hughes and Earhart in their flashing monoplanes. Moderne aluminum.

All shining dully. My mother always cleaned with steel wool, of course. A sponge wasn't good enough. Otherwise, things weren't clean. How would you know if something was clean unless you scrubbed it, scrubbed it with steel wool? I can never seem to get my pots and pans that clean, no matter how I try.

The coffee pot had a little glass hat set in the lid. You could see the coffee bubbling up. Little bright music, the tinkling of the lid seated just a bit loosely in the mouth of the pot. The black shining fountain, dancing in the glass, dropping down and bobbing up again. That's how you knew it was ready. Perking.

What did we have for dinner that night? I do remember we were all at the table. My brothers had not yet left for college. When we finished eating my mother cleared the table, as she did every night. She put up the coffee. Our house was not large, the kitchen was small. The range only a step away from the table. As she left her chair, I slid into it. When she turned back, she had the coffee pot in her hand. She turned quickly. Certainly she did not expect to find me in her seat.

I was in second grade. I was seven or eight. 1958 or 1959.

I guess it is not so very unusual that even the next day all memory of pain was gone. I remember everything else though, up to the moment when they put me under.

What everyone said, the weather, the ride through the night; that's all clear. No screaming though.

One of my brothers ran upstairs and returned with a blanket to wrap me in. One of my uncle's old blankets from the Navy.

My father yelling, "No. No. That will stick to him. Get a sheet. Bring a sheet downstairs. A sheet won't stick to him."

My mother was always deeply offended if one of her children referred to her as "she" or "her" in her presence. "I am not a 'she,'" she would say. "I am your mother."

And now they were back to talking about me as if I wasn't there. I was a 'him.'

How could a blanket stick to me anyway?

My older brother behind the wheel. My mother cautioning him, her voice rising, all the way to White Plains.

"Slow down," along Central Avenue to Hartsdale Avenue. Past Four Corners and then past the train station. "Slow down," over the Bronx River Parkway, along Fenimore Road, up the Post Road.

Suddenly bright brick walls and an entranceway. Swinging doors. Like nothing so much as a glaringly lit loading dock. Picked up and carried. But I'm far too grown up to be carried. Carried into the emergency room, past a room full of waiting people. They look terrible. Sick, dying. Patently expiring. Why are they sitting there, in chairs? They're sick. Really sick. Why isn't anyone taking care of them? I remember the deep embarrassment. I have no shoes, that is part of it. My cold, sweating, lisle-stockinged feet, the socks slipping down, my feet dangling in the air above me. And they were all looking at me. It didn't seem fair, going in ahead of all these people. Why shouldn't we have to wait like everyone else?

Then a long room with rows of metal beds. A crowd of grown-ups in white all around. A man speaks soothingly and I go to sleep.

A week or so after I got burned my mother took me to the doctor. As he removed the dressing, she told me to turn my eyes away. I looked instead. How could I not? Half my arm, and the side of my chest nearest, was all white, gleaming, pulpy. Uneven hillocks and rills; blistered and cratered. Streaks, fades, tinges of red.

Several years later, I was taken to a pizza parlor for the first time. Up in White Plains, on Main St. Gazing down at the presented slice on its slip of waxed paper, I was amazed.

I knew this stuff. The puddles of tomato sauce and the bubbling white mozzarella. The steam rising. It looked like me.

I walked about sporting a sling for a month or so. There was something to be said for that. Until some point in my late twenties, I could boast of some interesting scarring. It made for useful conversation when getting undressed with a girl for the first time. Not everyone gets to say their mother dropped a pot of coffee on them.

After a while, a few decades, it started to fade. Now, unless you know what you're looking for, you'd hardly notice a thing.

4.   *The Shapes*

The telephone sitting on its little table upstairs in my parent's bedroom. Black, heavy, blunt concave sides. That upright, stalwart Fifties model. You needed two hands to raise the receiver. Beneath the celluloid disc, the telephone number in the center of the dial. The *White Plains 8* pre-printed, the rest of the number roughly stamped in casual, random, uneven type.

Back then there was a great, overarching consanguinity among and between all the shapes in my world.

The telephone bore a visage. Did not all things have faces? The phone's receiver, resting in its cradle: the two ears framing the face made by the dial. It was not dissimilar to my parents' two-tone, blue and white Oldsmobile, its grill mouth, its headlight eyes. And that car's face, was it not repeated in the books that lived in my room: the little steam engine, the little train that could. That lighthouse under the George Washington, didn't they all have faces too? And the face appeared again on the yellow wallpaper in my room, with its bunches of balloons, in the expressions of the red and blue clown, perpetually gleeful, alternately dolefully surprised, repeated in the pattern, over and over.

By the same token when I grew a little older, there was a group of men: appearing over and over in Life Magazine, in the upside-down newspaper in my father's lap, fleetingly on the television. Those faces were all of a piece, they all seemed quite alike to me. There was Eisenhower and Churchill and Picasso and Khrushchev and Jack Benny and Jacob Javits too. And my father. Smallish men all, slightly older or just plain older, with round balding heads and ears that you noticed. And they seemed to smile a lot. Perhaps not Picasso. The era, when years and days were hazy, before I learned to tell time and it was hard to count or I didn't bother; that time seemed theirs.

Then, in 1960 or 1961 we got a new phone. Tan, trim, a color-coordinated cord. A receiver that was easy to heft with one hand.

5.   *The Miracle of Garth Road*

I put down my nickel and from the display beneath the cash register I select a pack. The first one at hand. The one on top. It didn't matter.

From the soft give, the ply of it, the supple accommodation as I bend it back and forth, clearly, this gum is still fresh.

If stale, the flat pallets of pink resound and crack. Jagged shards, a hazard to the dentine as you try to fold them into your mouth. Friable. Low, base tricked-up cardboard, the sugar going, distinctly somehow 'off.' But, this one gives nicely. The dusting of dry powder that coats the gum fairly leaping up to the taste buds. Only then do I bother with the five baseball cards lying there, face down, waiting, in my palm.

Old enough to go out by myself, but not old enough to go to camp. Nine or ten years old. 1960 or 1961.

I left my aunt and uncle's apartment, pushed the down button for the elevator and walked down Garth Road, past the rest of the half-Tudor, mock gothic apartment houses. Past the Plaza, where my mother used to drop me off on Saturdays for matinees while she had coffee with her sister. Past the A&P, that's gone now too. To the little stationery store sitting in the row of modest shops, halfway down the hill to the Scarsdale train station.

Hot. Past the end of the real season. Indian summer.

A few years earlier my father had taken me to an actual game. The thundering subway up to the Bronx. Dark green buses and black and green and white police cars. Soot everywhere. Emerging from the dark streets beneath the El, pulled through the echoing Stadium tunnels. Then the green revelation of the outfield. The incredible buoyant roaring. Jumping up from the seats. The pitcher, so near. The shouts for food. The close violence implied in every swing. Men in hats and suits. And Mantle hit a homer.

The beauteous, Indian Summer blazing-in-glory of the New York Yankees. A Yankees fan? Of course. So is everyone I know. Are we not but three towns north of the Bronx? It was not that many years ago that my parents moved up from there. And I was born there. Of course, it is more than that. It is natural to be a Yankee fan. The Yankees are to baseball as New York is to America, as America is to the rest of the world. This is the natural order of things.

I turn over the cards.

Right there, on the top: a Yankee team card. Each and every one of them, lined up, squinting at the camera, in front of the Stadium's cast iron-white picket ornament. All of them, our gods. Rising above them in the distance, the upper decks' girders, the painted I beams and rivets — like the IRT line, only taller, more noble.

I catch my breath. This is a card you wait years to get. If you got one, or had one passed down to you, you held on to it. It's for your children. I leave the store, stepping out into the hard sunlight of the fall afternoon. I want to go back and tell the grown-ups about my great fortune. This miracle. Not that they can be expected to comprehend the enormity of it, but there's no one else around.

First, I must thumb through the rest of the cards.

Nothing else in the pack can be worth anything, I know that, but it is foreign to my nature, to any boy's, to take a step further without seeing, knowing, having, and by eyeing owning, the rest of the cards in the deck. There's that greedy hunger, that necessity — I have to know. That eager, consumptive shuffle. Even the inevitable disappointment doesn't much dim it. You never know. Just not knowing makes it worth buying. All those second-rate Cleveland utility outfielders no one has ever heard of, the first time they appear in your hand, fresh, perfumed with the sweet musk of the gum, even they have an immense power, clean, new, the sun glinting on the black-out streaked beneath their eyes, standing with their bats cocked before empty Florida grandstands, or awkwardly crouching in a simulacrum of attentiveness. Knees bent, hands, gloved and bare, open, receptive, forever waiting for that screaming grounder up the middle.

I shuffle the team card to the back of the pile.

Bobby Richardson. The next card is Bobby Richardson. I gasp. I smite my forehead. Matrons passing by study me suspiciously. Bobby Richardson, the artful, the matchless, the small, sleek and errorless. The infielder nonpareil. That seeking, merciless glove. The precise, inhuman arm. The Yankee of Infielders. His neat, even, compact features, supremely confident, gaze back at me.

A Yankee team card and a Bobby Richardson in one deck. A wave of unalloyed, unearned bonhomie and shameless self-esteem washes over me: I shall be able to dine out, or the child's equivalent thereof, on this, this moment, for years, forever. I am a made man. I am compleat.

Bobby goes to the back. I have no expectations. I have been blessed enough for one day. I almost don't want to see what there next, looking up at me: his wracked and weary face, the beatific, accepting eyes, the discreet bulge of chaw in one corner of the jaw, cocking a jaundiced, knowing look beyond the camera. Casey Stengel. Casey, the Bunyon, the Runyon, the Durante of our, our — quick, I flip back to the team card — yes, somehow it is clear— these were snapped the same afternoon: the muss in the bristle of his crewcut, the way his jersey sags over his belt. He was ancient even then. He was always old. This was what managers were supposed to be. They wrote poems about him, he knew Ruth, played with Ruth, coached Ruth — something to do with Ruth. He was Casey, our Casey.

A quick fugitive thought: actually we, us boys, we ponder this often... how is it determined what cards to slip together into each deck? Is it random? How random can it be? What are the odds? And now I think: every once in a while, do they, whoever they are, some white coated types at Topps, do they purposely stack one deck, just like this? Put together one dreamy, immensely fantastical wonder of a deck, just to drive us mad, keep us buying, hungry, ever hoping, and somehow make sure it ends up in the right town? This deck would be wasted in St. Louis. Can they do that? Is it possible?

Then, unbelievably, the next card is Mantle.

Mickey Mantle, the sum of all our perfections. Our Apollo. The sun in his face. His sun.

Of course, he was a Yankee. What else could he be, a Senator? Those same modest American cheekbones and dimples. You saw them in every DC Comics hero. The tousled hair, the prototypical cowlick, the white teeth. That grin, abashed, a little crooked, modestly boastful, and who had more reason?

That flashing grace and hurtling, massive, controlled fury as the throw came hurtling back from the far reaches, past the cut-off man right down to the catcher's ankles, just in time. Or batting, like that time I saw him, as he swung and connected, and I stood, found myself standing with the thousands that flawless afternoon, as the ball rose and rose and flew off, slowing as it lifted, describing an arc that never seemed to fall, impossible that your eye could still see this tiny whiteness — if he had not drawn your eye along its path with his bat. As if he was saying to us all: look, here, this is where I am sending this one.

With Maris, that doomed, flawed, mortalled deity, the deck would have been perfect. Perhaps it was better without him. More fitting certainly. Poor Roger, that lost look in his small eyes, you could see it there even in that miracle summer when they battled. As if he somehow knew, saw it all unfolding before him. It would all be downhill from here.

The fifth card was some Brave or Cub or Tiger or Philly or some such lesser being deserving of little or no note. It was almost comforting, a gentle return to earth. I looked about me. The traffic on Garth Road seemed unchanged. The tailor down the street and the consignment store just past it, all the trim discreet shops, they all remained as they were, as they always had been, looking for all the world as if nothing had happened, altogether unchanged. Only I had changed.

And no one seemed to notice. My parents, my aunt and uncle, they just didn't seem to understand. And my friends, as I rapturously poured out the news, the words tumbling over themselves, at least the first few times I recounted the tale, they didn't quite seem to buy it, buy into it.

What were the odds of this anyway? I had older brothers and cousins, that was known. How much more likely was it that these had been handed down to me? Such things were not unheard of.

"But these are this year's cards," I expostulated. No one seemed to believe me. "Look. Smell. You can still smell the gum."

6. *White Horse*

Robert D. wasn't exactly a friend, though we played often. He lived in our neighborhood, at least for a while, at the far end, near the garden apartments. There was something always a little soiled about him. The cropped dirty blonde hair, the grimy jeans, something dun and unclean about his skin, the drawn cheeks and scraped chins.

When we were very small, he wasn't there, then he was around, and then, a few years later he was gone again. He had a mother. No father seemed ever in the picture.

In most ways Robert was all right. There was one supernal, redeeming quality about him, it hung about him like a glowing nimbus. Despite all else, this made him precious in our eyes. In his room there resided a fabulous, unearthly, terrifyingly mythy collection of old baseball cards. They were all from the early Fifties. None of us had ever seen anything like them. They must have belonged to an older brother, his father perhaps. While they looked vaguely like the cards we collected, the uniforms were the same and some of the players were familiar, there was something about them: the stock artwork framing the portraits, the way the stats were laid out on the reverse, the mincingly cute cartoons up in the corners, that was unnervingly unfamiliar.

It was as if you had been transported to another America, one where everyone drove turquoise Buicks and two-tone Pontiacs five or ten years older than you had ever seen before. You knew they were General Motors products but they somehow just a bit older than any models you had ever seen before. Like paleontologists on a dig, we only recognized them after extrapolating backwards from characteristics, fins and grilles, we knew and had always taken for granted.

Campanella, Williams, Robinson, Snider, Mays, DiMaggio, Lefty Gomez, Eddie Lopat and Mickey Mantle — as a gangling boy.

That was the good part of Robert.

Then there was the hurting that would flash from him. At the merest excuse. For no reason at all. A careless word or two. My downfall.

At the time, at the moment of incidence as it were, the last of our run-ins didn't seem particularly serious. I walked away from it quite calmly. Perhaps there was less blood. I remember the drops falling on the vinyl upholstery, in the back seat of the Plymouth, my friend Eric's parents' car. They took me around the corner back to my house. Up Marion Avenue, across Townsend, back to Healy and home. The emergency room was later.

No agony. No crying. No screams, no memory of any of that. Just another rock fight.

For some reason, there was a wait before we left. A wetted wash cloth was presented and I held it to my forehead. Were we waiting for an ambulance? When Eric's dad eased into our driveway there already was a crowd of neighbors in front of our house. Where did they all come from? How did they find out so quickly? What were we waiting for? There was muttering about the D's. They never fit in. Didn't belong. Such talk seemed patently unfair to me. They were talking about Robert after all. Too daunted to rise to the D.s' defense in the face of all those grown-ups, with an unquiet conscience, turning the cloth over, folding away the bloody parts, I stayed silent.

Three times, four. More. I always seemed to be getting into rock fights. They all broke out over there, down on Marion Avenue, and they mostly all involved Robert. Another time he hit me in the head with a metal rake. Kind of like a salute. A knighting. I crown thee... He didn't seem to put that much more force into the swing, albeit it was overhand. The momentum no doubtless helped. Maybe that was the last time. The thing is, I don't remember getting into a lot of arguments at that age. I'd tag along with some older kids. One thing seemed to lead to another. I know I liked to talk. Maybe they took it the wrong way. By this time, I had so many stitches in my head, my hairline felt like a swatch of corduroy.

My father was a joker too. Always making jokes. They were not always ones we had never heard before. One ready line was inevitably trotted out when, in the middle of some general family horseplay, my mother would start tickling him. When he tickled her, she would first make some vain attempt at scornful anger. Then try to push him away. When she would turn on him, he would deliver it, in between pealing yowls, in a mock-prudish tone that he never otherwise employed. From some ancient vaudeville routine?

"Don't touch me, you. Keep your hands off me unless you're a registered nurse."

In the same vein, his whiskey bottle, kept in the cabinet beneath the kitchen counter, always was dubbed by him with some patent medicine moniker.

While we were waiting my father opened the cabinet door and took out a bottle of White Horse. He started to speak. The line about "medicinal purposes" was on his lips. He stopped himself. Reaching up for a shot glass from the cupboard, he filled it with scotch.

"Go give that to your mother," he said.

A short set of stone steps ran down along the side of our house. They led to a bluestone walk which went from the garage, past a garden, to the back yard. My parents planted roses in that garden, along both sides of the walk. Bare, even in flower. The packed earth below. A place full of thin, spindly danger. A few years later they replaced most of the bushes with ivy and pachysandra. It made for much less work.

That summer afternoon my mother was sitting on a stone step with the roses around her, red, pink, bending, open. The other mothers standing near her, touching her shoulder, talking low, leaning over in their flowery sun dresses. I had never known my mother to sit down on the ground, not upon a beach or even a lawn. That's what garden chairs were for.

No ambulance ever came that day. Someone must have driven me to the hospital. Maybe Eric's father. My mother took the glass and drank it right down. She had never done that before, in front of me. It seemed she was trying to avoid my eye. And she was crying. Never had I seen my mother cry

And I said to myself: of course, I did all this.

7.   *The Gray Library*

Years later, as an adult, during visits to Ferncliff and those other
sepulchral marches, those endless downs, those vast, rolling demesnes
of the dead outside New York, in Westchester, actually not all that far
from where I grew up, making my way through the somber, echoing, dim
halls of their mausoleums, I would always find myself, to my surprise,
somehow quite at home. There was something comforting and familiar
about that vernacular, that vocabulary, the articles and prepositions of the
architecture thereabouts.

In a parallel way, was there not something awe inspiring about that
library? The library where I learned what books were all about. The
same cool gray cut stone planted in settings of treeless lawn. The bare,
unadorned walks.

Inside it was magisterial but not cold. Paneling, golden bookshelves, big
leather chairs. In the grown-up wings, to the right of the front door, there
were vast expanses of maple stacks, stone floors, a towering fireplace.
The card catalogs, row after row of them, drawer after drawer, each with
its neat little manila label, typed, centered inside its square iron holder,
each drawer with its little hooked, black iron handle. The banked rows
receding into the distance like an exercise in perspective. And quiet. My
damned shoes, even my sneakers, always squeaking, creaking. It was
quiet everywhere except where I walked.

My mother took me every week. Hartsdale was too small to have its own
library, or its own high school for that matter. When I was young the
town had some sort of arrangement with Scarsdale, the next town over,
allowing Hartsdale residents to make use of the larger, fancier suburb's
library. Every week my mother would gather up our library books from
their accustomed place: piled up at the foot of the stairs, atop the little
rounded extension of the bottom step that curled around to support the
pilaster of the banister.

The Children's Room at the Scarsdale Library, to the left as you entered:
a light filled procession of blond maple bookcases. In the center of the
room was a low row, two or three shelves high, and arranged in it were

all one hundred and fifty-odd lovely, sainted, enrapturing volumes of the Random House Landmark books.

These could not have been my first 'chapter books.' That's what my kids called them, a term I do not recall current in my time. But these certainly were the first books that I read in seriatim.

Here, I'm picking out the first one. Surely it wasn't the first in the row. No doubt I had to go back later to start from the beginning. Big and perfect bound. No illustrations. To all appearances a grownup book. The weighty array of them. The colophon — an obelisk, like the Washington Monument, as far as I was concerned it was in fact the Washington Monument, situated just behind the little trademark Random House house, like a Monopoly house, this one with a yard, a lawn, a picket fence. And the Washington Monument, as it were, stuck in its back yard.

One after another, they seemed so impressive, so intimidating, so uncompromisingly adult, an impression no doubt entirely intended. All those biographies: Edison, Lincoln, Lafayette, Grant; the story of the transcontinental railroad, the Pilgrims. All of it a kind of breathless swinging narrative. These are all wonderful stories, and you will like them, surely you will. And I did. And they were splendid tales indeed, all of them. Clara Barton. The Civil War. The Erie Canal. I devoured them. The painterly covers, mock primitivist. America, that vast and rich tapestry. And when I had finished with them by some lights, I had a pretty rounded education.

I digest the first few. I return with my mother and with each visit I take out several more. More each time, consuming them more and more eagerly, my reading skills, such as they were, increasing, I suppose, concomittantly. Until, towards the end, each book, each one the same, approximately hundred and twenty-five, hundred and fifty odd pages, each one which had each taken up a week's or at least a few day's-worth of reading, I found myself knocking off in an hour or less. And that, I found was an abiding pleasure. Finishing them. Being able to look at the row and tell myself, because no one else was particularly interested, that I had read all of them, all of them up to here. Now, up to here. Now, all of them. This row here, it belongs to me. These are my books. I've read all of these.

8. The Chairs

In my parents' living room there were two deep, soft, giving, easy chairs. Simple club chairs, drawn up to either side of the fireplace.

They were upholstered in a kind of rose-colored material I have never since come across: a kind of rough, nubby near-chenille, with a tight and closely cut pile, the pattern describing flowers of some sort. In summer they were slipcovered with a garden-y chintz. The low, wide arms were padded and gently yielding. There were flaps all around the base, from leg to leg, perfect for concealing toy cars and toy soldiers.

And next to each chair was a side table. Two identical side tables with antiqued fittings with some sort of jet inlay in each handle, each with an identical lamp sitting upon it. When I was small, five or six, the lamps were pineapples fashioned from a patinated brass. By the time I was older, in my teens, my parents had done some traveling, my father had been to Japan on business a few times with my mother, and now there were tall, delicate porcelain pots, with little, dark, wooden filigree bases. The chairs, however, aside from new slip covers every few years, remained the same.

Back when the pineapples reigned, and the candy my father brought home from the Barracini's in Grand Central resided in the side table's drawer by the right-hand chair, I would sit there, reading, reading for hours on end. Shifting position every once in a while, looking up occasionally as the afternoon faded in the picture window. Paging through Life, studying my picture books. Eventually, racing through the Landmark Books. Now and then scolded out of the chair to run out and go play. Go outside, get some fresh air. Then the teenage books, they didn't last long. Dark now outside, sitting sprawled. Sitting cross-legged, Indian-fashion we called it then, poring alertly, lolling, askew, propped sideways, sometimes in one chair, sometimes the other. Reading the World Telegram after my father returned from work, switching on the lamp when the living room grew too dim. Then, later, the Times, squinting down at the suddenly brightened, whitened page. Eventually reading the same novels my mother brought home for herself.

Reading there, always reading. An interlude, those dimwitted teenage boy books. Boys and their hot rods, *The Crash Club*. I brought them home from the library for a few months. And then, not much later, picking through the old Modern Library editions, from the Thirties and the Forties, lined up in the glass fronted bookcase near the front door. The thin hard covers, the faded spines and dun bindings. They seemed incredibly ancient then, though most of them couldn't have been much more than twenty years old.

After dinner peeping into the drawer where the candy was kept. Those fruit slices from Barracini's. Or a sampler box of chocolates.

Years later, dashing to a train on the Lower Level, back when the Lower Level still received trains, flying down to the gate, and there, just beneath the double stairway: Barracini's sad counter. How could this ever have seemed cosmopolitan? Those red boxes, the studied script. Then suddenly one day it too was gone, boarded up.

The chairs and their welcome. The benevolent cushions, the rough affection of the upholstery. I learned to read in those chairs, someone who learned to live in and through books. And there, in those chairs, conceiving the idea of becoming a writer.

I was so small that I could lie sideways in them. My head would rest on one arm and I could cross my knees comfortably over the other, reading on and on. Reading for so long my neck and legs would grow stiff. Laying my book down, reluctantly, upon the side table, upside down, forever unwilling to leave off, clambering down from the chair. Stretching my legs, twisting my neck a little. Then the climb back up onto the seat cushion. This time positioning myself opposite, my head where my feet had been, picking up my book again, finding my place, plunging back in. Returning to whatever world I had been briefly barred from. Escaping there again, reading on.

But the chairs, I remember them best. They live on, so much more clearly than nearly any of the books I read in them.

9.   *That Inscribed Sinking*

Kennedy had just been elected. So much dates from then, right then. Time, in a way, starts. Eisenhower versus Stevenson? Vague memories of campaign buttons. Our 1956 Olds — that's a clear memory. And the old Dodge before that? Certainly. Its dark navy paint job and the must odor rising from the seats. But that memory is from when, exactly?

After Kennedy is elected all memories now have time notations. The inaugural. The news conferences every Friday afternoon. Jackie's tour of the White House. And then, 1963 and that weekend — every hour in front of the TV becomes marked, entered: the scenes from the hospital, the jail, Air Force One returning to Andrews.

But before 1960, even a year before, time is so much hazier: Castro and Cuba. That was on TV, but precisely when? A fierce argument with my brother, fighting over the channel dial because Fidel is taking Havana at just the same time as Mickey Mouse Club — it had to have been at four o'clock in the afternoon or perhaps it was five o'clock, but when? Day and date?

After Kennedy we knew too much. And time, regular, even, wretched time, the continual diminution, the inscribed sinking, became part of us.

Grown-up time had commenced.

10.   *James Bond and Me*

My mother would bring them home from the library: *From Russia with Love,*
Dr. No, Goldfinger. They hadn't been turned into movies yet but the novels
were very popular. The President was said to curl up with one at the end of
the day.

And the two of them, James Bond and Jack Kennedy, were so alike:
debonair, slim, dangerous. The expensive accouterments, the naval
background, the unruly lock forever slipping across the forehead.

One day I picked up *Thunderball,* and started reading. Right there in the
foyer, there it was, at the bottom of the stairs. Upstairs to my room. I
shut the door. This was powerful stuff. There was sex here, women's
breasts, everything. The thing was, what was so astonishing to me
then was not so much what was in these novels, it was that my parents
condoned it all. The books came into the house and they read them too.
They knew what each contained. They saw me reading them. But they
never said a word.

Every week books from the library, four or five or six or more, sat quietly
there at the bottom of the stairs, where the banister curved around, waiting
for someone, anyone to come along, browse through, pick one up and
carry it off. If you wanted to read it you were welcome. In most things, my
parents seemed to have such obsolescent sensibilities. It was as if they were
living in another time, and were, in fact, trying to pull me back there with
them. Partly it had to do with the way all parents seem relics of another age,
hopelessly floundering in an era they were never meant to see. It was also
partly due to the fact that mine truly were old, much older than any of my
friends' parents. Despite all of this, in this one respect they hewed to a rather
remarkable policy and held it consistently, unwaveringly, not that I gave it
consideration at the time, nor for years accorded it, or them, the value that
it, and they, were due. They never once told me that some book or another
was too grown up for me, that I wasn't mature enough, that I had to wait.

Perhaps in this way too, they were a product of their time, a time when
reading, reading English, reading books of any sort, was seen as such an

unalloyed good, an imperative without qualification, that no child should be ever discouraged from reading, anything, ever.

These books would sit nonchalantly in the pile at the base of the newel post, with the rest of the books.

11.   Carl and the Mountain

Too steep to be buildable. Who owned this lot? We never found out. We called it the mountain.

Healy Avenue ran uphill from Central Avenue in Hartsdale, past a few houses including ours, then it described a curve into some woods and petered out into dirt road. When I was a child there were no houses at that end of Healy. That is why the town never paved it. In the middle of suburbia an unimproved, puddled, rutted track. No houses in sight, you could be anywhere. The Great North American woods. Forest primeval. And on your left as you made your way along the rock-studded track was the mountain.

The slopes of this little hill had to be close to 45 degrees. Looking up from the road it was just possible to make out the two paths, the packed-down dirt lines, perhaps they once were deer paths, sketched into the undergrowth, up either side of the hillock. One to the left and one to the right, each ending at one of the little rocky promontories, tiny Matterhorns, crowning our mountain. The sculpted sides of the tops. To us they were sheer faces, intimidating cols.

Just to get to the bottom reaches of the paths required no small measure of strength and mettle. Erosion or the road itself had eaten away the gradation of the last four or five feet of hill. It was a vertical bank there. You had to pull yourself up, scrabbling, the exposed roots as handholds. As if we were crew members on some B-17. Leaping up to grab a handle inside the belly of the fuselage, then like gymnasts, pulling up, as if through the little hatch, feet first, up and in.

For a long time, I was too young, too small, too weak to get up there. Standing, waiting at the bottom, watching the big kids gamboling about the heights. Then, the first time: dizzy with giddy trepidation, slow, wary. Sweaty hands, sneakers sliding on the smoothed path, taunts from the older boys up above, sounding somehow distant. The dirt road below already impossibly small. The middle slopes along the flanks were steep enough, but there were saplings along the way to grab onto. Just below the peaks though, the bare rock emerged and there was tricky climbing through tiny crevasses, vertical pulls in one or two places requiring main strength, straight up. Then the summit.

The heights were a good fifty feet above the road. You could see across the house tops. Our neighborhood, our world, reduced to a modest cluster. Down, off in the distance, Central Avenue, the traffic hum clear, but thinned. Beyond, past the next set of hills lay the country club with its green slopes and white patches. Snatches of the traps caught between the trees. Off to the furthest east, Scarsdale. To the north, White Plains. And if the wind was right, you might even hear the trains coming up from the city.

Between the two peaks ran a thin treeless ridge, traversed by another path. We dashed back and forth between them. How old were we? First grade, second grade at most. There was a little knot of us from the neighborhood, mostly boys. There was Carl and Eric and me and a few others, and there was Susan and another girl or two. Our mothers let us roam the neighborhood. None of them forbade us the mountain. We weren't to go down to Central Avenue, other than that we had the liberty of the streets.

Our Huffys and Schwinns would lie in a heap at the bottom, while up above in our aeries, like vengeful Sforzi and Medici in their towered hill towns, we wreaked all manner of havoc upon each other. What exactly did we deploy? We all had toy pistols aplenty and in each of our closets there were enough replica shoulder arms for a rifle squad. There seemed however to be a general reluctance to risk jamming barrels with dirt or scratching the stocks up there, on the rocks. More often we cocked our thumbs and emptied imaginary Thompsons at each other. Changing magazines every minute or so. Even at age five: clearly, automatic weapons were the way to go.

Our skirmishes blossomed into battles and our battles into wars. Disputes over who was hit, who was wounded, who was killed, themselves spawned endless, flickering conflicts. The dying fall was the grandiloquent aesthetic gesture of our play. I'm hit, I'm hit. Slow, not slow motion, that wasn't invented yet, but slow, slowly teasing it out. Playing it: the shock, the recoil, the grimace and the gasp, dropping to your knees, crumpling, and then the stillness. Embracing the rocky ground. That welcome rest. Dying was beauteous and magnificent, vastly more pleasing than killing.

Descending from the mountain was considerably more perilous than the ascent. The most sensible way to go down, though lacking somewhat in grace and, in more advanced circles, condemned as unredeemably infantile, was to sit down, slide down the path of choice to the bottom and, hoping for the best, leap the last few feet to the road. The more elegant exit consisted of a running dash down those same paths, heedless, headlong, reaching out lightly to the odd wayside sapling, not so much as a means of slowing one down as a serial of good luck gestures, stations of touchstones — yes, I am still on the straight and narrow — the feet dancing over the roots and the outcroppings, not fighting the speed or the pull of gravity, but accepting, eliding, trying to bend it all gently to the hoped-for end, racing full out down the slope, bounding from crag to crag, mostly in the air, flying, roaring and yelping, the odd rebound off into the desired direction, chancing to fate and that odd, inscrutable grace that somehow, usually, hopefully, attaches to the foolishness of children.

That was how Carl got hurt.

He didn't quite make it. It was an accident of course. No one pushed him. In this case it wasn't the result of one of our mock fights gone wrong, not one of those lazy, careless exchanges, the errant dirt bomb leading to the indiscreet epithet, the ones that would suddenly erupt of their own volition into something terrible, full of blood and tears. It was nothing like that, it was just an accident. Carl slipped.

His blood was running freely though. The scrape fairly covered the shin and knee, from the hem of his shorts to the top of his sock. Whether it was real pain and hurt, or the shocked realization of how far he had fallen, or perhaps an admission of a loss of face that had no other outlet, whatever it was, Carl was weeping openly in front of us. Now, we all cried a lot at that age. You weren't supposed to cry, of course, even if you were a girl. There was, however, an unspoken code: under the proper circumstances it wouldn't be held against you if you cried in front of your friends. Hurtling head-first from a bike onto the curb, for example. Or a tree branch whipped back in one's face, if it was thick enough. And then there would commence that particular sort of wailing that alerted us, you were hurt so much that you didn't care. You just didn't care. You didn't mind crying in front of your friends, that's how bad it hurt. Carl had taken a proper tumble. This certainly qualified.

He bent down, trying to staunch the bleeding with some leaves. We stood around him, no one saying much, faintly ill at ease. This was always a dislocating moment. Someone must have gone for his mother. After a few minutes Carl calmed down. The flow of blood was slowing. He was gaining some composure, starting to catch his breath, chatting again, a bit embarrassed at his momentary loss of self-control. Moving together, we made our way down the mountain. Helping hands, with a due amount of circumspection, eased Carl's way down towards the bank, the last few feet before the road.

Then Carl's mother arrived.

There was no chiding, no words of remonstrance. She didn't say anything. A slim, hurrying figure in a trim white blouse and a skirt and an apron. She held out her arms to him and he went sliding down the path to her. And as he slid, he started crying again. The wail rose up, you could hear it coming. It burst out of him. At just the simple sight of her. He was sobbing louder, more uncontrollably, ever so much more wildly than he had before. He had been doing so well until she showed up. All of his hard-won aplomb and carefully constructed face and instinctual uprightness as a six-year old went flying. Gone, completely gone. Carl landed at her feet, a soiled and scraped, wailing, red and white bundle of horror. We turned away. This we could not watch. His mother picked him up, examined his leg, felt his brow, perhaps she cooed once or twice, folded him in her bosom and took him home.

For the first time in my life, I knew the face of shame.

What a base charade. So plain, so transparent. This was nothing short of the meanest hypocrisy.

To engage in such weeping and carrying on. It was worse than eliciting; it was soliciting, it was suborning. Certainly, we all had consciousness of whining and acting, of acting up and acting out. It was part of our everyday lexicon. But this was different. Such outright, premeditated, consummate duplicity, and in front of all of your friends. That is what made it so insufferable, the way he had carried on in full sight of us, just as if we weren't there.

How could he do this?

I had no choice but to look at Carl differently from then on. It wasn't only the loss of respect. All of humanity seemed more capable, more dangerous from that day forward.

The truth of the matter never occurred to me, not for years and years. Not until I had a little girl and a little boy of my own.

Carl surely had every intention of maintaining a stiff upper lip all the way home. Now it seems obvious. Carl was not particularly different. He was no crybaby. This was not a matter of honor. It was his mother coming into view: the very sight of her, her eyes harrowed with worry, her arms raised to accept him. Just the outline of her against the background of woods, the source of all the balm he'd ever known. And then the bolus of hurt and fear and embarrassment, which he had largely succeeded in wrestling down, rose up and possessed him once more. He had no choice but to let it assume its power over him again, her presence urging it up anew. Only in this way could he rid himself of the pain. The process was beyond his control. His mother was there to take up the agony from him. First, he had to present it to her, so she could assume the burden.

Carl was just a little boy after all. As were we all.

12.   *My Days in Formula One*

There is a beautiful old blue rug lying now in my son's bedroom. It is deep and soft and still has its original, thick, horsehair pad. Ten feet by twelve feet. Something simple, pristine, something otherworldly about that perfect blue field.

It is dark, a saturated navy. A starless night, a stormless Pacific of navy.

A Bigelow, from back when that counted for something: *"A name on the door means a Bigelow on the floor."* The very first thing my parents bought when they set up housekeeping. It was in their living room in the Bronx for years, long before I was born. After the family moved to Hartsdale it was brought up to my brothers' bedroom. Then it became mine.

The old horsehair mat that is the carpet's mate is a few inches shorter, in each dimension, than the rug itself. And since the mat too is of abundant thickness, along each side where the mat falls short, the rug is bordered with a depression, a few inches wide, along which the rug lies directly upon the flooring.

It made a lane, a track, a straight, right-angled course for my Matchbook cars. I would lie on that rug for hours, the side of my face pressed against the pile, studying the look, the flanks and the foreshortened arrangement of the wheels and windscreens of my tiny équipe of F1 Ferraris. Frozen in a race of my creation, each caught up in a vicious four-wheel drift, one behind another, dicing ferociously, following the line around the apex of a stiff left-hander. Phil Hill dicing with Richie Ginther, with Von Trips closing in on them both.

Jim Clark was my hero. He was small, the smallest of the fraternity. There was an immediate identification there. He was quiet and shy, even after his second World Championship. That was me too. And he was the fastest. That, I always wished for. The Lotuses he piloted were never as powerful as his foes' machines, but they were the embodiment of the future. They were small, they were the first monocoque racers, the seats were tilted back, that in itself was deemed revolutionary. They made up in handling and aerodynamics what they gave away in horsepower. Sadly,

Matchbook didn't make Lotus 25s, or any other Lotus back then. My pretending had to go the extra mile.

Another favorite circuit was laid out right at the edge of the rug, around the frame of the doorway that led from the bedroom to the closet. There were more angles here, they were tighter. We were always halfway through the twenty-third lap of Grand Prix of Monaco. Around Gasworks turn, up the narrow Monte Carlo streets, past the Hotel de Paris and the Casino, through Tabac, down to the waterfront.

Wee Jimmie eternally just about to nose his Lotus past Graham Hill's BRM, stuck in that moment forever, or until I was called down to dinner.

13.   *The Cot*

I must have been ill. Or maybe it was yet another bloody nose. I used to get them all the time. I had been sent to the nurse's office.

There were two cots in the back room. They were canvas, covered with flat brown wool blankets and hard white sheets, no pillows at all. It was probably all surplus from WWII. I don't remember the nurse. I do remember being told to lie down and be quiet. The room was dark. She pulled down the tall yellow shades before she left.

I put my head down and waited. I didn't sleep. I lay there on the second floor of the Washington Avenue School, listening to the sounds of the building. Billowing screams and laughter of first and second graders. Teachers leading their charges from the gym back to their rooms, their massed scuffling feet resounding like reluctant regiments of poilus moving up to the front. Erasers being clapped and pencils turning in sharpeners. Outside, the muted traffic going up and down Hartsdale Avenue.

I didn't know what time it was. I'm not sure I knew how to tell time. I was told to stay there. I stayed. A little feverish perhaps but calm. I had never been sent to the nurse's office before and the novelty — the tall, white, glass fronted cabinets containing what? — was a long while wearing off. Eventually I grew a bit bored.

Suddenly the door opened. It was Mr. Allison, the principal.

He was a slight man, prematurely spry. A ready smile, a graying crew cut and a bow tie. He was surprised to see me. I don't remember exactly what he said but I had the distinct impression that I had been forgotten. Had he been making the rounds of the school before locking up for the night? We were certainly the last ones there. That was it: he had stumbled across me.

It was past four-thirty in the afternoon, hours after I was due home.

One source of Mr. Allison's popularity was his motor bike. Not a little Vespa or Lambretta but a noisy, smoking contrivance with full size wheels, halfway between a bicycle and a motorcycle. He would wave to us as he rode up in the morning, his briefcase strapped to the little rack behind him, that permanent half smile fixed on his face.

Mr. Allison ceremoniously locked the big front door of the school, gleaming brown shellac, studded with gothic rivets and bands, and we walked hand in hand down to the street. With a certain jovial deliberation, he sat me on the back of the bike, instructed me on the proper way to hold him about the waist, hopped aboard and kicked the bike alive. Neither of us had helmets, of course.

Suddenly we were flying down the hill to Four Corners. Tearing along at a breathtaking rate, nothing between us and the cars rushing uphill past us. Surprised commuters on their way home. The bike's tiny two stroke, to me a mighty roar. The pavement a blur just inches beneath us. I had never felt speed like this before, exhilarating, liberating, Bacchic velocity. Mr. Allison sounded his horn, tromped on the little accelerator, wove in and out of traffic. I held on tight, thrilled with terror and joy.

And then before I knew it, all too soon, we were home. I was deposited at my front door. My mother exchanged a few words with Mr. Allison and he was gone in a cloud of blue smoke. He never acknowledged that evening. My parents, perhaps my father was home already, never said a word about it. They never once chided me or berated me. They never asked me where I had been or what had befallen me. It was as if I had never been mislaid.

For years I assumed they just hadn't noticed I was missing. That was my explanation. That theory fit neatly in with other allied opinions I came to nurture about my childhood and upbringing. Why else that total lack of curiosity? As time went on it gained a sort of internal intellectual coherence and respectability. Like a conspiracy theory that's far too outré for anyone in authority to bother challenging.

When eventually I became a parent, one day in a store I turned around and the child I expected to be by my side was not there. My hand reaching down, purchasing the empty air.

It was just a few seconds. More than enough time for the nightmare, every parent's nightmare, to enfold me. Then I realized what my parents had gone through. Only then did I understand: it was a choice they made. They chose not to alarm me. They spared me their panic, forbore mentioning the frantic calls to school, to the other parents, the bus company. Keeping from me what they must have gone through for that hour or two.

Taking the fear, the dread, that matchless helplessness and keeping it close, bearing it away from me. Only now did I understand, they believed that to be their loving job.

14.   My Brothers' Things

There was mystery and grace attached to my brothers' possessions. Their room was a wonderful, half-explored land from which I was forever being banished.

Painted wood tennis racquets bound in wooden presses. Small, dark, deeply oiled baseball gloves. A little hi-fi; a portable. It only weighed thirty or forty pounds.

All of their things: charmed, refined, sort of hallowed, just because they belonged to them. And they were big, they were teenagers. It was the end of the Fifties, everything was beginning and what was ending had a beauty of its own. The everyday clothes, what they wore to school. V-neck sweaters. Gray sweat shirts. Thick Harris tweed jackets and chinos and Jack Purcells and moccasins.

And penny loafers.

Everyone still put pennies in their penny loafers. Dimes occasionally. Nickels were too thick. There were two kinds of penny loafers. Consequently, for years the world was divided into two sorts of people. Those who wore Sebago Mocs and those who wore Bass Weejuns. The Sebago Mocs featured those thick little bound-up scrolls of leather, like minute, cinched Tootsie Rolls, sitting along the seams, on either side of the cleft in which the penny was inserted.

Weejuns had no welt at all. A smooth plaque into which the parenthetically shaped incision for the coin was neatly slit. By comparison Sebago Mocs always seemed unconsciously slapdash, somehow crude, almost brutish. To look at them you knew they were the work of some fatigued shoemaker, annoyed that he was obliged to painstakingly cut a little frippery in the front of his shoe, to keep up with some fad he couldn't fathom. Just at the point of downing tools for the night, he notices the little bits of leather left over and, glancing up at the clock, decides to roll them up on either side in a welt instead of snipping them off.

Weejuns, on the other hand, were perfection. They were refinement, a quintessence of class. Those oxblood loafers, with worsted charcoal sweat socks, beneath a pair of gray flannels, or with a pair of white socks and well washed jeans, or with no socks at all and khakis. They verily embodied this era. The elegance, simplicity, the sculpted contours, a bare minimum of seam. Across the face, where the pennies might go, a passing nod to ornament, no more than that.

As if Raymond Loewy, cocking his eye at the bar crowd at the Racquet Club one afternoon in the Thirties, said to himself, "Yes, this is what they would wear on a Saturday. Something just like this," as he dashed off a few swerves on a cocktail napkin, then tossed it on the floor. "That is, if they had any sentience whatsoever," before wandering off down Park Avenue. And a few minutes later some nearly bankrupt Maine shoemaker fishes up the scribble from the lounge floor, stuffs it in his pocket and then hotfoots it back to his derelict factory in Waterville or Lewiston or somewhere like that. And the rest is history.

And then there were the Oxford shirts.

The highly textured broad cloth, trapping the light in its weft. In white, in blue, light blue, and in pink. The button-down collars. Buttons in the front and the back.

I remember when I saw for the first time a shirt with a collar that had a button at the back of the neck. I was transfixed. It was so wonderfully, beautifully, useless and perfect.

A bit later, there came along what we now call locker loops. Then universally referred to as *fag tags*. Yes, that's what everyone called them. We said that and thought nothing of it. In junior high school, eighth or ninth grade, a few of the girls collected them. They'd sneak up behind a boy and tear it off, half the time splitting the shirt open down the seams or across the yoke.

Then there was madras: shirts and shorts and sport jackets. The more you washed them, or your mother did, the more they bled, the better they got. A perfect material for the time: the casual formality of a plaid, yet, like a precursor to jeans and Levis and everything they came to communicate, its value increasing as it grew more faded. Entirely apropos for the end of the Fifties.

And garrison belts: thick, black. Squared, silver-finish buckles. Uncompromising. Vague overtones of juvenile delinquents. With dungarees. No other trousers had belt loops wide enough. The pant legs rolled up past the ankles, in wide flat turns, several inches each. This was the age of Lee and Wrangler. Sometimes the buckle sat off to the side, on the hip.

And there was one gorgeously blue soccer jersey, the possession of my middle brother, from Hartsdale Junior High School. Long sleeves, the gathers at the wrist elegiacally sagging, with a delicately frayed gold collar, some faded lettering across the left breast, and laces, not buttons or a zipper but white laces, like a pair of sneakers, through the placket, up to the collar, the ends flying in the wind.

And engineer boots and pea jackets and i.d. bracelets and cars without seatbelts and more things which are gone, and many more which are forgotten.

15.   *Right and Left*

In my friend Johnny's house there was a Grandma Moses reproduction over the living room sofa. Finely detailed, every little particle of the scene picked out. But perspective-less, flat.

That first day of school, it was raining. Just like a Grandma Moses painting.

All the boys and girls were in slickers, red, green, yellow, mostly yellow. My eyes still blurred with the tears I had been shedding from the moment my mother left me that morning.

At the end of that first day, as we were led out the front door I saw spread out before me a parade of buses. A row of them lined up, head to toe, in the parking apron. Some already leaving, going up the hill, up Hartsdale Avenue, some going down, towards town. But rendered without dimension: the children, the traffic, a few mothers with their umbrellas, all of it arrayed, flattened, pressed into a cutout. And every rain boot and lunch box, each glistening headlight picked out in unrelenting, vertiginous detail.

The halls of Washington Avenue School were endless, toweringly high. The classrooms were gigantic. Windows that loomed out of sight. Wide stone stairways rising in echoing wells. Huge doors with leaning, forbidding transoms above. It was built of dark brick, half timbered, with stucco. That mock-Tudor style, like so much of Westchester thereabouts: the stores and banks and firehouses and apartment houses, all laid out around the railroad stations at the center of each little suburb.

It was there, in the hallway outside my kindergarten classroom, with Mrs. Zirgler patiently correcting me, that I learned left from right.

I would turn the corner and stand looking down the hall. On one side was the water fountain. Yellow porcelain, gleaming chrome fixtures. It was still too high for me. The water fountain was my left. Opposite it was the door to our classroom. The tall, varnished, gleaming door, beyond it a glimpse of the sunny, colorful room, the little groups of tables and chairs, boxes full of blocks, construction paper shapes on the windows, that was my right.

A few years ago, I returned. Washington Avenue School had been turned into condominiums. My kindergarten class was now a show apartment. It wasn't that big. They weren't even listing it as a loft. It was just a studio. The playground was now the parking lot for the apartments, and our ball field had been sold off to another developer and transformed into a little curve of town houses.

16. *Upstate*

Before there was a Thruway or a Quickway or a Northway or a Tappan Zee Bridge. In the back seat of the Oldsmobile. It could even have been the Dodge. If we were riding in any of the cars that came along after the Oldsmobile, we would have been going to the Concord.

This was way before the Concord. Where were my parents taking me? It couldn't have been to the bungalow colony, a place where my aunt and uncle stayed. The bungalow colony was in the Catskills, on the other side of the Hudson. That would have meant the ferry to Nyack.

This time, we weren't going that way.

Onto the Bronx River Parkway, north, up, past Elmsford, past White Plains. Then the mighty Kensico Dam, its craggy, towering, blank visage, its own horizon. The formal lawns and circles laid out in front, like some kind of propitiatory gesture. All that water behind it, above us, unimaginable quantities of it, ready to burst out and drown us. The landscaping as an offering to keep the floodwaters at bay. Holding my breath until we were safely beyond. Past Valhalla and Pleasantville and on to Hawthorne and the vast milling, scarifying traffic circle.

Before Hawthorne we were on home ground. Our town or the next town or another town, just like ours. After Hawthorne everything was strange, different, foreign. The people, the roads, the signs, the sky.

That's where upstate began.

17.   *The Bumps*

My father would drive on Sundays. The only day of the week he got behind the wheel. Down the Bronx River Parkway. Sometimes to the Bronx, to see his parents. Other times, only a little way, say from the exit closest to our house, Fenimore Road, south for a few miles to Garth Road, and my aunt and uncle.

It was all of a piece. The gently turning parkway, easy curves beneath the tall trees, the rusticated stone overpasses. Those ever-present, planked guard rails. The swaths of park land on either side of the double roadway. The ponds and lawns, ducks and geese, paths and benches. The Tudor gas stations, with discreet little Mobil flying horses. All in keeping with the established tone. Along the accompanying parkways to the east and the west, the Hutchinson and the Saw Mill, there were similarly tricked out toll booths, with their small paned windows and overhanging woodwork and roughly applied plaster. Very bucolic, very English.

It all cohered. The half-timbered train stations that were planted every few miles along the right of way, right up the middle of Westchester: Bronxville, Crestwood, Tuckahoe, Scarsdale, Hartsdale, White Plains. The conductors' long plaintive litany that generations of commuters, now long retired to Broward County, still hear, echoing through their dreams.

As if Cornelius Vanderbilt himself, as he laid out the New York Central, plotting the stations along the Harlem and the Hudson and the New Haven lines as they ran north from Grand Central, the first Grand Central, through the Bronx and Mount Vernon and Yonkers and then further north; the Commodore decreeing, 'Yes, I like this, this will be the leitmotif for these suburbs.' That late Victorian, early Craftsman rustic look. In the facades of the stations, the grand, elaborate newsstands that once stood on the platforms, in the decoration of the waiting rooms too, before they were effaced, in the very frames of the signage suspended from the overhangs. It was everywhere.

You can still see it carried through in the built-up centers that were laid out near these stations. The apartments complexes originally meant for the superior sort of clerks and secretaries, who couldn't afford anything grander.

All of those buildings, with their dark, variegated, rusticated brick, have long since been converted to cooperatives and condominiums, their garages filled with moderately expensive Japanese sedans. No clerks or secretaries can likely afford to live there nowadays. But back then the only kids I knew who lived in those buildings, the ones near Hartsdale station, were kids who we could feel sorry for, because they didn't have fathers, or who we usually steered clear of, because they were rougher, and bigger, always up for a fight.

Along this particular stretch of the Bronx River Parkway, going south from Fenimore Road, that is, from the Hartsdale train station towards Scarsdale station, there was a stretch of roadway that ran right by the New York Central tracks. Here the parkway was essentially flat and straight. With two exceptions. One right after another. The bumps.

There must have been culverts beneath, old stream beds, something that the road builders were forced to arch over. They were little launching pads, twenty or thirty feet apart. And only on the southbound side. Perhaps a foot or so higher than the rest of the road. Ample warning signs, of course.

Most drivers, even if they hadn't been that way before, would have had the time and sense to slow accordingly. But we would speed up, our dad would, as we screamed and began the ritual anticipatory bouncing antics. Perhaps only I screamed. My brothers must have been too old already.

Giddy as we approached. Catching sight of the little angles of the guard rails where they went up and down, up and down in tandem, parallel with the bumps. "Faster, faster," I would urge. Taking a grip on the back of the front seat, for insurance. At the last minute my father would tromp on the accelerator.

That thump in the stomach as gravity suddenly fell away. For a moment airborne, the back seat sinking beneath me. Up in the air a good three or four or maybe six inches. But still in the seated position, knees bent, hands resting lightly along the gathered vinyl seam along the top of the front seat. Fingernails picking at the tight stitching, but the rest of me gone. Flying. Triumphant. Soaring. For at least a second.

Four or five years later, watching the news. The Mercury astronauts, in training. Floating for a moment or two in the back of an old DC-3, diving to earth from thirty thousand feet. Huge, silly grins on their faces as they push off the against the Vomit Comet's ceiling. Those beatifically raucous expressions. It all looked so familiar. That instant or two of weightlessness: defying, bettering, mastering the earth.

I had been there too.

And then the thump down. And, a moment later, the same thing all over again as we sailed over the second bump.

Though he was not a straitlaced or prudish man, this was the one wild thing, the only entirely unruly, uncivilized liberty I can ever remember my father taking. And it was for us.

18.   *Upholstered in Felt*

Gray dawn, waking before anyone else. The world upholstered in felt, cotton wool. A baffle of softness. Silence fashioned from a solitary, distancing comfort.

Then, the brave sorties into the numbing half-dark: to the bathroom and back, to the kitchen for a glass of water. Kneeling on the living room sofa, chin resting on the back, studying the empty street through the picture window. Waiting for the streetlamp to extinguish itself for the day.

To the spare room with the television.

Sitting cross legged on the carpet before the set. Turning the volume down so no one would wake and intrude. Pulling out the On button, gently, softly, waiting for the click, hoping it would be muffled.

Waiting the endless moments for the tube to warm, the anticipatory crinkle and sparkle as the electrons began their dance. Spinning the channel changer, setting it atwirl, flicking it, whirling it, a roulette, deliberately ignoring my mother's insistent complaint echoing in my head: turn the dial slower, you'll ruin it. It would be years before anyone heard of remote control. And we did, we ruined several dials on that poor Zenith.

On most channels the test pattern only. Those wonderful test patterns: complex, compound, as fabulously intricate as a dollar bill. The most abstrusely convoluted design any of us could conjure, but perfectly symmetrical. You could regard it sideways, or stand on your head, we often tried to, and the test pattern looked exactly the same. Or else a static-softened Stars and Stripes flying over a gray U.S. Capitol, waving vaguely in time with a jerky, indistinct *America the Beautiful*.

One or two channels would have something on. *The Modern Farmer.* Or better yet, *The Big Picture.*

Its title sequence alone: the booming narrator and that wonderful, monumental, 3-D lettering. The kind of lettering that only filmed versions of the Old Testament rated. You knew something big was coming. And it was, it was very big, it was *The Big Picture*.

The unarguable advantages of our battlefield nuclear artillery: Big John. Long John, Honest John? Then, there were the awkward scenarios that all seemed to be filmed in Germany. The occupation troops, for that is what they certainly still were, in their shining helmet liners and Sam Browne belts, bloused fatigue pants and spit polished boots, self-consciously shouldering their M-1s for the benefit of the Defense Department cameraman. They would pretend to assault a good solid Bavarian farmhouse, masquerading as fortified position. The voice over droning on. The milking barn dressed up as a pill box.

Just to have the TV on. That was the important thing. That is what consumed the time. Soon it would be time for breakfast, for school, for someone else to take responsibility. Just as, years later, ten or more years later, the weekends would stretch endlessly before me with nothing in them, nothing to do, nowhere to go. Nothing.

The terrible expanse of Saturday. Every week, it loomed up like some lumbering, doom-y Japanese monster. Overshadowing Wednesday and Thursday, quite blotting out Friday. Nothing to do. Nothing ever to do. No books worth bothering with, no magazines, nothing left but the television. And there all longing and desire and expectation came to be housed.

The way hope gets parsed out. Even as children we learn to live on air. Anticipation becomes a staple, to be chewed up and discarded and then hungered for again. All manner of deprivation becomes merely a run up to — to what? And the slightest excuse for relief becomes the base line that all waiting gets measured along.

Mutual of Omaha's Wild Kingdom. The World Series of Bowling. Painting with John Nagy. Anything as long as the television was on. The gray, unblinking bath. That same light that shone on me, at 5:00 am, at five years of age.

61

19.   *The Drills*

There were fire drills, they didn't count. The real drills meant ducking under your desk, or going down to the basement, standing in line, waiting. There we were all together: children, teachers, your friends. It wasn't so bad.

There were other sorts of drills, though. I remember being at home, more than once, alone with my mother. The sirens from the fire houses all sounding at once. The Hartsdale firehouse up near Four Corners, the Greenville firehouse a mile or two south of us, and others, further away, all screaming out. And then, no cars on the road.

The trees were bare. I could see clearly: nothing, no cars moving on Central Avenue. The road usually so busy even then, back in the Fifties. People pulled off to the verge. A few sedans, a pickup truck, a Railway Express van, a tow truck. Nothing moving. Suddenly alive to the lack of sound.

That background to all our days, constant, endless, that hum rising up from the road. Whir of tires, thrumming engines. It was such a part of our life we never noticed it. All gone. And all I could hear was the wind. The inauspicious blowing. That baleful breeze for five minutes, ten minutes, forever, until the sirens cried again.

And then, other times, on weekends, in the summer, there were long convoys of army trucks. The National Guard on maneuvers.

We would ride our bikes down the hill to the stop sign at the bottom of our street. They rolled past, going north. Truck after drab green truck, some pulling little two-wheeled trailers, some pulling cannon. Jeeps, stake trucks with canvas backs, staff cars, every now and then an ambulance. On and on, for half an hour, for an hour. It seemed endless.

That wasn't scary at all, it was entertainment.

But before the first jeep appeared, hours in advance of the rumbling, with no warning at all — there, I saw one. In the car with my mother, doing errands in town. Is that what I saw? No, now he's gone. But no, there's another one. Are my eyes playing tricks on me?

All the way up Central Avenue, from our house to Four Corners. As far as we would ever travel that day, every quarter or mile or so, a soldier. Helmet, rifle, pack, web belt, canteen, sheathed bayonet. Standing at parade rest, just standing there. Guarding the route, I suppose. They would be there in the morning, appearing out of nowhere. No one else seemed to notice them. Stationed along the road, in front of Shoe King Sam's parking lot, in front of Carvel, in front of the pumps at Dom's, where we filled up. Stolid, expressionless intruders in my world.

They would be there all day and then they would be gone. They frightened me.

20.   Miss Ethymiou

This was third grade, and we were boys, real boys now.

I can't even remember how to spell her name. She was beautiful, tall. Lissome, that's the word that sticks now. Light brown, honey colored hair.

I don't remember much about that year. Giggling a lot. What did we learn that year? Subtraction? Multiplication? It is all hazy. But Miss Ethymiou: her twin sets, her pearls, her divine outline.

And best of all, she had that car, a red and white Austin Healy. A vision in the parking lot. It barely came up to the fenders of the other teachers' Chevys and De Sotos. The body so taut, curving over the tires like a tight skirt, not an inch of wasted sheet metal. The little badges on the grill and the trunk lid. Amazing, gleaming wire wheels with their deadly-looking, chromed, knock-off hubs. They really were wing nuts, they actually had wings. The white body work insets that swooped back behind the front wells, the marque's trademark. The antithesis of the panting reptiles crouching in our driveways: those Impalas, Imperials, Galaxies, with their vast, awkward, overhanging chrome ziggurats and pediments and ogees and follies. This modest, minute British roadster, like a pursuit plane, an interceptor waiting for the scramble klaxon, a stinging rebuke to every other car on the road, a glove across the face, just sitting there in the parking lot. It was everything we wanted.

To see her gather herself into that car. Leaning down, easing herself into the little bucket seat, swiveling her hips, folding up her thighs, tucking in her legs.

We were little but we knew what we were seeing. This summed everything up, the whole wonderfully terrifying round of existence, what more could one hope for: a British sports car and a beautiful tall woman. Certainly, I was in love. So were we all.

Where are you now, Miss Ethymiou? I was eight. You were twenty-five, thirty at most. This was so long ago, ago. You are old, old now.

Waiting for the bus at the end of the day, watching you, with all the other boys. How could we not? How could you not notice us? You push down the recalcitrant black canvas top and button the tonneau cover over it, tie the bright scarf under your chin, fire her up and with a little over-the-shoulder wave to us, throw her into gear and roar away.

21.   *Go Away*

I could make the world go away.

I could sit on my bed and look across the room, my closet to the left, set into the wall opposite. In the middle, my brothers' desk, mine for a while now, with its barrel chair before it, reupholstered too many times to count. The ancient, brown, fluorescent angle-arm lamp leaning over the desk's battered blotter.

It is not that everything would disappear. I could simply make it go out of focus.

My bedroom was twelve feet long. Without shifting my gaze, I could move from staring at the unfinished homework on my desk and my two Matchbox Ferraris half hidden beneath the sweatshirt lying on the floor next to my closet, to seeing virtually nothing at all.

That's not really true. My vision would shift from focusing on an object to focusing on the intervening air, six feet away. I would still see the object, whatever it was, the flag hanging next to the classroom's blackboard, the dim eternal light suspended above the ark in the front of the synagogue, the sloping driveway across the street in an empty afternoon rain, but with a moment's work they were reassembled, stripped of their distracting detail, reduced to their chromatic, crepuscular essences and removed, essentially and definitively moved off into a special place, over there, out of the way, like some sort of reserve or keep, where they could be safely studied, or ignored, as I wished.

The world would get warmer then, at least somewhat smaller, not so loud and insistent.

And the wonderful thing was, I could do this anywhere. Bored, anxious, brushing my teeth, riding on the bus, waiting for dinner to be put on the table.

"Michael. Michael? Michael!"

The marvelous, un-focusing seemed to have an auditory component as well.

My mother certainly had cause. Ample premise. Manifold, aggregate, frequent and plenty. I offered up to her a bounty of cause: that simple, bottomless, worry-wonder of all mothers.

Then, one day, again, in my room again, once more gazing idly across the room, I had occasion to remark to myself that it had been quite a long time since I had engaged in that sort of behavior. I didn't call it 'un-focusing.' Since there was no reason to mention it to anyone, I never had any reason to name it. So, I looked across the room and made my eyes un-focus and reassured myself that, yes, that particular place, that yielding and welcome world was still there. I could still visit.

Then, it must have years later, in high school, something happened. What? Was I dazzled by the sun driving home one afternoon? A street lamp arcing? Something, some visual disjunction, whatever it was, was thrown my way, and it gave me pause. It occurred to me that I hadn't done that, tried that, been there in, how long? I couldn't remember the last time.

I didn't wait until I got home. At the first traffic light, I tried. I tried to make my eyes un-focus, but I could not.

Many times, in the years that have gone by I have tried. I cannot make it happen. There, I tried again. The room grows a little blurred. It is not the same. I remember what it was like. It was not like this.

Now the world will not go away.

22.   *Our Stephanie*

She had the most beautiful name of any of us.

I didn't know a single other Stephanie.

And her surname was truly magnificent. It was a remarkably English last name. Pre-Norman. It was all Angles and Picts. You saw thatched roofs and wild downs and serried ranks of shaggy men armed with staves and long bows.

Sometimes we played a game: Cooties. To start it off, a designee, typically chosen by popular acclamation, would be deemed in possession of the cooties. It was like tag. When you were cornered and that someone laid a hand on you, instead of being *it,* you got cooties. Now it was your turn to pass along the bug. Stephanie never played that game with us. What was the point? She had them all the time. Besides, no one wanted to touch her.

There was something long and coltish and as yet unfolded, unready, unripe about her. Yet, it was clear to me then, with a certainty I could never acknowledge, but which, somehow, I felt inside of me with as much force as I knew anything, that this girl, who clearly was as smart and witty as any of us, if not more, who we submitted to unremitting shaming and continual, endless shunning because of her looks, just because of her looks, and who bore it all with a dignity that was to some an even greater incitement, that she would turn out to be a beauty.

There always seemed to be something wrong with her face. She never stopped breathing through her mouth. And her nose was forever streaming. Her damp blonde curls always stuck to her forehead. Her eyes were too big and there was something lame or halt about her. Now I think she was simply shying away from us.

That wide open mouth probably turned into a beautiful pair of full lips. At least I like to think so. I am sorry now, of course. I have been for years. Maybe it is wishful thinking to claim that I knew then that there would be a happy ending.

Was there ever any question that she was deserving of our scorn? She was so different, so awkward, so blemished and snotty, so goggle eyed, just so blessedly ugly. The fact that there was nothing mean or mean spirited about her was entirely beside the point. She had been picked out, tagged, embossed with the imprimatur. She was the one. It stuck with her all the years I knew her.

There were other scapegoats and outcasts. Rejects. Some were different, one glance could tell you. Others had difference thrust upon them. And the teachers and the parents? What did they see, what did they do about it? Did they ever step in? Did they keep their distance or were their interventions so occasional, so tentative, so extraneous to our lives and what we knew, what we believed, that nothing they did or said made the slightest difference? Is that why I can't remember any grownup ever saying anything to us about her?

There was not a single doubt among us: Stephanie deserved her fate. And she understood it too. She could see plainly that she was not like us. If she did not deserve it, certainly she could make sense of it.

I haven't laid eyes on her since I was fourteen or so. She was as ungainly and blotchy and blundering then as she had been in fourth grade, but still there was something about her, something beyond the matter-of-fact Eleanor Roosevelt plainness, that shone out from those huge wet eyes of hers, that made it clear that she would live to see us all sorry.

I can only assume that Stephanie flowered into the beautiful young woman I believe I saw waiting inside that put-upon child. But that presumed efflorescence, perhaps it never came to pass. We might have succeeded. Perhaps she came to see the truth in our argument. In the end did we convince her?

23.   *She and Her Sisters*

By the time I was born my mother had already had her fortieth birthday. For my part, I must have been at least ten years old before it occurred to me that she was in fact a woman, and not just my mother, with a life of her own and a youth behind her. By then she was fifty, more than fifty, and by then already moving beyond middle age. I was a love child, that's what some said. There was a good ten, twelve years between me and my two brothers, and there was a similar distance between myself and just about everyone else of my generation in the extended clan I was born into. My mother came from a large family. There were four sisters and a brother; there were many, many cousins.

As for my brothers, they spent much of their childhoods in the Bronx, before we moved to Westchester. Now and then, we would all sit on the couch, gathered around the Noguchi coffee table in the living room, looking at family pictures. That huge, heavy Noguchi table, its impossibly thick green-sided glass slab, it took three of us to lift or shift it. Its base, dark-stained wood, biomorphically suggestive, like a Moore nude. It was always there throughout my childhood, a dangerous handhold as l learned to stand, to walk; a natural obstacle for my little race cars. As we sat there it would become clear as we looked at the pictures: I was the outlier, I'd arrived late, very late. Perhaps indeed by accident.

And then when I was a bit older, as we would sit in the dark while my father clicked through his Carousel slide shows, it was even clearer. My brothers knew everyone. They remembered the streets, the old neighborhood, the buildings and the parks, the splendiferous, leatherette and chrome Bronx delicatessens and the dignified, tiled kosher bakeries. They remembered the blintz factory down the street, the subway stations and the garages, the apartment houses and the underpasses. I could call on vague memories, drawn from early, very early-on trips back to the old neighborhood to visit grandparents, but I'd been so little, so young, back then. Fugitive memories, fleeting.

And years later, decades later, when we gathered in my parents' condominium in Florida to divide up what was left, to decide what to consign to the dumpster and what to box up and take back to our own lives up in New England, where all three of us now lived, we went through those pictures again.

There we were again, once more sitting around the Noguchi coffee table. There were so many of these pictures, of course there were, as if we needed any reminder, my father was in the camera business. As usual, as we used to do in the old days, we thumbed through the prints. There they were, all of our third cousins and second cousins by marriage I'd never quite known. Their names still bore a particular assonance, a certain weight carried from hearing my parents and my aunts and uncles refer to them so often. These distant relations who'd struck off for Los Angeles or North Carolina or Hawaii or Miami or had been discovered twenty or thirty years after the war ended, in Israel or Argentina, not lost in the camps after all.

Then there were some other pictures.

I'd never seen these before. Little prints. And not a format I was familiar with, I who had put my time in as a sales clerk in photofinishing departments in big camera stores. How old were they? Here was a pretty girl. A lovely girl. Dark, longhaired, sixteen, astonishingly good looking, in a simple white blouse, already grown into her womanly figure, looking away from the camera, shyly looking down; shy but somehow already clearly aware of herself, the power of her affect, the impact she could have on others, whether she liked it or not, on boys, on men.

Who is this, I asked?

Are you kidding, they said. That's Mom. She's sixteen or seventeen there. And, yeah, that's what she looked like. I looked closer. That was my mother? She was beautiful. All of my aunts were attractive women, but they were my aunts. They were aunts. Here was my mother, as a girl. It was a lot to take in, especially since she had just died the day before.

Here she was, a teenager, walking down Jerome Avenue, strolling along the Grand Concourse with her girlfriends, she must have had to beat the boys off with a stick. And of all the men who no doubt been circling about, she'd ended up with my father. My little father. That too was something to conjure with. The longer I studied the picture, though, the more I was drawn back to the cast of her eyes, the way they seemed to be focused on something away, away and below. What was she looking at, or looking away from? And the particular set of her mouth. Not a smile, or not quite a smile. She wasn't happy. And then I remembered the other stories, about how something had happened to her, when she was a young woman. She'd had to go away. Wasn't it something like TB, or was it something else?

I now know that my mother had some sort of breakdown back then, and she'd ended up going away for some good amount of time. And when she came back, she picked up her life and went on. She got a job, she worked in an office at Altman's, the department store. She worked there for a good number of years. She got married and raised three sons. She and my father survived the Depression. These two children of immigrants who'd grown up in Harlem, who were born into poverty, real poverty, built middle-class lives for themselves and their three sons in the suburbs.

And perhaps what was so remarkable was that she managed to do that despite the fact that *that* look never left her face. That somehow, somewhat, discanted expression painted across the face of that lovely sixteen-year-old girl. Always, in some way, looking away. Howsoever she contrived to convey it, never, in a way, entirely with us. It seems to me now that she was, forever, never quite able to join us, in our pleasures or foibles or vanities, as boys, as teenagers, as men.

24.   *The Parable of the Olives*

I have long been of the opinion that it all comes down to a single turning point, one moment at the crossroads. That is what sets a person off on the path that becomes his life.

Tommy was a big kid. Not the biggest in the class but big enough to have something of the bully about him. Though, in ways that only the conscience of a young boy can compass, Tommy was capable of generous acts of compassion and comradeship.

A wide, crooked smile. Always with a half-healed cut on his forehead, an unruly lock of hair hanging down. There was a wild streak, a strain of vagrant syndicalism, a cock-eyed willingness to go just a bit further than the rest of us, and, of course, a great deal further than a timid soul like me, combined with an astounding creativity in channeling that willingness down avenues hitherto undreamed of by grown-ups or children.

There was nothing remarkable about the lunchroom at Hillcrest School, nothing out of the ordinary about the lunches served there. Except the olives.

There was the hot lunch and there was the cold lunch, or your mother made your lunch. The hot lunch invariably came with two small black olives on the side. I don't know why. Maybe the purchasing agent for the school district had a Greek brother-in-law. An arbitrary value had been attached to these olives, a gourmandizing halo, for some reason we found them particularly savory. They didn't taste all that great. Perhaps it was because, compared to the rest of the fare, only they had any taste whatsoever.

The fourth grade all had lunch together. Over the year we had developed a lively trade, a kind of curb exchange, in such items as Cheez Its, Fritos, Ring Dings, Devil Dogs, Eskimo Pies, Creamsicles, Fudgsicles, the odd Flav-straw or Atomic Fireball. Tommy had hitherto displayed only a fair grasp at the intricacies of this market. That day was different.

The hot meal was some substance, some material, long strips lying of it there in an ominously shining puddle, gray mist rising, alleged to be roast beef. Accompanied as usual by a cratered thwack of pulverized, not mashed, potatoes. The pool of clotting gravy disappearing without a trace into its middle. Some wilted green beans. Something utterly wrenching for dessert, like tapioca. Milk, of course. And on the side of each and every plate, sitting primly next to the conjectural roast beef, lay the two regulation black olives.

What possessed Tommy that day? All of us at his table sensed immediately that he was engaged in a special mission. Most of the hard-bitten haggling was passed by the board. Perhaps it was the novelty of the quest. Even the girls gathered round to watch him bargain and wheedle. By the end the whole lunchroom was cheering him on.

Tommy was trading everything on his tray for black olives. Not only the entrée, the dessert, the vegetables, but even the milk, under normal circumstances a fungible commodity in which there had never been a secondary market. Towards the end the silverware went and, to climax it all, the napkin too.

This was triumph. This was an Olympian achievement. Tommy had traded his entire lunch for forty-nine black olives. A sum that seemed stunningly incalculable to us. They lay there on the plate, blackening it completely, a few spilled onto the tray. We stood in a circle, applauding. A crooked, modest, glowing smile creasing his guileless features.

And then, Mrs. Bennett, swooping down from nowhere. She had lunchroom duty that day. No one liked Mrs. Bennett. There was something corpulent about her. Her swollen features like some mid Fifties Buick with those thrusting, aggressive, bullet-like bumpers. And that large mole on her chin. Mrs. Bennett was the least popular teacher in school. After this, not even her own students would stick up for her.

She took Tommy by one hand and his lunch tray by the other. She marched him to the back of the cafeteria. There, before the assembled grade, in a ceremony that gave away nothing to the breaking of Dreyfus in that hollow square, she forced the weeping, protesting Tommy to dump the entire contents of his tray, all forty-nine miraculous, gleaming black olives, in the garbage. Then, deaf to our jeers, gripping him by the shoulder, slowly, with a horrible stateliness, she guided him back through the lunch line and picked out for him a regular lunch with milk, napkin, straw, one entree, one vegetable and two black olives.

Tommy was never the same.

After ninth grade we went off to different high schools and I never saw him again. I wonder how he turned out. Every time I pick up a Wall Street Journal, I half expect to see that odd, askew smile of his on the front page, picked out in the paper's trademark illustration style, all those Benday dots, instantly recognizable after all these years. I just can't decide whether the article will be covering some takeover Tommy has engineered or the stretch in Allentown he's just been sentenced to.

25.   *The Sphinx of Lieberman*

Compared to Hillcrest School or Washington Avenue School, the junior high was vast and noble. A nominally Norman-style brick and stone pile from the Twenties, back when schools were meant to impress. Everett S. Webb Junior High School sat in front of a generous spread of playing fields, on a little rise above Central Avenue. There was a huge marble and stained-glass entranceway and long high halls with the odd Winslow Homer reproduction stuck way up above the lockers, nearly out of sight.

It was as if the things of childhood were to be put away. Now we had home rooms and we moved from class to class. We had schedules. And in sixth grade we had Mr. Lieberman. Mr. Lieberman, with his unruly, receding hair line and his dun suits and his Tail Gunner Joe five o'clock shadow. That heavy-set, earnest air, a kind of Thirties, City College look about him. The chess champion turned union organizer. He was rumpled and spirited, spilling over with exhortations and cautions.

We were talking about the Sphinx.

I know that must have been the topic of the day because Mr. Lieberman had asked me to spell *Egypt*. I was the know-it-all. The great speller. I stood up, squeezed shut my eyes, took a deep breath and proceeded to spell it wrong. I immediately then became subject to some considerable disapprobation at the hands of my classmates, far more spirited than others might have endured, largely because of my inflated reputation as a speller. This was a reputation that Mr. Lieberman himself was responsible for, he and his not entirely well thought out broadcast announcement of some flukish, beginning-of-the-year standardized test scores.

Maybe that was what set me off, what put me in the mood. As if that sort of shifting, flitting, evanescent, fugitive, capricious, boy-born mood could be said to have some root cause or, equally, to be the cause, in and of itself, of what was soon to ensue.

I made some joke about the Sphinx. A massively erudite pun linking, by means of a not particularly elegant figure, the word Sphinx and the

76

word 'stinks.' A good section of the class heard me and emitted the appropriate titters. Mr. Lieberman acknowledged the interruption with good grace.

A few minutes later the second bon mot tripped lightly past my lips. This one was even more learned, drawing on the deep pattern linguistic relationship between Mummies and Mommies. It suggested itself to me, and at the same moment, the very instant it appeared on my consciousness, there I was, sharing it with the entire class. It just popped up and popped out. I had no control over it. I was just the vessel. This talent for humor, I was humbly convinced, was a gift. It was far bigger than me. This little beaut garnered even more laughs from my classmates. It received, however, a decidedly different reception from Mr. Lieberman.

He thundered. He ranted. He shook his massive forefinger at me. There was always something Old Testament about Mr. Lieberman. I immediately realized I had gone too far. Then came the dreadful command, "you stay right there in your seat after the bell. I want to talk to you."

I'm not sure if this fate had befallen me before. Perhaps not. If it hadn't happened to me personally, I'm sure I had seen others similarly condemned. The line on Mr. Lieberman was that his bark was worse than his bite. I knew if I played my cards right, I might still be able to make the bus and avoid having to walk home. The bell rang. Everyone else scampered out. Mr. Lieberman slowly gathered his books and papers. Finally, he looked over to me and with a not intolerant expression he said, "And don't you think you have better things to do than sit here like this, after school?"

I looked down at my folded hands. I looked up at the flag hanging next to the clock. I looked down at my blue three ring binder, the little sweat stained crescent along the edge where my palm gripped it, the three dimples in the cover where the rings were pushing through. I looked back at Mr. Lieberman. He was waiting for an answer. I didn't know what to say. What did he exactly mean by that? Was this a trick question? Did he mean, wouldn't I rather be outside, running free, sauntering around town, heighing myself to the candy store at Four Corners and putting my five cents down for a Three Musketeers? Of course, I would. Or, was he asking me if I didn't think it was more important for me to be sitting here than enjoying myself outside? Wasn't more profitable for me to be meditating penitently here upon my misdeeds and lapses of decorum, my lack of respect for my elders, the general paucity of self-control that had landed me in this fix?

What to say? He was still waiting for a reply. What a quandary.

I decided to pay it safe, "I guess it's better to be here."

No sooner were these words out of my mouth than Mr. Lieberman erupted in a rage the likes of which I had never seen before in a grown man. He threw his books on his desk. He started screaming. He hurled malefactions at me. He balefully predicted only darkness and disaster for the rest of my days. Who did I think I was? What did I think I was getting away with? He had known my brothers, both of them. And my parents too, they were good people. How had I managed to turn out like this?

He went on and on. I began to weep. But even as the tears were dropping, syncopatedly, left, right, left, soaking into the azure fabric of my notebook, a separate part of me sat back and coolly observed that all this was quite elementary. I had simply selected the wrong answer. I had offered up the perfect, the most consummately inapt response. I had meant well. I had just put my money on the wrong color. Now I had to pay.

He stormed out and left me to sit in the silent, darkening class room. Sit and wait. Nothing remotely like *this* had ever happened to me before. I had never driven anyone unrelated to me by blood to complete distraction. I was scared. I never cried for so long in my life, at least not since I was an infant. I sat there in that classroom, shuddering and sobbing, alone for close to two hours.

Eventually Mr. Lieberman returned. He sat himself at his desk and started marking papers. Gradually I stopped crying. He ignored me.

Finally, he stood and motioned me to the front of the room. We put on our coats. He drove me home.

I recall Mr. Lieberman offering some cautionary words during the ride down Central Avenue. Perhaps he tried to make me understand that this had been the last of a string of bad choices on my part. That this, for him, had been the last straw, that all the sass and back chat and raillery had inevitably led to this. If he did try to make that point, it was lost on me.

What looms there, undiminished by the decades, is that ascending trill of terror as I realized that I had just picked wrong. Very wrong. And now there was hell to pay. All over a few words.

26.   The Strikes

I had Mr. S. for English the year newspaper strikes started. We were reading the Herald Tribune in class every day. He was teaching us to read the newspaper.

My father used to bring home two papers from work. The Times, which he would never finish on his way to work; that was for my mother. And the Telegram, which he'd pick up for the train ride home. There had always been so many newspapers at the newsstand at the train station in Hartsdale, at the stationery store nearby where we got the Sunday paper, at the candy store at Four Corners. Ones that we never read, like the Post or the Daily News or the Journal American, which my parents looked down on.

Then came the strikes. After each settlement the paper he brought home would be a little thinner, the name on the banner a bit longer. Eventually they became too much to pronounce. And no one was sure how to break them down. The Herald Tribune was easy, everyone called it The Trib. But what did you call The World Telegram & Sun, Incorporating the Journal American? If that was indeed how they strung it together.

Some of the boys in our class were already as tall as Mr. S. I suppose one reason I found Mr. S such a sympathetic figure back then was that I was small too, just about the shortest boy in my grade.

He was always so neatly dressed, nearly dashing. Brooks Brothers wash suits, snowy collars, immaculate cordovans. Slight, slim, crew cut. Those alert, expressive eyes. Those blazers with the narrow lapels. He drove a white VW Beetle. You'd see him sitting upright, a little stiff, leaning forward slightly as he left school. That was in seventh grade.

Many years later, a quarter of a century later, one October, I moved to a new apartment, in the West Village. I hadn't given him a thought in all those years but I caught sight of a man on Hudson Street and without a moment's hesitation, I immediately said to myself, there goes Mr. S.

I began to see him not infrequently. I think it was him. I'm sure it was. Still slim but not so erect, whitened brush cut, hurrying down West

Fourth or across a windy Abingdon Square. Invariably in an oversized topcoat. Not altogether that often, every few months or so. He surely was retired already.

I had the sense that he saw me studying him, though I don't ever remember him actually returning my gaze. Of course, he was gay. Had I realized that back then? I never went up to him on the street. We never spoke.

I had the impression that while he thought he recognized me he wasn't sure who I was. Where to place me? At least that's what I told myself. On the other hand, perhaps he recalled exactly who I was. It made sense. I could have been no more than a drab little boy who hadn't been interesting enough to merit any particular attention at the time, much less twenty-five years later.

27.   *Soccer Hooliganism*

I always thought that Billy was my friend. In ninth grade we sat next to each other in biology.

There is a childhood science of appraisal. An unsentimentally accurate, often unforgiving discipline. Over the years, through junior high, Billy and I came to acknowledge each other roughly as equals when it came to school work. When it came to everything else, sports, girls, or any combination of the two, like showing off in front of girls, there was no question. He had it all over me.

Our junior high school had a soccer team. I had never tried out for any team. The thought never crossed my mind. But the summer before ninth grade I had kicked a ball around with a young French guy who was the chef at the restaurant up the hill, near the mountain. There was a huge old house up there, close to where Healy Avenue turned into a dirt road. At that time, it was a French restaurant. He drove a white Mercedes Benz 300 SL roadster, a Gull Wing without the wings. I was just old enough to be properly impressed. All summer he tore up and down Healy Avenue. He taught me a couple of moves with the ball: how to kick it with the side of the foot, how to trap. That stunt: kicking it with one leg coming out from behind the other.

The first week of school Coach Tarbox held soccer tryouts. I had nothing to lose. He stuck me somewhere on the front line of one of the teams. We started scrimmaging. Suddenly, I was transformed.

I took the ball. I passed. I dodged around the defenders at will. I stole the ball from the other guys. I scored. Two times, three times, four times. It was unbelievable. It wasn't me. I didn't feel the ground. I couldn't do anything wrong. Even crusty old Tarbox, that hard-bitten sod, was affected. The customary laws and the accustomed limitations and impositions, in a moment they fell away. I was a different boy. Sure, cunning, swift.

We must have had away games and the season no doubt went on for weeks, but all I remember is that first game, against Scarsdale.

The opening kick, then a flurry of feet and confused shouting. Their maroon uniforms everywhere. The ball spurting down field. We race after it. It's like flying. There's no effort. The ball rebounds off an opposing knee. We're catching them flatfooted. Now, suddenly, their goal is right in front of me: an open, green, inviting place. And it's all mine. I am open. No one is in front of me. None of the opposing backs. Not the goalie, he has fallen yards away, well out of it, supine, helpless. Billy feeds me the ball, a quick, flat, short, cross-field pass. I stop it with my right foot, not breaking stride, dribbling it before me. One long racing step, then another. Setting up.

I am ten feet from the goal. I'm ready. There's shouting behind me and from the sidelines, it sounds miles away. This is a shot I can make with my eyes closed. Anyone can make this one. I set the side of my foot against the ball, just like I am supposed to. I am careful, I want this to look just right.

I aim. I shoot. I miss.

The ball sails over the goal and bounces towards Central Avenue. The force of my rush sends me right into the net. I hang there, my fingers meshed in the webbing. The groans and screams are all around me. I want to stay there. Forever.

Perhaps we lose the game because of that flubbed goal. I don't recall. It doesn't matter.

Now it is open season. It is as if I'd forgotten my place. I had been acting uppity, taking on airs. In those days or weeks since soccer tryouts there hadn't even been a grumble. No one could argue with the facts, as hard they were to believe: I was, after all, good at something. They had to accept that. Now that I've made a slip, all hell breaks loose. And not just a slip, an error. A fatal error. I choked and we lost.

The next morning, after gym class, it starts.

We've returned to the locker room, getting back into our clothes. I'm pulling on my trousers when they jump me. Billy takes my combination lock, it must have been hanging loose from the handle while I'm changing. Two or three of them hold me down as Billy reaches up and locks it onto the metal safety grill that surrounds the light fixture in the ceiling. That's not so bad, I think. I'll just stand on the bench and reach up, but my fingers can barely touch the dial. Before I can get the lock free, they grab me again. They start pushing me towards the door. One or even two of them I could take on, I'm wild now. That desperate, uncaring flailing when you don't care what you're doing, who you're hurting. Even the biggest boys try to steer clear when another kid goes crazy like that. But there's too many of them. Everybody is shouting and pushing. They don't just throw me out of the locker room and shove me down the hall. They push me into the girl's locker room. Screams from the girls, white slips and underwear. Then laughs and high-pitched jeers. Hands over mouths and fingers pointing. The boys lean on the girl's door from the outside, keeping me from escaping.

Billy is the most ferocious. The most betrayed. I can hear him shouting through the door, pounding on the wood.

Soccer, of course, is an autumn sport. This was only September, the school year has barely begun. In the days and weeks that follow things get better for a while, then worse. I am outside the pale now. Fair game. Several fights, beatings really. Thrown into the shower once. It is like that until June. As for Billy, at least he has the good grace not to act like my friend anymore.

28.   *Curry Chevrolet*

Every boy was infected. It was in the water. We were all crazy for cars. In the beginning it was any kind of car, sedans, station wagons, American cars, anything. Later, we grew more discriminating.

The Auto Show had just come to town. Several of us, with someone's hapless dad trailing behind, trooping up and down the Coliseum, gaping at the models in their gowns on the turntables, smiles painted on, elegantly gesturing, their opera gloves describing arcs, drawing your attention to this or that feature, a Continental kit, an array of louvers, their cars' ridiculous fins. Wolfing down the fearful hot dogs, returning laden with complimentary shopping bags bursting with brochures. It was the year Ford got back into sports car racing. At the Ford stand: a gorgeous GT40, the one that had almost won at Le Mans. White with the thick, double blue stripes over the hood and the top and down the back and the three little blue stripes — thin, thick, thin — along the rocker panels, just like the ones that would appear on Mustangs next year. The engine was in the back and it was astonishingly low. Even for a slight boy, the roof only came up to my hip. That was the fantastic thing. It could go two hundred miles an hour and it was no taller than a go kart. All the other racing cars, the Ferraris, the Jaguars and the Maseratis were big and front-engined and suddenly, old, ungainly. This was the future.

There was a kid in school, a couple of years younger than us, his existence had no significance whatsoever save for the fact that his father was Allie Sherman, the football coach. A week or so after the Auto Show, in the middle of the afternoon, with an hour to go before the end of the day, there he was. Allie Sherman himself, in front of Everett S. Webb Junior High School. His appearance alone was not particularly noteworthy. The Giants were not having great seasons back then.

It was what he was driving: a Ford GT40, ticking over, right there next to the flag pole, burbling gently through its twin pipes. In street dress, no racing stripes, a relatively sedate silver blue, but no license plates. No license plates at all. Ford must have assumed that no cop would notice it, it was so low, or that if he did catch sight of it, barely as tall as the door handles of the Biscaynes and Polarises and Valiants that kept blocking his vision, he'd be too flummoxed to try and ticket it. Why they would lend a car like this to the likes of Allie Sherman was a question we didn't trouble ourselves with.

I had never witnessed anything on the order of what next ensued and would not again until my freshman year at college. The complete breakdown of authority.

Every boy rushed to the windows. Mrs. Latour, the French teacher, vainly calling us back to our seats. And then one boy, maybe it was little Sherman, appearing on the lawn in front of the school, tentatively touching the Ford's fender. Then another, and another, and then we all were rushing down the stairs. Every single boy in the school, crowding around, elbowing and shoving for position. And we weren't there for Allie Sherman's autograph.

That was a miraculous event. A visitation of the sort that is forever befalling schoolgirls in Portugal. Instead of the Virgin, our vision was of the fastest sports car in the world. But the fact was, we were entranced with almost anything that moved, any kind of car, especially if it was new. Riding home every day in the bus the boys would all crowd into the left row of seats, so we could see the oncoming flow of traffic, and we would 'call' the cars passing the other way.

"I've got that Bonneville."

"That Electra is mine."

"No, mine!"

"I called it first!"

Naming them made them ours. And, after a point, the cars up for grabs didn't have to be particularly choice. When the fever came upon us even a Dodge Dart or a Rambler American would do.

Back then, the term 'model year' had some meaning. All the cars were new every year. Usually there were just little changes: tail light treatments, the grillwork slightly altered, new wheel covers. Just enough to be able to tell that this was a brand-new Buick Special and that other one, in your neighbor's driveway next door, though mechanically identical, was now old, one year old, two years old, or, if they had no sense of shame at all, three years old.

Just because they were new, that was enough. We understood the language of cars. We understood what it meant to add a line of chrome, to scallop a fin. The cars spoke to us. We understood the family relations. The lines of descent. The consanguinity linking a Falcon and a Fairlane, a Chevy II and an Chevelle. And every fall the anticipation would grow.

In early September, even before the breathless commercials announcing the new models aired, before the first episode of *Route 66* ran and Martin Milner eased himself into his brand new Corvette — somehow, every autumn, he'd roll into the first episode at the wheel of a new Corvette — my friend Eric and I would play out our annual ritual. We were old enough now to take our bicycles onto Central Avenue. We would ride the few miles down the road to the nearest dealership, Curry Chevrolet, in Edgemont.

Two boys on bicycles. It is amazing how little notice people give to boys. Way in the back, parking lots where no one was meant to go: there they were, rows and rows of new cars. The new model year. The colors just a bit off, not what we were used to, for the paint schemes too were altered each year. In dull ranks. They weren't even cleaned yet. We would coast up and down the rows, calling out our finds to each other. These were the cars we knew, the Biscaynes and the Novas and the Monzas and the Sting Rays, but they had changed.

And those minute, thrilling, unsettling alterations made all the difference in the world.

29.   Richard Q.

Richard never fit in.

He played the French horn and the flute, he had a vaguely English accent.

He was my friend, in a rather distant way, even though or perhaps because he was just a little odd. The two-tone National Health Service eyeglasses didn't help. Then there were those prominent teeth and the spiky crewcut.

A big, cheerful, uncomplicated kid who for some reason, much to his unending confusion, woke up one day and found himself here, in Hartsdale, New York. Deposited from another world. What or where that world was, exactly, we never found out.

I assumed his family had lived abroad for some time. He was tall and gawky, entirely unathletic, at least in any sport we recognized. At first, he couldn't even throw a ball. Alarm bells went off immediately. Foreigner. He threw like a girl. Or, rather, like an Englishman. Someone who hadn't grown up throwing things: baseballs, snowballs, rocks. That was part of his undoing. A permanent besmirchment.

He and his brother and his parents lived in an odd house up at the top of the hill, past the upper end of Healy Avenue. It was a big old house, older than our suburbs, a relic of another time, a country house from the turn of the century. Perched on a hill that once must have had a sweeping view of the long valley down the middle of which Central Avenue now ran. An appropriate weekend house for a Gilded Age cotton broker or the assistant general manager of a steamship line or a minor Tammany leader. The house sat at the end of a long drive that now was lined with a row of unlovely little post war salt boxes. It was a graceful welcoming late Victorian. Clapboard, a minimum of gewgaw, with a warm lintel and a dignified staircase and views out the back over the wooded drop.

Richard was a gentle boy, full of artless enthusiasm and puppy intelligence, even more unlettered in the arts of war, of fighting, than me. When he was sufficiently provoked, however, and he lost it, simply by virtue of his size, for he was a large child, he could wreak some juicy havoc.

The flute and French horn: both seemed to us odd choices for a boy. In third grade music started. Music class several times a week. Lessons. Band. We were all given the choice of instruments. As in, "your choice of weapons." I picked the drums. They seemed the loudest. My parents were not happy about this and they let me know. They gave me the impression that it was a low, rather unintelligent, somehow lumpen choice. But they dutifully bought me the sticks and the practice pad. Richard had already been playing his instruments for years.

Sometime later, in sixth or seventh grade, in some doomed exercise in collaboration and self-regulation and responsibility, our music teacher decreed that we all had to pair off and, on our own, rehearse and then perform a duo for the rest of the class. Richard and I, as the appointed outcasts of the grade, naturally ended up together. No one else wanted to be associated with us. I don't remember what we picked out, some piece from the band's repertoire. Something wildly inappropriate for drum and flute. Whatever we were playing had been intended by its composer to be the background for some saxophones or clarinets that were nowhere to be heard. The shame we both felt. Pushing on to the end. Speeding up to bring it on quicker. Standing there in front of the class.

Richard had a younger brother, Alex. More than two years younger, two grades behind us. Where Richard was all elbows and Adam's apple, Alex was compact, muscled, fluent instead of squeaky. His accent had disappeared long ago. We all waited at the same bus stop in the morning, at the corner of Marion Avenue and Townsend.

It was one of those predestined fights. We were bound to fight it. Like an arranged marriage.

The manifold law of our kind, boy children, moved us to that spot of lawn after school, Alex and me. The laws of precedence had been violated. He had stepped out of line or refused to accept some taunt I had tossed off. I have absolutely no memory of how, or why. Some challenge? A third party's derision? Richard was out of it altogether. I was the smallest ninth grader. Alex was the strongest seventh grader. Did someone coax him into calling me out? The only satisfaction for this matter of honor was fists and half nelsons by the traffic light at the end of the school's driveway.

Some fights were all blows, and some were all wrestling. There was no discussion beforehand. They developed organically. This one was both.

All afternoon knowing that this was coming, knowing there was no way out. The last bell ringing. A braying ring of boys and girls around us. Bloody nose, aching ribs. Cheek burns from the pebbles underfoot. Five minutes, ten minutes, the rage giving way to the dull rhythm of a degrading intimacy of pain. He knew I could not decently give up. Not yet.

I don't know whatever happened to Alex. The following fall I was attending a different school, where almost no one knew me. In time I almost forgot all about Richard, about them both.

Then, one morning in 1979, I opened the paper and there he was. An Iranian hostage: two hundred days, three hundred days in the embassy. Then he alone, just him, set free by the Revolutionary Guards. A compassionate gesture. There was something wrong with him. It wasn't quite spelled out in the Times. The kind of disease you can live with for years, or forever, if you have the right medication. But without, you go downhill fast. His waving hand and wan, smiling face as the stretcher bearers carry him down the boarding ramp at Wiesbaden.

Maybe it was another Richard Q. I don't think so. There was something familiar in his expression. Mere survival transmuted into triumph.

The Foreign Service, that was fitting. Maybe for Richard that meant going into the family business. Sitting on the packed Lexington Avenue local on my way to work, wondering: had junior high turned out to be a kind of a boot camp for him? Toughening him up for the months on end of blindfolds, beatings, mock executions? Or is there only so much you can stand of that sort of thing? During those years when we were small, what had been done to Richard? Had his reservoirs of resistance been drained? Is that why the mullahs let him go early?

30.   *The Mighty Zalooms*

The mighty Zalooms appeared in huge, quart sized waxed paper sacks, like the bags that Eight O'clock Coffee was sold in at the A&P, but larger. This was the good stuff.

My family was mad for pistachio nuts. All of us. Even the meanest, smallest, most cheaply dyed red rejects that left us looking like painted women out of de Kooning. None of those tawdry little cellophane tubes ever lived to see the dawn in my house.

Eventually, a guy who worked for my father started coming across with the goods. Zaloom Brand, straight from Iran. Lightly salted and delicately roasted. Undyed, of course. Someone he knew, or was related to, was an importer.

By now both of my brothers were long gone to college. It was just my parents and me. After dinner my mother would do the dishes, my father would go into the living room to read the paper and I would go to my room to finish my homework. Except for the nights we played Scrabble.

I don't remember my parents ever playing cards, or any other board games. Scrabble was their game. Fast games, two or three a night, rapid fire.

Years later, ascending a grimy staircase in Chinatown one Sunday morning, I found myself suddenly struck by the most bizarre, yet fugitively familiar, sound. The building itself was roaring. A frenzied, unfolding, careening thunder echoing from floor to floor, seeping out through every closed doorway I passed. The Chinese men were playing mahjong, it was explained to me, and they were gambling. Then I placed it: it sounded just like my parents playing Scrabble.

An old maroon box, held together with masking tape. And old gray felt bag for the letters, from some lost piece of stereo equipment, meant to hold a mike perhaps. Some slips of paper and small pencil, for scoring, and the tile holders, fancy ones with scoring holes on top and pins, which we never used, intended for cribbage. And we always had to have to have something to eat. Some fruit, a cookie, the candy my father would bring home from Barracini's. Often it was ice cream. No matter how much I complained, my mother always bought the Van Choc Straw. Or we might be blessed with pistachios. Big, ripe succulent pistachios.

They were ranked according to some sort of grading nomenclature, like olives, like American bombers from World War II. The smallest were Large and they went up from there. There was a little chart on the back of the bag. Our Zalooms were at least Super Colossals, maybe even Jumbo Dreadnoughts.

The delicate, shimmering chartreuse of them. The fragile paper-thin skin between the shell and the meat, almost every single one ridiculously easy to open.

It was the first time I found myself unable to stop, simply unable to stop myself from doing something. I could not push them away. Aware that control was slipping. Alive to the realization that the ecstasy of the first bite, of the first crack of the first shell was, incrementally but inevitably, diminishing with each additional nut. Nevertheless, entirely helpless to stop myself. One after another after another. Searching the dish, a quick aerial survey, then the swoop, the snatch, the snap between the thumbnails or the longer, sweeter, crack between the molars followed by that unearthly pleasure.

The rough, slightly misshapen pod of meat: rolling it around on the tongue. Easing off the crackling skin, sometimes having to pry it from the roof of the mouth. Then milking the nut dry again, extracting the last of the juice, sweetly perfumed, lightly salted, finally biting into the intoxicating core. Sometimes latitudinally, usually along its axis, splitting the nut into its constitutive twins. The doubled, slightly concave interiors of them, taut yet luxuriantly smooth, like the stretched stomach of some delightful being I was years from stroking. Then biting down, impatient, finishing them off, first one, then the other, grinding the fruit down, pulverizing it between my teeth, releasing the last of the goodness, then swallowing. Gone.

Then a sip of ginger ale. My mother allowed only ginger ale in her house. No other soda. Yukon Club ginger ale. Unless it was a birthday. Then what we called flavored sodas were allowed: cream soda, root beer, cola, but Yukon Club only. Only house brands in our house. Yukon Club, of course, the private label at A&P. Something left over from the Depression, I always assumed. No Coca Cola or Seven Up or Dr. Pepper, ever.

A quick sip, then another pistachio, and again that thrill, once more commensurately diminished. Opening up another sweet one, and the concomitant tinge of... what? Anxiety? Of knowing that I could not stop, that I didn't need another, that each was just that much less pleasing than the one before. Perhaps it was a function of the salt, deadening the taste buds, and not some more metaphysical satiety at work. Knowing, accepting, that this one was nothing like the last, much less the first, but I was just as incapable of stopping now as I had been a moment before. I had to have another. A feeling I came to know many times over the years, with many other things I held in my hands, gazing down at, then raising to my lips. But this was the first time.

Eventually my father would bang on the table, "Go. Go on, you're taking all night."

My mother would halfheartedly pull away the bag of nuts and the clinking, overloaded ashtray, muttering, "You'll make yourself sick with those. You never know when to stop."

And all too often the best I could come up with would be some pathetic single letter tacked on to someone else's word: a T added onto G-O, for a measly three points. At least it wouldn't be my turn anymore.

As we lay down our tiles, each of us had our own way of expressing the merriment or despair, as appropriate, that accompanied our turn. My father's unmitigated glee, his war whoop, his whole face worked up into a beaming smile, his round eyes squinting in triumph as he laid down his coup. My mother's deceptively modest and retiring smile, as if this was just another dinner of pot roast and mashed potatoes she was serving, setting the plates on the table, as she quietly plunked down some stultifying seven letter, triple word score with a Z, a Q, and two Ms in it.

As for me, I always got embarrassed. It was always easier when I had a poor hand, when all I could summon up were those feeble two- and three-letter combinations, T-I-N or H-A-D or F-A-T. Three points, seven points, five points. Then there would be no comment and the game would move rapidly along. But now and then, almost despite myself, I would look down and see, swimming up from the jumble of characters on my slate, a long, intricate, fully formed word, some charming, stylish creature.

S-Q-U-A-L-O-R, say, or S-Y-Z-Y-G-Y.

The first pairing, S-Q, would suggest a word, a word I might not even be certain the meaning of. Then the hurried swapping of tiles and the rush of pleasure as the letters sorted themselves out and indeed, it was so, a word entire, right there. Then, another dampening. Where can this go? Where can it fit in? But, yes, I find a place for it. It can, it can go right there. Hoping no one else will snatch away the opening before my turn comes round. Waiting, trying not to stare at the beckoning, alluring, all too obvious space. Any one of us at the table was entirely capable of tracking the others' eye movements and making a purely defensive, spoiling play, just to ruin another's set up.

Whiling away the intervening moments, surreptitiously adding up the potential payoff. Trying to act cool, bored, unsatisfied with my letters. Shifting them about some more, putting them out of order, as if I was continuing to cast about for some combination, fruitlessly. And then, miraculously, it is my turn and the space is still there, waiting for me. And that is when I would get red in the face.

I never knew what to do. I would deposit the letters. The first one, and then the next, and then another. And as I kept on going, laying them down, my parents' eyebrows would start to go up. When, finally, it became clear, my mother would pronounce it out loud. "QUORUM," say, with a little wonder in her voice.

"Ah," my father would echo as he toted up the score, "QUORUM."

He'd pronounce the word with that same wonder. As if it was some rare monster, like a sailor's legend. Or a precious alpine sprig, long believed extinct, I'd borne back from the far ends of the earth and laid before them on the kitchen table. And I never knew what to say. Face red, looking down, waiting for play to resume.

And then, when I was around thirteen, we sat down one night after dinner for another fast, furious game of Scrabble.

As this game wore on, I knew it would be close. At the end my father finished the scoring, debiting the remaining letters from those who had tiles left when the first of us, it might have been me, got rid of all his letters. He finished the sums in his tidy, precise accountant's hand, running the pencil point quickly up and down the columns, checking his addition, which never needed checking, and then he looked up.

He studied me with a marvelously gentle smile on his face.

"My son," he said, "You have won."

I had won. I had beat my parents. Now I really did not know what to say.

My mother let out a little, "Ah," of joy.

My father was still looking at me, his eyes shining. My mother got up and kissed me on the forehead.

"No more nuts for you," she said, putting the bag away.

31. *Please Smile*

He had beautiful cameras of his own. There was a gorgeous black Rollei with its twin lenses, over and under, one a bit larger than the other. The black crackle finish, the raised silver lettering, the rich, ribbed, fitted, mahogany leather case. Then later, a big Nikon F. Black too, shiny, with an awkward, banging crew of extra lenses, each with its own carrying case swinging from the neck strap.

As I was growing up, as far back as I can remember, every time I turned around my father had a camera in his hand. Some were his, some were borrowed, but every weekend he was armed. Throughout his working life, every weekend of my childhood it seemed, he was bringing home new cameras from work, trying them out: Canons, Olympus's, Konicas, Bronicas, Mamiyas, Pentaxes, Contaxes, Leicas, Hasselblads. Every weekend I was pulled, unwilling, whining, scowling, out to the front yard and steadied in front of the dogwood tree.

Posed in the backyard with a rake.

Positioned in the driveway with my new bike, the front wheel turned just so.

Made to kneel with the white German shepherd from down the street.

Prodded into position standing next to the grand foyer steps of the Concord, or the big glassed-in pool in back of the hotel with a bored Buster Crabbe.

Posed at camp with my hand resting on the canoe rack.

Picked out high up in the third row at junior high school graduation.

Accosted in the living room while I was minding my own business, reading Fitzgerald next to the fireplace.

How I hated it. Every time I saw a camera pointed at me, I donned that same sulking scowl. Eyes fixed off in the renegade distance. Never returning the gaze of the camera, or the photographer, never looking up, never smiling, not once.

I hated cameras. I hated posing. I hated the freezing nakedness, waiting for the shutter. Observed. There for the gazing, by anyone passing by. My father standing there in front of the entire ninth grade of Everett S. Webb Junior High School, all of us in white dinner jackets and white gowns, posed on bleachers in front of the school for the official portrait. There he was, Nikon in hand, smiling, waving, crouching down, calling my name, working for my attention, trying for a smile, as if I hadn't noticed him, as if the entire graduating class wasn't staring at him, smirking as he waved his short arms, gesticulating, capering. I refused to look at him, refused to recognize my father, who only wanted to take my picture.

 He had his revenge, of course. I have been left with a suitcase of pictures. It is stuffed full of transparencies, glass slides, two and a half by threes, three by fives, five by sevens, the little booklets with the matte, pastel covers with the scalloped edges into which photo finishers used to bind up rolls of snaps.

A surly boy: at seven, eight, nine, ten, eleven, every year, and on each face that same expression, resentful, closed, just waiting to flee.

32. The Little Label with the Sheep

As if there had to be something better than this.

If only *this* was different, or *that*. If only we lived in a bigger house, or, better, in a big, big house, like one of those homes on Mamaroneck Road or a house like Bobby had. If only there were those lovely labels on all of my shirts and my jackets.

To the best of my recollection, it all started with a red vest. My mother took me to that consignment shop on Garth Road, in Scarsdale. On the same block as the stationery store where I purchased the divine deck of baseball cards. Not Scarsdale though, not really. If it was Garth Road, it was surely Eastchester, an important distinction. I don't remember why we were there. Was there was something special she was looking for? It was not like her to be interested in anything used. Used clothes or used cars, or antiques or flea markets, all held absolutely no interest for her.

But there she was with a red vest in her hand, holding it up to my chest. Brass buttons and four pockets, two on each side. And then she was purchasing it and we were taking it home.

I don't actually remember wearing it all that often. There are a few photographs of me in it. What I remember most, what intrigued me and enthralled the most, in the most literal sense, enslaving me in a very real way, was the label sewn into the collar. It was a small white label with blue thread, or blue ink, picking out the words and the image. The vest was from Brooks Brothers. It was the very first, and last, item I owned that came from there, until I was living in New York City and old enough to go shopping there myself.

There was something about the label. Even now, especially now, there is no little embarrassment in admitting the hold it had over me. The little fat lamb hung up in the sling.

It didn't matter that it was used, that it had been worn by and discarded by someone else, or someone else's mother. I finally had something from Brooks Brothers.

Of course, everything my friend Bobby owned, absolutely everything he wore to school every day, seemed to have come from there. That was one of the differences between us.

There was a refinement to that vest. An ineffable, effortless, artless charm adorned those clothes, and those that wore them. It was palpable. Like a nimbus around them. And if only I could have them, wear them too, then I too could move in that world.

It's so easy to describe now, so easy to denigrate those naive fantasies and motives. That Brooks Brothers label doesn't do a thing for me anymore. For a few years after coming to New York, when what money I had for clothes, I often spent there, as well as some money that I didn't have, or that should have gone for other purposes. Even then, the power of that image, and that remembered life, that aurora of enchantment, was fading, but back then, standing in that consignment shop...

33.   *Taking Walks*

My father and I would go for walks around the neighborhood. Across Townsend Avenue, then up Marion and then back, maybe along the back side of Healy, where it became a dirt road and passed beneath the mountain. It would be Saturday, or it was Sunday, neighbors would be out working in their yards, mowing their lawns, washing their cars. My father would stop and talk to every single one. These grownups treated all manner of weighty subject: the school budget, the latest newspaper strike, the damage the dismal, rainy spring weather had wreaked upon the dogwood and the pachysandra. My father would assume a pose, arms folded, one foot up on the curbing and he, along with whichever father or mother it was that we'd come across in the midst of their weekend chores, together they would dispose of the topic at hand, and one or two in addition while they were at it, all the time taking a kind of pleasure, this was clear, even then, even before I necessarily understood what exactly it was they were talking about, I must have been small, rather small since I know there was no way I would have had allowed myself by the time I was ten or eleven to be seen by my friends in the neighborhood taking walks with my father, they were taking an undeniable satisfaction in the simple engagement, the plain and simple neighborly connection they were making.

And for my father, I could see, this was something that gave him great pleasure. It was as if these uncomplex interactions invested him with something. It wasn't just an opportunity for him to be clever and funny, though, clearly, he took pleasure in his unquestioned, and this was obvious to me even then, his assumptive ability to do just that. It was more than that. He took pleasure in the interactions themselves, in hearing people talk and being able to react, to connect with them, to them. He was energized by these contacts. I know it, because I can see myself doing the same, drawing satisfaction and energy in just the same way, from just the same sorts of interactions. The subject matter matters not much at all. It can be the weather, the latest blunder by the board of selectmen, the latest office tittle tattle. The pleasure is derived, is generated, from the sharing, the bond, howsoever apparently trivial or temporary. It is the conversation, that is where the value, the human nexus, inheres.

From my perspective though, as a little boy, these conversations went on forever. These grownups just liked to talk, all they wanted to do was talk, and it was about nothing. There was no content. It was all affect and altogether unrelievedly dreary. Who cared about what the Board of Regents was up to now? And though, in a very real way, if this was a conversation about the Regents and how in the name of racial integration, some said, that Hartsdale was being perscecuted, what they were talking about was in fact my own future, for when it came to that topic, that is, kids like me, the young white kids of Hartsdale, New York, and where we were going to go to secondary school, was right then being fought over at the municipal level, at the county level, the state level. So, it so happens, such a topic was indeed at no remove whatsoever. Nevertheless, to me this was the epitome of adult blather, and I could not wait for it to come to a close. I pawed at the ground. I shot my father pleading looks. I'm not sure I didn't tug at his elbow from time to time. These conversations went on for so long.

And then, finally, my father would extricate himself, reluctantly, with many closing interjections that extended the conversations even further, some additional point or rejoinder always needed to be addressed, but then finally we'd be back on the street again, headed to the next house or, better yet, headed just up the road, to the unpaved portion of Healy or perhaps, even better, the further, yonder extension of Healy Avenue, where it went up the hill, past the dead end where Richard Q's family lived and then, further on, where it reached almost as far as Yonkers, an exponential extension, our little, organized street becoming something else, shooting out, transforming itself. It was a kind of exercise in scale: this little street, it so happened, had turned out, by accident of history and the quiddity of post-war development, to run on and on, to go on for what seemed like miles. There was a summer camp at its further reaches. An Italian restaurant looked out at Central Avenue beneath one of its supernumerary extensions. It just kept going and going.

And, if I could tear my father away from our neighbors, we, the two of us, would walk. We would walk. We'd talk. And, somehow, over time, this conversation of ours refined itself. The subject matter of these chats coalesced into a single topic. We ended up having the same conversation over and over, every single time.

I'm not sure how we got on to this. I'm inclined it believe this too is a story that had its naissance in a photograph, in imagery. Images that came out of a trip my parents took, by themselves, down to Miami. I couldn't have been more than five or six then, which meant that this trip occurred several years before my father and I had these conversations. I think they likely took a number of vacations down there, but there was something special about that one. That trip produced some remarkable pictures: my parents posing, first my mother, then my father, then them both, in front of a fantastic, throbbingly vibrant red-and-white Corvette convertible, its top down. It was a '54, or maybe a '55 or a '56, one of the first years in its production run, and it was spectacular, with those contrasting white curving insets flaming out behind the front wheel wells. The two of them looked so handsome and beautiful. What a couple, tanned, smiling, easy in their sport clothes. A white, mid-century, Collins Avenue hotel, the Fountainbleau perhaps, spread out behind them. For years I thought they'd rented that car for the vacation. It wasn't until much later that I learned the truth. It was just a car they'd espied, parked along the street, which they'd pressed into service as their backdrop and prop. But it was beautiful and it betokened, at least it seemed to me at the time, an awareness of fashion and mode on their part.

Whether those pictures were what led to these conversations, I'm not sure, but these conversations with my father were all about Florida. All about Miami, a place I'd never been to and wouldn't set foot in for years. In these conversations my father and I would pretend, would act out, a vacation of our own. Just him and me. We would discuss, we would plan, we would comment upon and act out a jaunt down to Miami. Just the two of us. First, we'd pack, then get to the airport; to Idlewild, not Kennedy. There was no Kennedy yet. Then we'd check in and board the 707. Was it Eastern Airlines? It must have been Eastern, unless it was Northeast. We'd talk about what kind of meal we'd be served on the flight and what we'd read to pass the time. Then we'd discuss getting from the airport to the hotel, would we rent a car? And what would we do that first afternoon? A jaunt across the street to the beach seemed always in store. I would lead the conversation, prompting him for details as I paced the narrative, letting him add some color from time to time.

We'd have these conversations over and over. We would take off on these fantasy jaunts over and over.

Among the unvarying elements in this father-and-son wanderspiel was a small point, a minor point. We covered quickly and then moved on with alacrity. Each and every time it would come up and would then be promptly dispatched: for some reason, whenever we went on these trips, and in a sense we went on them every weekend, for some reason, it was a mystery but there it was, it kept happening every single time: my mother would be unable to come with us. For some reason, it always ended up being us, my father and me on the plane, checking into the hotel, stretching out on the sand. Just the two of us.

Why was that? Whose idea was that? Who brought it up the first time? I can't recall. I do remember my father gravely assenting one time that I expressed regret that she wasn't going to be able to join us. Where did this come from?

34.   *The Eyebrows Have It*

Perhaps it is something genetic. My father could do it. My brothers, both of them, too.

I was staying with my brother and his wife in their apartment on Hancock Street in Cambridge. A beautifully run-down floor-through. Walls of books, crumbling plumbing. A decaying brick row house on a snowy Cambridge street. Everywhere you looked: students and bicycles and Volkswagens and girls in turtlenecks. It was 1963, maybe. This was everything I wanted. Down Massachusetts Avenue the Orson Welles was showing Bergman and Kurosawa every night. A few blocks further along was Harvard Square. The crowds flowing across the street, in and out of the Coop, up from the subway. The preppy pomp and the beat, intellectual frump.

It was heaven for a boy like me. I was older now, maybe twelve. It was the antithesis of suburb. If this was not the kind of person I was, I was sure it was the one I would become... someone who belonged here.

That evening they took me to Brigham's. A damp, chilly Boston winter night, not particularly propitious for ice cream. We walked to the Brigham's up Mass Ave, towards Cambridge Town Hall. The place was dark, paneled with dark wood, dark booths and mirrors, and dour waitresses. As I worked away at my sundae, I noticed some people in a booth across from us. They were college kids, two girls and a guy. The guy was nothing special, thin, untidy hair, glasses. But the girls were obviously entranced by him. They were hanging on every word, laughing at his little jokes, pretending to be scandalized when he leaned towards one or another and whispered in her ear. They were all sitting rather close together in their corner.

As far as I could tell there was absolutely nothing out of the ordinary about this fellow, except for his eyebrow. This total nonentity, this Pfc. Wintergreen of the Sexual Revolution was doing something with his eyebrow that I'd never noticed any man do before. Every now and then he would turn and cast a doleful look upon one of them and then, a moment later, he would arch his right eyebrow, while the other remained immobile, stationary. It would turn his pitiful expression into something arch and devilish. To me it seemed hopelessly bogus. Sad, pathetic effrontery. The thing was, it seemed to be clicking, just clicking. These girls were, if it doesn't sound disrespectful to say it, eating out of his hand.

Right then and there I resolved to do what I had to do. As soon as I got home from my weekend in Cambridge I set about my new regime. Every spare moment I spent positioned in front of the mirror on my father's dresser. I would poke my index finger up into my right eyebrow then raise and lower my eyebrow. Up and down, up and down, practicing, it seems, for years. Thankfully I was never caught.

It only occurred to me later, much later, that since my father had been raising his eyebrow in just the same way, occasionally with grave interrogation, often full of soft mockery, for as long as I could remember, perhaps I would have come to possess this ability without all those years of drilling in front of his mirror. And if only I'd known that, perhaps I might not have been so sorely disappointed when I saw what a failed technique it proved to be, for me.

35.   *The Idea of Another Life*

I can always blame my parents. If they hadn't insisted on such an early bedtime none of this would have happened. Every school night, I would lie in bed and try and try, willing myself to sleep. For hours, for what seemed like hours, I would stare at the ceiling, the shadow that the divided window threw against the shade, the fan of yellow from the hall light, spread out on my floor, seeping through the crack between the not quite closed door and the jamb.

Thinking about tomorrow, what could go wrong. A challenge on the bus. An ambush in the playground. Danger was everywhere. Sometimes I knew what was coming, some threat that had turned into a promise, some invented retribution in the cafeteria. Then sleep would never come.

I hated getting up in the morning. I hated school, I hated my life. I hated myself for putting myself through this every day. I hated myself for the lack of imagination or courage to do anything about it. But the nights were the worst. In the morning at least I could busy myself with getting dressed, breakfasting. As the day wore on, I could attempt to defend myself. I could always try to run. At night there was no escape: there was nothing else but the conjuring of the day to come.

One evening, trying to sleep, trying to keep myself from thinking, I lay there in the dark, tossing and turning, envisioning new torments for myself, the kind that had the nasty habit of coming true. Then, somehow, no doubt under the influence of Ian Fleming or perhaps an *Our Man Flint* film, the next thing I knew I had forgotten my troubles. I was constructing a pretty little fiction for myself. I could be a spy: me, myself. And why not? I too could be the owner of a high-spirited roadster and a splendid flat, some gallant haberdashery, an evil looking automatic. I could have women hanging off me. I could engage in all sorts of dangerous and ethically arguable deeds. Suddenly, the black oppression of the night bed was lifted, I was free. I could fly myself anywhere, and the darkness only made the journey easier.

I was some sort of secret agent. I owned a splendid Lotus Europa, British Racing Green. Under my armpit, in a chamois holster, nestled a stubby gray Webley. Not that I had ever seen a Webley in my life. James Bond favored them, along with Berettas. That was good enough for me.

I never did anything. No adventures. No rescues or assassinations, no daring espionage, nothing. I would get dressed, mentally survey my splendid house, don my blazer, arm myself of course, then hop into my English sports car and roar off. That was it, that was enough. If I was still awake when I got to the end of my private lane, I would start all over again.

And soon enough I learned to summon up the scene and the scenario at will, making myself ready for sleep. Though I embellished it slightly, the little tale I told myself never changed, not for years. The Lotus was traded in for a Ferrari 250 LM, but the outline remained the same. It worked every night. The idea of a life, the sketch of it, the lineaments, the most outward of its trappings, that was enough.

Where was I going when I accelerated away? I never got there. I never found out.

36.   Climbing the Jewish Alps

It seemed as if we had always been going there.

As the years went by the Concord seemed to get bigger, to grow and expand apace with me, as I grew. The wondrous thing was that nothing was ever done over. Nothing got renovated or replaced, the place just kept spreading. Walking through the endless lobbies and hallways: always that anxiety, afraid of getting lost, suddenly the highway of carpet I'd been idly studying as I wandered along, trying to step over the borders of the pattern that were just a little too short or too long for my gait, would abruptly come to an end, and a new course of marble tile would begin. There in front of me would stretch a whole new wing, door after door disappearing into the distance, maids laden with towels, luggage carts parked in corners. On our last visit, a month or two previous, all this had been part of a fairway.

It was immense and white, like the new white brick apartment houses rising in Yonkers. Thousands of chaise lounges, in endless ranks, drawn up at the edges of the vast indoor pool, in its own echoing wing, glassed-in, like a monstrous car dealer's showroom. And Buster Crabbe. You couldn't get away from Buster Crabbe.

There was an indoor street of shops and several nightclubs. In the big room where the headliners, like Martin and Rossi, played, a set of xylophone mallets sat on each table. Instead of applauding, if you liked what you heard you were supposed to bang on the table with your mallet. One night for some reason I was up late and from the hallway beyond I heard the room. A song ended. There was some light applause quickly drowned out by an eerie thunder of blows, wood against tabletop, going on and on. Some menacing ritual being played out.

Every morning there was a freshly mimeoed schedule of activities. Groups and lessons and outings and of course, Simon Sez. The Concord's Simon was very famous, at least that was my impression. There were several sessions a day. Simon Sez had a hat, a silly peaked, Robin Hood affair. You were supposed to buy one. Or you could win one from him. No one ever seemed to win. He was good, very good, quite fast, and he made everyone laugh, including the grown-ups. Some of his routine was in Yiddish, only the adults laughed at that. And in twenty minutes or so it was over, he was gone and again there was nothing to do, except wander the halls, venture up to the scary, misty steam rooms buried in the oldest, windowless middle of the complex, wander back past the shops and the pools and the bustling front desks and sit on the curving steps opposite the front door and wait, like everyone else, for the next meal.

The dining rooms, one after another, each one a sea of huge tables, each table gleaming with silver and china. Each with its little table number sign, in its little silver holder in the middle of the table. A three-digit number, that is how big those halls were. For an entire generation of American Jews our first introduction, in fact, the bulk of our exposure to keeping kosher, was at the Concord. We certainly didn't eat like that at home, no one did.

It was as if those endless courses, the tottering towers of challah, the gigantic platters of stuffed derma, the mounds of herring in cream sauce, all the things we rarely if ever ate elsewhere, and all served up in those stupendous quantities, were somehow intended to placate these virtually completely assimilated Jews who were being forced to eat no meat during this meal and no dairy the next. A make-good for keeping their half and half from their coffee, their butter from their bread.

One visit there was a band playing in one of the smaller rooms. Bill Haley and the Comets. I successfully lobbied to be allowed to stay up and attend. Afterwards we went backstage. I collected an autograph and my father told Haley that I played the drums. In front of all these adults, one of whom was famous, really famous, I hadn't the presence of mind or the wherewithal to issue the proper demurral. That is, to mention that while in fact I had been playing the drums for several years, the kind of band I played in performed at assemblies and Memorial Day parades. While I was respectable on the snare drum, decent with a bass drum, competent with a pair of cymbals, I had never played them all at the same time — that is to say, I'd never sat down at a drum kit, like every drummer in every rock band since the dawn of man.

The next afternoon the band was playing again, a sort of jam session out where Simon Sez usually had his stand. At one point Bill called for volunteers. He remembered me. The little kid who played drums. He pulled me up on stage. Suddenly there I was, sitting in with Bill Haley, swiveling on the drummer's stool, trying to bang on the cymbal, tap on the tom-tom, rattle the snare and treadle away on the high hat and the bass drum all at the same time. I should have just stuck with the snare and swiped away at the cymbal a few times, no one would have noticed. I thought I could do it all, I thought in a bar or two I could get the hang of it. I'm sure in a day or two I would have. I was a decent drummer. I had a feel for it, as much as you can feel a drum. But there was no way it was going to happen then and there.

The rest of the band threw uneasy glances at Haley. On his face the quick disappointment wiped away by a masked annoyance. I had gotten over on him, the expression said. Quickly he ushered me off the platform. That was my moment in the limelight. The faces in the crowd looking away, embarrassed. They'd wanted so much to enjoy this: a little kid banging away at the drums, feeding the rock and rollers that back beat.

I stood at the rear of the crowd for a while. No one noticed me leave. I went back to the halls and my walking. The pool to the pool hall to the pro shop to the gift shop to the dining room. Eventually the weekend came to an end.

37. The Books in the Basement

By the time I was reading nothing but grown-up books, when I was eleven or so, both of my brothers were out of the house, off to college. As time went by their visits home became shorter and less frequent. At the end of every semester though, they would deposit a carton or two of books in the basement. It was painted cinder block, the old bedroom and dining room furniture piled up in a corner, the dark furnace room with its great gray burner and my father's neat, neglected worktable. It was always cool in the basement. Sometimes, in summer, during long heat spells, my brothers would grab some pillows and go sleep down there, a privilege always denied me.

Usually, the pickings when it came to their books were exceedingly slim, some Ayn Rand, some Dreiser, *The Encyclopedia of Sociology*. As I kept digging, however, it got more interesting: some Margaret Mead paperbacks that included some suggestive scenes of sex education among Pacific islanders. And then, one day, at the bottom of a box, a breathtaking find: a copy of the Evergreen Review. Tattered yellow covers, and, inside: Sartre, Terry Southern, Beckett, Ginsberg. All of them together in one issue, as if giants walked the earth, with, and this was the best part of all, advertisements for the Olympia Press interspersed throughout.

Then, beneath it, in the same box: Henry Miller. *The Rosy Crucifixion,* all three Grove Press volumes. Suddenly I was transported to another plane. I had of course heard of Henry Miller. I had been reading the Book Review in the Sunday Times for a while. I knew where to place him. But those books, the language, the writing itself was something else.

Some months earlier I had come across a copy of *Fanny Hill,* in one of the other boxes in the basement, or perhaps it came into my hands from a classmate, eventually to be returned. But this was different. John Cleland seemed like so much high-class smut in comparison, though I certainly was not complaining. But, Henry Miller, wow, this kind of writing I'd never come across before. It was New York, a New York I recognized. A heroically soiled place, Twenty-third Street, Sixth Avenue, Fourth Avenue. The Els, the Automats, the men in shabby hats and shiny suits.

But his sentences were so flat. Like someone talking, just talking. Talking out of the side of his mouth. There seemed to be no art whatsoever. He described walking the streets, working in the telegraph company, taking the ferry, just the same way as he described sleeping with his best friend's girl.

He wrote so much. There were so many words. And it took so long to find the good parts.

38.   *Found in The Woods*

Behind our house, below the back yard, there was a wide swath of woods between us and the ceaseless traffic of Central Avenue. There were a couple of little ponds in there, a stream, open grassy glades and paths.

The woods were a relic of another time, just like the mansions, abandoned and not, dotting the more elevated parts of town. While walking in those woods one day I came across a stone wall, nearly drowned in the brush. I returned again and again, running along its length, laying atop the warm stones. This wasn't some tumbledown farmer's wall, like you see everywhere in New England. This was massive, with dressed stone on top, and still in good shape. Whoever built those mansions, before the subdivisions had transformed this town, back in the Twenties, further back perhaps, was responsible for this too.

These woods, threaded with their old, overgrown paths, stretched for a mile, two miles, three miles, parallel to Central Avenue, almost all the way into the middle of Hartsdale. As I got older, I gradually discovered more and more of them. My pal Eric and I would walk to Four Corners, for candy bars or baseball cards, never once having to venture out onto the road, ambling along, one path leading to another, strolling, occasionally running, now and then dashing like commandos through the trees.

Among the grassy little dells that dotted these woods was one that had about it a kind of quiet, retiring, recessive, eerie charm. There were a few widely spaced low trees, apples run wild, and scattered here and there a number of odd little sink holes. Some were carpeted with the same long soft grass as the rest of the glade, others, a bit larger, say five or six feet wide and three feet deep, with deep, soft, sandy floors. Those became our fox holes. We would run, take flying leaps and soar into them, all the while emitting blood curdling cries, like the Screaming Eagles of the 101st Airborne, leaping into the night sky over Normandy.

One day we tumbled together into one of the sinkholes and landed upon a small, old, fiberboard suitcase. What was this? When we opened it, it was like unwrapping that blessed, miraculous pack of baseball cards all over again. We never figured out what it was doing there. Aside from this discovery, in all the years we tramped along these paths we never once saw another sign of human presence in these woods. But someone must have put it here. Lost it? Dumped it? Why? Some wife who'd stumbled across her husband's little hobby; determined to get it out of her house but too mortified to put it out with the rest of the garbage?

As far as we were concerned there was only one possible explanation. It had dropped from heaven. The suitcase was filled with dirty pictures.

There was so much. It was stupefying. This was some guy's collection, it had to be. His loss, our gain. We, who'd treasure every single issue of Playboy we got our hands on, pass it from hand to hand until it was falling apart. We had struck a gusher. And like James Dean in Giant, we whooped and danced, showering ourselves with the stuff, tossing it up in the air, letting it fall back on us. Then we sat there for the rest of the afternoon, thumbing through it all, silently, passing the pictures back and forth. At the end of the day, we were so dumb struck, so unnerved, so suddenly superstitious and suspicious that we pushed it all back into the suitcase, snapped the lid shut and left it. When we returned the next day, it was all still there. Then we went ahead and divided it in half, Eric took some and I took some. We never brought any of it into school, never mentioned it to anyone else. Who would believe us? And, I think we were still a little frightened that the rightful owner would track us down and wreak some terrible vengeance. I don't remember what happened to most of it. I think eventually I threw them away, though I'm not sure how I decided to accomplish that surreptitiously.

It wasn't real pornography. There were no acts depicted, no couples. Nothing that Playboy wasn't showing us already. There were just scores, scores upon scores of naked women. Black and whites, some Kodachromes. Women in cheap bedrooms, in backyards, on the beach, in bathtubs, on toilets, atop desks, lounging on easy chairs, lawn furniture, unmade beds, scratchy looking rugs, in the back of pickup trucks, in hallways, in kitchens, on sagging plaid sofas in front of paneled walls, knotty pine.

Some of the women in the suitcase were beautiful, many others we'd never have looked at twice if they hadn't been naked. Nude, they possessed power. How *pretty* these women might be was only a part, a small part, of their hold on us. There was their face and then there was the rest of them. The symmetry and imbalance of their shapes, one after another of them, hundreds of them; as we pored over these pictures, the body parts composed themselves into a taxonomy as variegated as a dictionary of faces, faces in the street. But here, of the bedroom. It seemed surpassingly strange, even then.

39.   *These, Here*

Getting away was a great part of it: for a few minutes or hours, to be gone from everything that I woke to. All that made me shudder as I rubbed my eyes and remembered where I was and what I had to face that day, in my house, on the way to school, the banal horrors there, the hours until I could sleep again.

Another part of it was the congratulatory part. How grown up I could feel, and seem to others, if anyone happened to look close enough to see what book I was reading, or carrying, or purchasing, or taking home from the library. I read as fast as I could, as much as I could, for as much of the day as I could. First those old Modern Library editions in my parents' bookcase: *The Sun Also Rises, Gatsby, Fathers and Sons*. And then, every Hemingway, every Fitzgerald. One right after another. When I was finished with one, I would move onto the next: Tolstoy to Flaubert to Chekhov to Turgenev to Ford to Joyce. Stacking them up.

Those old Scribner's paperbacks with the gray bamboo covers. The old Signet paperbacks with the white covers and the simple cover art, like *Animal Farm*. The matte, buff covered Anchor paperbacks, like *The Wanderer*. The old Avon paperbacks with the corners trimmed off into curves, like *Call It Sleep*.

The accretion, the accumulation. These, here, these are my books. That accounted for a great deal of the pleasure right there.

40.   Eight Jewish Korean War Veterans

That one Pauline moment: I was old enough to bike down Central Avenue, a good three or four miles, down to Korvettes.

We were always so proud of E.J. Korvette. You could hear it in the parents' voices. A big department store chain, and Jewish. Built by men like them, their generation. Gimbels, Orbachs, they were Jewish too, but that was different. Eight Jewish Korean War Veterans: that's where the name was supposed to have come from. When the chain went out of business, in the Seventies, you could feel the air going out of people. It was another reason to head for Florida.

Back then, when I was a boy, Korvette's was smart, it was new, and it was right down Central Avenue. There was a big toy department, with lots of model cars and slot cars too, and a big record department. A few years later I bought Sgt. Pepper there and Tommy too. I suppose back then, at that age, I was halfway between the toy department and the record department. And then there was that day, when I had that moment, as I walked into the store.

I was going through the doors. They were eight or ten across, a double set. First the outer doors and then the inner doors. Brushed aluminum, rubber matting on the floor between the doors. Then the white linoleum beyond and the white Formica fixtures, the chrome hangers, the overbearing fluorescents. The jewelry department was just to the right as you gained the entrance. The piled-up women's wear in front of you, the escalators beyond. But I wasn't there yet. I was still on the sidewalk, under the overhang. My hand was on the door handle, the gum machines and kiddy rides on either side. I was pulling the door towards me when, for some reason, I said something to myself:

You are going to remember this moment forever.

You will look back at this moment for the rest of your life.

You will remember that it all began here.

This is when you realized that you were special, that you were different.

The banality of the setting was not lost on me. Why here? Why in front of godforsaken Korvette's? Even then, I was learning to disdain my surroundings, already considering avenues of escape. And as for being different, I had known that for years.

And, the fact is, I have never been able to forget that moment. It keeps bobbing up. Like one of those Joe Palooka dolls. The inflatable ones, with the weighted bottoms. The harder you hit them, the quicker they bounced back up. Slap happy, punch drunk. Always game for another drubbing.

And then, a second later, as I congratulated myself on the decisive way I'd declared my fate, a declaration that has, somehow, for one reason or another, proven to be true, another question suggested itself. A question I have been forced to ask myself ever since. Being different and being special are not one and the same thing.

What is it, exactly, that is supposed to make me so special?

41.   *This Is the End*

The Doors were on the air every few minutes and the Young Rascals and the Lovin' Spoonful and Herman's Hermits and Paul Revere and The Raiders. The summer we turned sixteen, Bobby had his own car. A vast, elegant, white Buick Electra. A coupe, with two doors, two huge heavy doors. It had been his mother's car. She was driving a Cadillac now. We'd roll down the windows of that Buick and go, just go, anywhere, up the Taconic, into Connecticut, pushing the buttons restlessly back and forth, from WABC to WMCA and back again.

That was the last summer it was the same for us. He was now a private school kid. I was attending a high school a few towns away. He wasn't really Bobby anymore, now he was Bob. He was running in what I thought was a fast crowd. It included a kid from the family that owned Barneys. And there was the kid whose father was a big shot at the Times. One of them had been given a Jaguar by his father, I can't remember which. We did stay friends though. Nothing happened to us, between us. We were just setting off, each on our own way, into the respective narratives of our lives. After high school we didn't stay in touch quite as much. Years later, in New York, we saw each other from time to time. After joining his family business, he became Robert.

Evening coming on, the evening was always coming on.

Gliding down the cool, darkening, tree-lined streets in Scarsdale, calculating precisely how long we could stay out. Like me, Bob had a junior license. We had to be off the road no later than one half hour after sunset. The sun went down at a quarter to nine, eight-thirty as July passed into August, eight-fifteen, eight. It was like the summer was impatient, hurrying us, chivvying us to its close. The battlewagon Buick, the radio on, always on, Jim Morrison moaning about seminaries and horses, our hands trailing out the windows, fingers loosely rising and falling against the airstream, gliding past the Tudor manors and the Georgian mansions and the expanded ranches and the tennis courts and the pools.

Bob had a girlfriend by then. Her name was Michelle and she lived in a huge contemporary in Scarsdale, not far from the Post Road. It was low and gray, all glass, sliding doors and skylights. Lots of Japanese landscaping, expanses of raked gravel. We would roll past the Scarsdale library on the way on her house. By then it already seemed small to me, prim in its gray stone, set back on its plain lawn.

Michelle's father owned a very prominent womenswear brand. His full-page ads were in the front of the Times Magazine every Sunday. Like Bob, Michelle had a best friend, we'll call her Ellen. By default, the two of us were thrown together.

Ellen's house was not far from Michelle's. It was not particularly smaller, though in terms of its aesthetics, it was of an entirely different time and place, a two- or three-year-old mock Federal decked out in shockingly new red brick. Four tall white pillars out front. A lawn barely deep enough for the obligatory circular driveway.

As warm and friendly as she was, Ellen made it clear that no sort of peer pressure or desire to keep up with her friend would be sufficient to yield to my charms, such as they were. There was something truly wonderful about Ellen though. But it had nothing to do with her. It had to do with her house.

That summer *Good-bye Columbus* was being filmed on location in Scarsdale. We all knew the book. Some of us had even read it. The world Philip Roth depicted was ours. We knew it. We were living it. There were sightings of Ali McGraw and Richard Benjamin everywhere. But what was really marvelous was that Ellen's house had been chosen, plucked from the striving, contending multitude of pretentious Scarsdale piles, to serve as the exterior of Ali McGraw's parents' house, the epitome of Jewish suburban, high-echt, conspicuous consumption.

It was not as if her parents were unaware of the derision that this attention might entail. We all spoke freely about it. It was as if we were subjects of a documentary which we ourselves were reviewing for some newspaper. It was a morsel to dine out on. And if I had been dining out then, it would have been well worth the accumulated humiliation, not to mention frustration, for Ellen never let me do much more than kiss her neck, and that not more than once or twice, that fleeting summer Bob and I rode through those delicious, leafy and shadowy streets.

42.   *Eastern Standard Time*

I don't recall exactly much courage I had to screw up. I asked her to dance and unbelievably enough, she assented.

R. was blond. There were a lot of blond Jewish girls back then, and she was one of the most beautiful girls in the high school. This was 1966, late Fall. She looked like she had all the making of a cheerleader and in due time she did indeed don the minute white skirt and the big white sweater. She had a pert, flawless face, dimpled chin, high cheek bones, the properly turned up nose. A slim, boyish figure, and that straight, shoulder length blond hair, parted in the middle, usually held back with a headband.

Gloria over and over.

Whoever was in charge of the music — that term, 'd.j.' wasn't part of our vocabulary yet — was playing it every five minutes. The whole place shouting along with Van Morrison. As if none of us had never heard the word before. G-L-O-R-I-A. As if it wasn't some worn suburban name but a thing divine, formed from gold and fire, a kind of kyrie eleison. Inside the vaulting, splendid hymn, there was something liturgical, high church, Marian even. No matter. It took us over. The driving, mounting jubilation bursting out of us all.

It was hot, close, sweaty. They were serving flat soda. Tired crepe paper hung from the rafters. None of that mattered. Kids spilling out onto the parking lot for fresh air. Billows of cigarette smoke.

It was a new school for me and I hardly knew anyone. I didn't realize at the time how much that worked to my advantage. There was only one girl and one other boy from Hartsdale. Three of us in all had started off that fall at White Plains High School. Stewart's mom drove us there that night, Barbara's mom picked us up. My father was going to Japan on business often at that time. Occasionally he took along my mother. That week they were both gone. I had been left home alone.

The dances were run by the town's recreation commission and held in a big green barn, or what was once a barn, behind the parking lot of our synagogue. Originally part of an estate, the barn was another relic out of the past, that long-gone, semi-rural, genteel Westchester, half hidden back there behind the gigantic Fifties brick and glass temple.

Later that year we started going to a club called the Cheetah, down the street from the Westchester County Center, near the White Plains train station. A few months after that we started spending more and more time in the city. But that fall, at the beginning of tenth grade, we went to these dances every Saturday night.

At beginning of the evening, I stood around with Stewart and Barbara. After a few minutes Barbara went off with some girls who she'd struck up a friendship with and not soon after, as I recall, Stewart wandered off as well. Then I caught sight a girl I had seen in school, striding, regally erect, through the halls. She was standing with a group of giggling girls as I approached.

I don't remember what she was wearing that night. I do remember she danced the second dance with me. And then she stayed with me and danced with me for the rest of the evening. I went to get her a soda and she was still there when I came back. She hadn't disappeared, she hadn't been surrounded by her girlfriends, she was waiting for me.

There was a language of courtship back then. It was mute and dumb. I don't know if it still lives but it was a powerful, intuitive means of expression which, for all the joking, instinctive buffoonery and braggadocio it engendered, was, in its way marvelously fluid, subtle, articulate. It had to do with where a girl would put her hands when she danced with you, behind your neck, along your back, fastened behind your waist, where she would put her head or her thigh, how much weight she decided to lean against you. There were gestures of acceptance, both fine and coarse, that did not need to entail any more than the most tentative acts of touching. There were statements of trust comprising no more than a tilt of the head. Diffident complicity, complaisant rejection, were signaled equally with simple smiles. Indeed, with a virtually identical smile.

By the end of the evening, it was clear that we had decided, jointly and severally, that we were a couple, albeit provisionally. We would try it on for size. We had done enough talking, about school, about the other kids, about the music, to know — along with our other conversation, the one our bodies had been conducting — to know that something could happen. I could be amusing. At least I must have been somewhat amusing. I felt confident when it came to dancing with a girl. After all, I had been going to socials at camp for years. She wrote down her telephone number.

At the end of a song, at the end of a slow dance, and we were dancing the slow dances so close together, the music would finally end and there would be that little ritual: looking into each other's eyes as you slowly disengaged yourself, keeping your eyes locked onto each other, pulling your damp clothes away from your back, as you shyly smiled. They also played *Norwegian Wood* a lot that night. McCartney letting loose at the end of every refrain with those inhalations. Or perhaps they were exhalations, supernally expressive. At the time, those sighs seemed to us, us boys for sure, girls too I think, the absolute height of lubricity.

The dance ended. I think she kissed me, I'm not sure. That's not particularly central to the memory. I went home, let myself in the dark and empty house and promptly went to sleep. A happy boy, brimming with anticipation.

The next morning, Sunday, I came down to the kitchen to make myself some toast and juice and looked up at the clock over the window. It was then I remembered that it was time to change the clocks. Daylight Savings Time was over. I didn't have a newspaper in front of me, neither the radio nor the television was on, but I remembered anyway. I was proud of myself. It was quite early, not even eight o'clock, but I went industriously around the house, upstairs and downstairs, adjusting the hour hand of every clock we owned. After I came back to the kitchen and finished my breakfast, I decided to telephone R.

It was just about nine o'clock, not too early to call. I unfolded the little white slip with her number on it. I dialed. It rang and rang. I must have dialed the wrong number. I hung up and tried again. This time it was answered on the second ring. It was a woman's voice, a grown woman. She didn't say hello, there was no greeting.

All she said was, "Who the hell is this?"

Despite, or perhaps because of the fact that nothing ever happened between me and R., that our relationship died before it could be born, I found myself thinking of her from time to time as the years passed.

During my freshman year of college, the bus that was taking me and fifty of my fellow stalwart protesters on the way to Washington, to one of the Moratoriums, made a stop at Goucher, and I ran into her. We chatted and she seemed much warmer, decidedly friendlier, than she ever had been during high school, at least after that night at Brass Tac. I think I had it in mind to give her a call, perhaps during the next vacation, but I never did. Then, years later, after college, long after moving to New York but when I was still of sufficiently modest means that my chief source of entertainment consisted of walking up and down the streets of Greenwich Village, I ran into her again. She was coming out of one of the fancier apartment houses on West Twelfth Street, a building with a doorman. A prosperous and harried looking husband was loading big canvas L.L. Bean bags into a Peugeot station wagon, and there was R, with a baby in her arms. We chatted. The husband was introduced and the child presented. She still seemed quite warm and cordial though they were clearly rushing off somewhere. The thing was, R rarely came to mind from then on. It wasn't that the idea of a station wagon or children seemed in any way repellent. A life like that did just seem so distant to me, foreign and impossible. I came to stop thinking about her altogether, eventually.

To this day I am still not sure whether R refused to talk to me for a year or so, and then only deigned to recognize my presence chiefly to mock me to my face because I had been so entirely out of touch as to turn my clocks back instead of forward, thus waking up her entire household at six forty-five in the morning, rather than ringing at the decent-ish hour of eight forty-five, or because I had so little presence of mind to not only attempt to engage her poor mother in conversation at that ungodly hour, but instead of hanging up without a word, I'd actually provided my name, first and last, when she asked, "Who the hell is this?" Stupid me.

43.   *Drinking*

Every night when my father got home from work, he did the same thing.

After taking off his jacket and tie he went to the cupboard beneath the kitchen counter, next to the stove, and from it withdrew a bottle.

A bottle of White Horse or J&B or Johnny Walker, or Dewars, occasionally Chivas. Or Seagram's Seven, or Canadian Club.

From the cupboard above he took down a shot glass. Ceremoniously he would pour himself a shot. He seated himself at his place at the head of the kitchen table and then he downed it.

Not all at once, but it never took him more than a few sips.

He would smack his lips with a not-unsaucy appreciation, make one of his three or four jokes about taking his medicine, lay the glass in the sink and put the bottle away, out of sight. He would have one drink and one drink only. Occasionally he made a real joke of it and poured the booze into his grapefruit. Growing up I don't think we sat down to a dinner that didn't start with grapefruit, or a piece of melon, honeydew or cantaloupe, and his shot of whisky.

No one in the house seemed to give it a second thought. This was entirely normal. It was just what was done, what Dad did. What all dads did, for all I knew. It seemed a fitting and proper way to end one part of a day and commence another. As I grew older, I heard the mutterings about one or two fathers in the neighborhood. That they drank, that they stopped off at that bar near the station every night on their way home from the train. Those men had problems. My dad was nothing like them.

Behind the left-hand door in the credenza in the dining room there sat a dusty and lonely collection of Manischewitz. Bottles of Concord Grape that survived miraculously from Passover to Passover, none of them ever quite emptying. Sad fifths of <u>Kahlua</u>. Dark sticky cognacs. Presentation bottles of bourbon opened once, upon arrival. No one drank in our house, except my father, one drink a night, and only after he had put in a long day of toil in the city. It was not until I was much older that it occurred to me how singular was this habit.

Once I mentioned it to my mother, well after my father had retired and they had moved to Florida. I was surprised to hear her speak of this in the same way that I had come to think of it. It was a terrible thing to have to live a such life, she said. Day in and day out, for twenty, thirty years, to have no other way to make a living than one which drove you to have to have a drink every night. To me too, it seemed to sum up everything that was wrong with that way of life. I was resolved never to live that way, to paint myself into that corner.

In fact, for some time I managed to convince myself that I'd cobbled up a life for myself and my family that avoided at least some of the fears and drudgeries my father willingly submitted to on our behalf. Then, the time came when I couldn't make that argument to myself anymore. That's another story. But, when it comes my father, it does occur to me with increasing frequency that a quick shot, it wouldn't even have to be a cocktail, just a little neat one, maybe sour mash instead of scotch, right at the end of the day, just after walking through the door, might not be such a bad idea after all. I think sometimes that he was onto something.

44. No License

My parents were away again, Europe or Japan or Israel. It was my junior year and I had a learner's permit. In passing, as they left for the airport, my mother said to me, "And be sure you don't drive the car."

I'm not sure the thought had ever occurred to me before that moment.

A learner's permit meant that I wasn't allowed on the road, unless I was with an adult, someone who held we called a senior license. In fact, as far as any of us were concerned, that pretty much summed up the definition of adulthood: possessing a senior license.

They were gone for two weeks and for the first week the car, our 1966 Pontiac Le Mans sat quietly in the garage. Every few days I would turn it over and let it run for a few minutes there, making sure the battery didn't go flat.

Then one day after school I looked in the refrigerator and realized that I was out of milk. There was a little convenience store at the bottom of the hill. I could have walked, I usually did. But that afternoon something clicked. I would be traveling on Healy Avenue, our own quiet little street, nearly all the way there and back. I'd only be on Central Avenue for a hundred feet or so. It seemed almost entirely without risk. I got the keys. I had never driven the car by myself before. At first, I felt not drunk, but somehow altogether much too alive to the moment. Was a cop car lurking on Townsend just out of sight? Would any neighbors notice? How could they not? Then the car reassured me with its familiar responses. It sped up, it slowed down, it leaned in the turn, and I relaxed. It was a piece of cake.

Over the next few days, I grew bolder. Soon I was driving to school. No one seemed to notice. I would park, go to home room, proceed through my day and then drive home. No one said anything, no one noticed, no one cared. I still had nothing to do when I got home, aside from reading. Having wheels did not change my life.

A few nights later my parents came home. The airport limousine brought them to the front door. They dropped their suitcases at the bottom of the stairs, they kissed me. My mother checked the mail, asked me who called. My father disappeared into the garage. A moment later he returned with a scrap of paper in his hand, a wrathful expression on his face.

"Why are there a hundred more miles on the odometer than when we left?"

What? A hundred miles? Me? How could that be? Was he bluffing? It was years before it even occurred to me that the scrap of paper might have had nothing at all written on it. To this day I'm not sure. He sat me down in the kitchen and proceeded to interrogate me, bringing me to the verge of tears. While I was fully aware that he was using the same techniques that he employed on shoplifters and light-fingered clerks, by the time he was finished with me, I had confessed to a vastly inflated number of sins, many more trips to the Chinese restaurant and to school and back, than I had in fact committed.

My mother had long since sat herself in her accustomed chair. Her hand over her mouth, her eyes fixed on me. They had both heard enough. Right there, on the spot, they meted out my punishment. They did not ground me. That wouldn't have meant anything. I never went anywhere anyway. I didn't go out at night or on the weekends. Where was I going to go? I sat home and read. They decided that I would not be allowed to get my license until I was seventeen. No driving on my own until I was seventeen, and then I would have to pay for my own insurance.

So that summer I got my first job, as a stock boy in the boys department at Alexander's in White Plains. And every day that summer I rode that foul, smoky bus up Central Avenue to White Plains, past the County Center and past the train station, up Main Street, past that pizza place and past Macy's and the RKO Keith. Every day, sweating in the department store's dark, airless stockroom, choking on the fumes rising from thousands of pairs of boys' Wrangler blue jeans, from the starch or the permanent press, whatever it was. It stank like an oil refinery. Wrestling the clothes racks into the freight elevator, through the dim, dirty, streaked back halls out to the selling floor. Trying to keep the piled-up trousers and T shirts and sweaters from sliding to the floor. I was in hell now. That's what I told myself. I had been banished to the dark place.

Sweating, cursing, cursing my fate all the way from July through August and into September. I did spend some of that time reflecting on what might have been. I could have been cruising down those leafy summer streets as the sun slowly slanted.

45. Northwards

Central Avenue as a continuum, a continuation, a kind of extension of, say, the Grand Concourse.

The Grand Concourse itself, in a way, maybe, an extension of Park Avenue.

Central Avenue's real name: Central Park Avenue.

Park Avenue to Central Park Avenue. The spine upon which it is all hung.

My grandparents sailed into the New York harbor and settled in the Lower East Side. That was closest. Around the time the Lexington Avenue line was laid north of Grand Central, they headed uptown, to Harlem. Due north. That's where my father lived when he was a little boy, my mother too, before they met.

When they were a bit older, both families ended up in the Bronx, the South Bronx, not far from where the Bronx River Parkway starts. That's where they finished growing up and courted. There they married and started their family.

Then came Westchester, Hartsdale. Straight north, not far from the Bronx River Parkway, just a couple of miles from the New York Central's Harlem Line, just off Central Avenue.

Now, it's the third generation. We've kept going. We're up in New England now. I write this not far from where the old Harlem Line ends. It was not until I moved up here that I deduced that the Harlem Line wasn't named for Harlem, as I always thought. It must have been named for the Harlem Valley. That's the end of the line on that line. Nor are we far from the Taconic, the Taconic State Parkway, in its own way a kind of continuation of the Bronx River Parkway. And the Taconic, it turns out, is named for the Taconics, a little range of hills, up here they call them mountains. I look up at them every morning as I drive to the post office.

Park Avenue to Central Park to the New York Central to Grand Central to the Grand Concourse.

North, always north. Is it some sort of class thing or is it in the blood? Will we be visiting our grandchildren in Labrador or Newfoundland in twenty or thirty years?

46.   The Harlem Line

Every day my father would take the train down to Grand Central. Every morning with his Times, his briefcase, dutifully fishing out his monthly ticket as the conductor swayed past, for years, for a good twenty years, until the day he retired. And every morning, if he sat in the righthand row of seats, as the train picked up speed as it left the 125th Street Station, not long before diving down beneath Park Avenue at 96th Street, if he looked out the window he would see, not what I would see, just a row of tenements back in the 1960s, with grimy, broken windows, some abandoned, perhaps he would notice all that, perhaps not. But he would also see the window of the bedroom where he grew up. For there, looking out onto the New York Central tracks was the apartment he lived in, with his brother and his mother and father, and an occasional boarder, as a little boy in Harlem.

I never probed too much. Occasionally I asked him what came to mind when he looked out that train window. He would admit the reminiscence, expand upon it a bit, stories about his bachelor uncle who lived with them awhile, describing some of the mischief the boys got into in the outdoor market nearby. He always mentioned the Marx Brothers, who had grown up a few blocks away. They were a few years older and had belonged to a different gang.

One of his earliest memories, he told me: going with his father to Madison Square to see the parading troops returning from World War I. He was nine then.

I wonder what he thought now. In his fifties, his sixties, a businessman, an executive with a big company, the house in Westchester, traveling the world on business. Every morning, looking up from the financial pages and seeing the grimy window of the humble bedroom where he grew up. Did that past seem unreal to him, I wondered, or perhaps was it this present? But maybe that was just me, I thought, and the kind of questions I would ask.

47.   Our Correspondent in Upper Volta

It was huge and brutal and fast. I don't think they ever fully understood what they were putting into my hands. Were they trying to make it up to me for keeping me from driving while I was being punished?

A big chrome and vinyl bucket seat, like some menacing barber chair, a massive Hurst shifter on the floor just asking to be jammed up and down and, sitting on top of the flathead 409 V8, a yawningly vast Weber carburetor. It said 'Weber' right on it in raised letters. I was driving a car with Webers, me. Webers were serious. Ferraris had Webers. This was great. I only had the nerve to floor the car once or twice in all the time I drove it. Floor it, that is, enough to open up more than one or two of the Weber's four barrels.

I was almost a senior when my parents bought me a car. Barbara and Stewart, the other two kids from Hartsdale, and I all ended up getting cars so our mothers wouldn't have to drive us to school and back every day. What was not typical was the car my parents bought me. It was a 1964 Chevrolet Impala SS coupe, with a rakish sham convertible roof, its angles described with slight ridges picked out of the sheet metal, gesturing at the ribs of the hypothetical ragtop roof. And best of all, it was black.

My parents had another reason for buying me a car. Now my mother didn't have to drive my father to the train station. My father took that 7:41 every morning, six mornings a week. In fact, she didn't have to make us breakfast anymore. She didn't even get out of bed. My father made us breakfast. One of my mother's flowered aprons tied about his waist, humming, always humming, singing some little tune, some unidentifiable snatch of ditty he'd made up. At the time it drove me crazy. It was as if he couldn't stand the silence. He had to fill it up with music, with happy cheery undertones. How often I wished my mother was there just so they would talk to each other instead.

Then we would be in the car. Down Central Avenue, past Tung Sing and Carvel, the world's first Carvel, past Shoe King Sam's and down to Four Corners. Then east on Hartsdale Avenue down to the train station.

The mock Elizabethan, half-timbered little station with its huge round radiator in the waiting room and the high barred ticket windows, back then still open for business, at least occasionally. And a newsstand on the platform, not yet replaced by the soiled row of battered, chained up newspaper boxes.

My father would get out of the car, go over to the newsstand and buy two New York Times, give me one and say goodbye. He didn't try to kiss me anymore.

The problem was that I was always early.

If I dropped my father off on time and headed straight for school I'd arrive before eight o'clock. No one got there that early, not even the kids who had nothing else to do, not even the earliest bus, not even the teachers, much less any member of the crowd I fancied I belonged to. At first, I would park in one of the school's lots near my homeroom and sit there, but that was no good. Everyone coming in could see I had been there before them. I came up with another solution. I would park next to the green barn where the Brass Tac dances were held, behind the synagogue. No one would see me there. I kept the motor running, so I could listen to the radio. I sat there and read the New York Times.

I would read the paper for half an hour, at least half an hour, every day, just so I wouldn't appear unfashionably early at school. The fact is, in actuality, as opposed to in the realm of my anxieties, no one really cared. People were now a little more grown up. They just left you alone.

For at least half an hour, I made myself read. The international news, the national news, the metro news. The editorials, the sports, the book review, the theater review. That is when I acquired a taste for obituaries, for the advertising column and the patent column, the real estate news, the daily piece on the Treasury markets.

I was already a habitual reader, addicted, hiding from so much of the world, hiding behind books, behind the printed page. That course was set already. In that parking lot, sitting behind the wheel of that idling, wildly inappropriate muscle car, I pushed my loneliness, or rather, my fear of exclusion, of outsider-dom, the kind only a half-outsider knows, pushed it, coldly disciplined it, forced it like some winter bulb, trained it like some ruthlessly pruned shrub married to an espalier, into a habit that has persisted, I have to say, for the rest of my days. I cannot face the morning without the New York Times. It has been decades since I tried. It's not necessarily anything to be proud of. I don't think it is such a great habit, not especially cultured or worldly. Being able to rattle off the former name of the Democratic Republic of Burkino Faso is not all that it is cracked up to be.

48. *All Get Out*

The aimless circling. To go, to get out, to get away. Away from the four walls. But never going anywhere, circling. The idea that there is a place to go, to be able to say to yourself, now I have a place to go, I'll go there. I no longer have nothing to do, I have something to fill up this terrifying, stultifying day.

I'll go for a ride, I'll go for a walk, I'll get in the car and drive. I'll go *there*, yes, that'll be nice. I'll go down to the backyard and look for that tennis ball. I'll go up the hill and see if that German Shepherd is home.

I'll ride my bike down the Pipeline to Scarsdale village and check out the little ponds and the paths by the edge of the parkway. I'll take the bus up to White Plains and go to the bookstore. I'll go to the Windsor Shop and look at the shirts.

And years later... I'll walk down to Old Town in Schenectady and get a slice of pizza. And then, a year later, I'll walk up to North Bennington and have a drink at the Villager. And then a few years later, I'll take a walk up to Union Square, maybe over to Park Avenue South. It's Sunday and I have nothing better to do and that'll be a nice walk.

And so, I would go, get out, go anywhere just to get away from those four walls. But that's not really true. Not just anywhere. Each time it was a fine, little, curdled destination. This will be nice, this sounds good. But it never was. It was cold and alone and boring. A way of doing nothing without standing still.

Little lost places.

A tiny triangular cul de sac, no more than six feet in any direction, freshly paved, virtually invisible, set behind a row of stores near the train station in Hartsdale. A new store had been put up, not quite plumb in line with the end of the older row it was joined to. The facades were melded, but in the rear there now was a little space between the old and the new, just a few feet wide, almost invisible, neatly and freshly paved. Now, decades later, riding that train up to the country, I can almost see it as the train pulls out.

Another one: an old forgotten walking path next to the stream that was once the Bronx River. When the landscaped procession of parkway and park and stream and pond was laid out in the Twenties this walking path was no doubt a well-promoted amenity. Most likely it extended the full length of the parkway from the Bronx to the Croton Reservoir. By the time I came along, it had disappeared in long stretches, lost to improvements in the roadway, mud slides, debris scattered from the generations of careless track workers on the New York Central Line, a few yards away. But in bits and snatches, for twenty or thirty yards at a time, it abided. A wonderfully thoughtful, curving, civilized promenade. Part and parcel of the humming road, only a few feet away, but completely apart. Entwined with the forest, the stream and the occasional pond. Certainly, all equally artificed. This sad old path, the worse for wear, all the more piquant for its decrepitude.

Years later, in the Seventies, now in New York, walking the streets, weekends wandering the empty commercial avenues. The grimy side streets of the Twenties and the Thirties, the loft buildings and the dispirited travelers' hotels. The lost old warehouses below Canal. The inscrutable, twisting old Dutch byways east of Maiden Lane. The generations of grime. The haphazard, thoughtless signage.

And then, every once in a while —

…Between the old Gimbels and Willoughby's, my father's old store on 32nd Street. And, also, between two shiny insurance towers on Madison Square. And there, between two classroom buildings at Hunter, just off Lexington. And between two old National Biscuit Company buildings, which eventually became Chelsea Market, high above Sixteenth Street. Among and between the neat, trim, cream and green Jehovah's Witness buildings in Brooklyn Heights, too. And, most improbably, hidden above an alley behind an old American Express office on Hudson Street, years before it became a temporarily famous nightclub, a tiny, shuttered thing, connecting a modest Greek Revival office building to its stables…

I would look up and there would be an amazing sight: bridges in the air.

Tunnels of steel burrowing in the air between streets, linking buildings. They were minute, miraculous rebuttals to the city. Connections between contradictions, between two places that never were meant to be joined. And there they were, some seemed abandoned, some downright hazardous, but they remained, aerie despites to the darkness below. And best, or worst of all, they seemed entirely ignored. No one ever talked or wrote about them. They were invisible.

So, I began to search them out. Exploring new neighborhoods, Inwood, Rockefeller University, always hunting for new ones. I took pictures of them. The pictures ended up in collages and the collages ended up in my first book. But eventually, those walks too grew empty. The air bridges did not change, they did not care. The walks themselves became familiar aimless circles. Up around and back, back to another four walls. No money and nothing to do, no one to do it with, nothing, until another day, another week of work would start, with its different sort of emptiness.

49. The End of the West in Front of the West End

1968. The promising, simple unaffected spring air. Falling in with two or three other boys from White Plains, crossing the Columbia campus, the odd, instantly recognizable institutional decay, the sagging woodwork in the dowdy lecture halls. Something tantalizingly free and licentious in the very air.

For everyone on the staff of our school newspaper, the undisputed highlight of the year was the Columbia Journalism School conference. For a week every spring, Morningside Heights was overrun by hordes of high school kids. Editors and assistant editors and assistant publishers and executive publishers from high schools around the country. There were competitions, and announcements for competitions which all of us had entered months ago, and there were seminars and talks on a host of topics of interest to budding journalists. Every morning for a week we'd board a chartered bus for the ride down to the city. Was it different that year? Surely it was.

There was indeed something in the air. Earlier that year, along with a couple of other kids, I approached one of our history teachers, a young woman. We asked if she'd be interested in serving as the faculty advisor for a SDS chapter at our high school. She was amenable, I remember that, but nothing came of it.

I don't remember a thing about a single seminar at that conference at Columbia. I don't think I sat all the way through even one. Even their titles were unutterably boring. I didn't particularly have any interest in the school paper, or writing for newspapers in general. It was a social thing. Everyone I knew was on the school paper, so I was too.

That afternoon in front of Low Library we came across some men. They weren't really men. They were freshmen.

But to me, with their hair, longer than anyone I knew, their sprouting beards and their impossibly cool eyewear, one was sporting a pair of mountaineering sunglasses, they seemed impossibly exotic and sophisticated. One of them, Mr. Sunglasses, was a friend of the older brother of a member of our group. They stopped and deigned to chat with us, joking easily about the riots that had shook the campus, the city, the entire country, not many weeks earlier. They were so neat, nonchalant, mocking us, mocking themselves.

"This is what cops do," one said to us, "They have their job, and we have ours. Their job is to split heads, our job is to take off our hats," or maybe it was, "Topple the state." I can't quite recall. In their easy banter I sensed, bound up with the words, in the pauses, carried along in the grammar, the most erudite political analysis I'd ever come across.

That was the problem. All the leaflets and other revolutionary ephemera that was scattered and plastered everywhere, and those apparently bona fide radicals who we caught sight of, putting up posters, mouthing off at some befuddled campus cop, they — SDS kids, maybe. Maybe not. Who knew? — each and all, carried with them the weight of unshakable authenticity, an indisputable certitude, unassailable, not particularly for the ease with which the cant ran off their tongues, much less any compelling aspect of their argument. It was simply because they were clearly and obviously so much more with-it than anyone or any other group or idea that tried to compete with them.

They had the momentum. It was their historical moment, regardless of the veracity of their claims or the acuity of their critique. If you fancied yourself a sentient being, these people were where it was at. Some of them in this group chatting with us actually claimed to know Mark Rudd, and the rest of them spoke offhandedly, banteringly, disparagingly of him. And they all dressed like him.

They were cool and we wanted to be just like them.

That is why, towards the end of the week, we ventured off campus, crossing Broadway around 114th Street. We were headed to some bookstore on that block. Our days on campus had made it clear to us that carrying the right books, Marcuse for example, or Fanon, was very important. As we crossed over the median in the middle of the block, against the light, a speeding cabby heading downtown, probably running red lights himself, suddenly veered from the righthand lane and made directly for us, accelerating from a fairly illegal clip up to what had to be close to sixty or more, the driver all the while hanging out of the window, screaming incomprehensible imprecations at us and shaking his fist.

We stood there in a stunned, frozen clump. At the last minute he veered away. Then he was gone.

Breathless, we looked upon each other, amazed. Then we scampered the rest of the way over to the west side of Broadway. Leaping, crowing, springing past the West End. Alive, spared. Fancying ourselves bold and brave and defiant, we bounced among the indifferent housewives lugging home their shopping in the chill late afternoon.

He'd taken us for lousy, lazy, commie college kids.

That seemed so aspirationally apt. That was precisely what we were aching to be.

And in those dark pre-revolutionary days, roiling clouds of repression on the horizon heralding the cataclysmic storm that was surely only months away, it seemed quite natural that this misguided member of the petit bourgeoisie, for we were certain he must have been an owner/driver, would take it upon himself to commit such a rash act of provocation.

We felt elevated, exalted, downright ennobled.

50.   *Decisionless and Right*

What was more attractive about Ramparts, the magazine's politics or the graphics? It was easily as good-looking as Esquire in its day. And so witty, wise, so cynical.

I often wondered though, where did they get those story ideas? Who decided? Without any warning, with no stories buried in the middle to prepare the way, out of the blue, there would be a lead story on, say, the environment. On the cover a tombstone planted in a barren field, marking the life and death of the planet. Earth was to have died somewhere in the Eighties, from corporate greed of course. Then, right after the Six Day War, another cover story. The Israelis were the new Bull Connors and Lester Maddoxes and the George Wallaces? Wait, how come we never read anything like that in the Times?

But, somehow, over time, Ramparts came to seem too palatable. The graphics, the color, the clever banners and catchy covers. I started reading the National Guardian instead. Had I picked up an issue at Columbia that spring? Perhaps I saw an ad in the Voice. The National Guardian was different. There were no gestures towards the marketplace, no tongue-in-cheek satires. There were no vestiges of bohemian Village life. No Feiffer cartoons, no Shel Silverstein or Jill Johnston or Jonas Mekas. The art direction was nonexistent. The only ads seemed to be for the Monthly Review.

Shortly after I began subscribing to The National Guardian there was a split in SDS. On the one hand there were the Weathermen, they hadn't yet decided that 'men' was unacceptable. On the other, there was Progressive Labor. The Guardian, as I recall, tried to hew a relatively balanced course between them, for a while. The stern, stiff Progressive Labor folks went around with little Stalin pins stuck in their lapels, didn't they? They did dress well, in a way: sturdy work clothes, construction boots, plaid shirts and two-tone science major glasses, twenty years before they were cool. The Weather people, on the other hand, were obviously clued in on what was going on now. They were into rock and roll. They were into drugs too, weren't they?

And then, there was that last SDS national conference, and the Days of Rage in Chicago. After that the Weather people went underground. And then, less than a year after I started college, they blew themselves up in the townhouse in Greenwich Village.

What I found most compelling, or perhaps most frightening about the Guardian, for the year or two that I subscribed to it in high school, was how clearly it communicated the sensibility of the people who put it out. They had no desire whatsoever to make it look good. They just didn't care. The grainy, posed photos reprinted from the North Korean press agency were not just hokey, not just stodgy, not just tricked up and staged, they betokened an aesthetic that I had never come across before, breathtaking in its assurance. It simply did not care what it looked like. All that posing, primping and pretense that seemed everywhere all around, that was part and parcel of our world, even in Ramparts, all of that had to be smashed. And when those sorts of people decreed 'smashed,' there was no metaphor involved.

And for a while that absolute, sweeping lack of compromise — what did it matter if we all had to end up wearing the same blue jackets buttoned to the neck? What the hell, I look good in blue — all that had something powerfully attractive about it. Decision-less and right.

51. The Writing Life

It was without a doubt one of the worst poems ever to be set in type in the English language. It was called 'Death Is Left,' and about all that could be said for it was that after reading it you were very likely so depressed that you were only too happy to agree. There was indeed nothing left but to get on with it.

It didn't help, of course, that every line ended with the same refrain: "Death is left." As in, "When you are tired of all and sundry, death is left." Or "When you think it cannot get any worse, death is left." It went along like that for quite a few stanzas. I haven't set eyes on that national high school anthology for years, thankfully. There very well may have been something along the lines of, "If you find at the end of the afternoon that you are out of ginger ale, death is left."

I was made senior editor of the high school literary magazine. All that meant: I was the editor for the senior class. It meant nothing. The only reason I got that spot was because the faculty advisor had taught me in a creative writing class the year before. And, no one else wanted the job.

What strikes me now is not how cheaply my poem's despondency was tricked out, nor the effrontery I displayed in offering it up exposing any hapless reader who might innocently come across it to such acute discomfort and embarrassment. What is striking is how my parents forbore from using 'Death Is Left' as all the excuse they needed to bundle me off to the nearest sanitarium. Instead, they proudly displayed it to family and friends. Perhaps they were finding excuses to show off few and far between.

"Look, Michael has gotten something published."

I don't recall any odd looks from those other adults as they duly read the proffered page. Just cheerful encouragement. I wonder, did my parents and aunts and uncles ever look back and remember that wretched scribble and ponder what would have happened, if only they had raised a ruckus then. This was several years before I went about telling anyone who asked, and many who didn't, that I intended to become a poet. All the squandered years and the wasted talent, for that is doubtless how they see it, that could have been avoided. If only.

52. On the Way

The guidance counselor had a list for me: Syracuse, Temple, places like that. I didn't say a thing. I could feel my face turn red. Was that my fate? Was this what I had to look forward to? He must have seen my distress. He asked me if I had any ideas of my own. Now I blushed again, this time with embarrassment.

He was the expert, and he knew better.

"The ultimate decision is up to you, Michael, of course."

And then his work was done. Our fifteen-minute chat about my future was ended and he moved on. Next.

As it happened, I did end up applying to Syracuse and to another of his suggestions, Clark University. And then there was Union College. I knew a kid who had an older brother who went to school there. This kid had a Union College sweatshirt. And while there was certainly nothing unusual about a college sweatshirt being paraded around our high school, there was something very special about that one. It was the Union College seal that adorned it. Unlike most, there was no lions rampant or quartered shields, just a fair line drawing of the goddess Minerva.

I don't remember the interview at all. I have some memory of where it took place only because this was the college I ended up attending for a year and a half. And I owe it all to a sweatshirt.

I also don't remember waking up ill that morning, nor feeling particularly out of sorts during the interview. Perhaps I was disconcerted that my mother had dispatched me there by myself. I had never before driven alone so far from home. For whatever reason, that day, on my way back to Hartsdale from Schenectady, returning from my interview, driving alone in my aging Impala SS, I realized I was coming down with something.

Somewhere near the Harriman exit, I found myself dreadfully, desperately ill; in the grip of a throbbing, all encompassing, jealously embracing fever.

It was a sensation I had cause to grow familiar with in years to come, those first years in New York. Then a full meal meant a grilled cheese sandwich and a bag of chips. An entertaining night out meant meeting a buddy at a Blarney Stone where, if we were feeling rich, we could splurge on two shots of Heaven Hill each. Then, a walk home down Lafayette Street in the snow. Followed not at all that infrequently by a nice dose of flu. But this was the first time. I had never gotten sick like this before.

Before I knew it, I was going eighty-five, ninety, ninety-five. Past Suffern and Spring Valley. Down past Nyack. Sweeping across the approaches to the Tappan Zee. It did occur to me that this was excessively foolish and dangerous. I could easily be letting myself in for all sorts of horrific punishment if I was caught. The bridge's great looming towers rising up before me. The hazy skyscrapers of Manhattan off to the south. To the north, the undifferentiated mass of Ossining and Sing Sing.

And, onto the bridge now, craning my neck I found myself looking around — like I do today, still expecting to see the World Trade Center downriver — but, that time, seeking the long, neat ranks of mothballed submarines and destroyers and Liberty ships left over from WWII that used to be tied up there, just south of the bridge, row after row of them. My mother pointing them out on long ago trip to the Catskills, just her and me, before there was a bridge, on the ferry. And they really did look mothballed, all bundled up in white, lots of white where the guns should have been. They hadn't been there for years, but every time I crossed the bridge I always checked.

Then, I realized I was veering off to the right. I had crossed all the lanes, from the passing to the breakdown. I was only inches from the guard rail. Finally, I slowed that Chevy down. Ninety-five to eighty-five, down to seventy-five, to sixty-five. And sixty-five felt like crawling. Like I could open the door and step out and keep up without breaking into a trot.

Was it the flu or was it something else? Somehow was I almost ready to throw it all away rather than accept less than what I thought I deserved? It could have all stopped right there. My future nearly gone before it had a chance to unfold.

53.   *What Wasn't Vanity?*

There were two closets in my parents' bedroom. One closet was good-sized, capacious. You stood before it and could see at a glance all it held. It was wide but no larger than the closets in the house's other bedrooms. The other closet was different. There you opened the door to a small room. It had its own window, directly above the front door, the driveway stretching out beneath you. The builders intended this closet for, as it used to be said, of the lady of the house, surely. But in our house, this closet belonged to my father.

My father had suits, lots of suits. This grand walk-in held a vast array of haberdashery. My mother would remark from time to time, not all that often but not infrequently, upon the irony, or was it the injustice, of this state of affairs and how chafing were the compromises which flowed from her grudging acceptance of this arrangement. For, indeed, my father, otherwise, and in every other dimension of his life the soul of fiscal probity, discretion, conservatism, nay near-parsimony, so completely had he been formed by the Great Depression, was a man who did own a lot of suits. He had dozens of suits, beautiful suits, each cut and fitted for him by a master tailor down at Barneys. My mother never complained about the cost, at least not in front of us, but she made it clear that, to her mind, it was simply frivolous. Since she was always so well turned out, especially when they were dressed up, I know she was surely not insensible to sumptuary demands, but there was something about my father's attention to his appearance that she could never cotton to. It smacked of something, of preening vanity, of some sort of materialism perhaps.

When I was little, my father took me along with him to Barneys for fittings. By then he must have been going there for his suits for how long? Twenty years? Thirty years? Longer? Had he been going there since Barney Pressman himself paced the floor, chalking hems? By then there was no more esteemed nor fashionable men's wear retailer in New York. The salesman greeted my father with respect, the tailor offered a muted deference. My father stood before him, perched upon the little platform in front of the three-way mirror.

What I recall most clearly is the tailor, small, saturnine, balding, even older than my father, in shirtsleeves and some sort of smock or apron, or perhaps just his own suit. There was his respectful yet familiar tone with my father, they discussed drape and drop and other things unfathomable to me. What was clear to me was how my father, and perhaps the tailor too, following his lead, made no effort whatsoever to hide from me just how misshapen was his poor body.

The deafness I knew about. When we walked together, I always had to stand on his right side, because he was stone deaf on the other. Or, was it his left side? God forgive me, I cannot remember.

But, aside from, in addition to his deafness, he was lame, and his back was curved. One leg was longer than another, all a product of a poverty-stricken, disease-ridden youth. There had been TB, and polio too. A spell, two, at least two, on what was then called Welfare Island, now Roosevelt Island, in the state hospitals. And yet he had survived, married a beauty, the love of his life, raised a family, thrived, and now here he stood, on a tailors' podium at Barneys.

Barneys had, in its own way, over the same span of years, grown and prospered, evolving from a rock-bottom hawker of closeouts and remainders to a luxe ornament of its industry. And this lovely tailor knew my father's body. My father accepted his hand tracing its chalk across it. To how many other depression-era executives was it that fellow's practice and pleasure to provide suiting?

There were the various Barneys house brands, and Hart Schaffner and Marx, and Oxxford and so many others. My father had many, so many, of each, and they were all tailored with such faithful attention to his frame, his slight and bent frame. Of course, to my mother was it not all venal affect, morally specious waste?

So, should any of this have been any surprise when the three of us, Jack Gottlieb's three sons, now in their forties, fifties, sixties, found ourselves there that day, in our parents' Florida condominium, our father's clothes laid out before us. He'd just died.

Almost nothing fit. He had been so small though he towered, this I remember, over his parents. He was a tiny man, stunted by the Depression. And, even if they fit, so much of what he left behind we'd never be caught dead in. Our father, our dapper father, had turned into a white-shoe-and-white-belt Floridian. As we stood there and picked items up, put them down, fingered them and then let them fall back on the bed, it became clear that the dashing executive, that intrepid fellow in elegant worsted, lived on solely in our memory. There was none of that left here. We selected a few pieces: some socks, a belt; one or two polo shirts which were kind of appealing, with an ironic charm that likely would have been incomprehensible to him.

Then I saw them. I stepped over to the now-empty closet where my father's clothes had hung, pulled them all off the rack and laid them across the bed. They were my father's hangers.

We'd never paid a moment's attention to them over the years. Over the years, he'd bought suits, expensive suits, as expensive as he could afford. And over the years, every time he bought a suit, it came with a hanger, naturally. Sometimes a very nice hanger. And, while clearly, those suits, those suits which for years upon years had expressed, denominated, articulated I think, who he thought he was and who he wanted to be, were long gone, he'd had no need for them for decades, no doubt my mother had enforced their expulsion from their home, the hangers, the hangers upon which all of those suits and so many of his values and realities had hung, those hangers remained. For some reason, surely it isn't difficult to understand, he'd held onto them.

We divided them among us. It wasn't a difficult exercise, not for us, at least. For our mother, it was something else. She didn't understand. This was absurd. Why on earth why would we pay all this attention to *this*? This was important? She was affronted. The appeal of these items was absurd, and, as we persisted, she was never less than astute when it came to reading others, or, at least, reading us, as she came to countenance our unalterable focus on these icons, these relics of our dead father, she came to deride our estimation of them in, shockingly, the very same words, the same adjectives and conditions, the same modifiers and terms of art that she'd used so many years ago to slang our father himself. This attention, our appreciation, our father's predilection itself, was banal, trite, trivial, effete, corrupt. And yet, we persevered.

I still have mine, of course. They are weathered, aged. Old-wood now, virtually works of art, antiques, antiquities even. The wood is dried, darkened. One or two have broken, split apart, but I can't see throwing them away. I hold one in my hand now. Now that he's been gone for so many years already, how many things that were his, that he touched, aside from me I suppose, do I have left?

This one bears these words burned into its faded wood:

Perfect Laundries

Launderers & Dry Cleaners

Where could my father have come across this? What kind of cleaning job did he need that could have obliged a launderer to provide a wooden hanger? It beggars the imagination. Beneath those two lines, a phone number of its own, a redoubtable, respectable number: "CH 3900." How long ago was it that telephone numbers in New York City were expressed not as seven-digit numbers, as we recall they were until area codes were introduced, but — along with that two-letter exchange, CH for Chelsea — but not seven, instead: a four-digit number? The 1920s? The 1930s?

And, Chelsea — the Manhattan neighborhood where I sit and write this now, decades, decades and decades, later.

54.   *That Eternal World*

I was driving through Hartsdale. It was the middle of August. In a few weeks I'd leave for college.

Despite my carefully tended cynicism and preternatural bitterness, I was excited. I was going off into the world, I was going out on my own, though not too far. I was busy buying clothes, books. Amazingly enough, I was actually looking forward to something.

For some reason I found myself on Washington Avenue and as I came up to my old elementary school I pulled over and stopped. It was still a school. The condominium conversion was years off. The late afternoon sun was starting to sink, though the day was still very hot. It was as if the dark brick building was sleeping, the tiles on the roof shimmering in the heat, lost in that hibernation schools retreat to every summer. There was the old playground, the leaning merry-go-round, the asphalt crumbling a bit here and there.

A couple of kids were twisting idly in the swings. They were a little on the old side, a bit too big for the seats, dragging their feet in the dust, revolving in a drowsy, slow, bored, spiral. Letting the torsion of the cables or the ropes turn them first this way and then that, a little slower each time. I remembered that lazy sway. I could feel myself turning in the same gyre. I wondered, when had I last been swinging on a swing? Then I realized that these boys, fourteen, fifteen years old, maybe, were living in a different world than me. It looked like they were getting ready to leave theirs, though they were still its denizens.

There is a separate world that children dwell in, I realized then. I lived in it too, once. It occupied the same rooms and lawns and streets as my nearly grown up, going-off-to-college world, but it was distinct, different, apart.

And it never aged. It is still here all around us, you and me. A world that made of rhymes, games, songs, words, curses, blessings, terrors, discoveries. It is not our world, this world I sit in now, writing this. Our world changes, that world does not. And it has almost no substance. It lives their minds.

152

It was there in their minds, those kids on the swings. And now, grown up, likely with their own kids, it lives on still in those children, surely.

It lives in children and in what memory and memories they have. Its scribbled runes, the hopscotch chalk, are washed away daily. Its artifacts, the Mother's Day cards and holiday pottery ending up in attics, or discreetly deposited in the trash. All that is manifest about this world is entirely ephemeral. Yet, despite all that, it endures, unchanging: the same nursery rhymes and taunts chanted every day, year after year. The same invocations to the cracks in the sidewalk. The same divinations of true love as the petals are torn from the dandelion. And all the while the populace of this world shifts, every year, every month. Every day a few more citizens enter and a few more, scornfully, impatiently, depart. Going on to greater things. That's what I saw then. These boys were on the cusp, they were departing.

And not so many years after leaving, we come to forget almost all its terrors and its joys. Even the tales we manage to remember, that we carry about on our persons, like these, they barely limn the outlines.

If we become parents, perhaps we can glimpse it again. But only at a distance, tolerated, like tourists at a tribal rite. But that world lives on, passing from child to child, unaltered, eternal.

55.   This Lost World

Though I pass through Hartsdale often now, on my way back and forth to the country, I hardly ever stop.

But a few years ago, I found myself there. I was returning from a funeral service for an uncle. A sweet gentle man with a full head of white hair. He always had white hair and he always seemed old to me, even when I was small, and he had been younger then than I am now.

He served as a Seabee in World War II. His Navy blanket, soft, ivory, his name tag still stitched in the hem, covered me in the winter when my regular blankets just weren't enough, and then there was time when I had to be taken to the hospital. And when I went off to camp, I stuffed my sneakers and my baseball mitt into his green duffel bag. His name stenciled on the side, faded a little, right above the Seabee's insignia: a cheerily ferocious bee, unshaven, a stogie jauntily jammed in its jaw, armed with a shovel and a machine gun.

This aunt and uncle lived most of their lives in California. She died suddenly, in her seventies. Within a year he followed her. The service was in a chapel at one of those vast, sprawling, endless cemeteries, cities themselves, girdling New York City, this one in Hartsdale. After the service we all repaired to the home of another aunt and uncle, a few miles away.

I drove down the old familiar streets, down Ridge Road, down Hartsdale Avenue to Central Avenue, past Healy Avenue. The streets where I had grown up, riding in the back seat of my parents' car, on my bike, in the school bus, in my friends' cars, behind the wheel of my first car. Some of the suburban landscape, the streets, the houses, the stores, was changed utterly, entirely unrecognizable. Some was altogether unaltered. I rode past a house that had not changed a whit in thirty years. A few yards further on was a brand-new strip mall with the celebratory bunting still hanging over the vacant store fronts, blowing in the light breeze, slightly tattered.

I was thinking about my parents, my aunts and uncles. How immensely different was the world they were born into. How unlike any of this. And so much of that world they grew up in was gone, vanished from this earth, except in their memories. That world of Jewish immigrants, the Lower East Side at the turn of the century. Harlem during the First World War, the Bronx in the Twenties, the Depression, World War II.

Then I looked around me. That is, I saw what I had been looking at while I had been thinking about our parents' world, and what I saw around me was yet another world. This world that was once the universe to me. The miraculously unaltered shoe store where that soldier had stood. A truncated bit of woods at the bottom of our street remaining, where the secret paths once ran. The garden apartments re-stuccoed, now condos, but otherwise the same, where Robert D. and I fought our battles. And along Garth Road, the storefronts were the same, though the stationery store and consignment store were long-gone.

Despite the unchanged, apparently unchanged bits and snatches, I knew that this world was gone too. It is as far from the here-and-now as my parents' world. And as close, I suppose. That is when I decided I wanted my children to know. Maybe it will make things easier for them. Perhaps it will assuage, at least a little, the terrors that may come their way. Though it may wrong for me to assume that growing up will be that hard for them.

I hope they find them comforting, heartening maybe. All those snaps of me when I was little, their age or younger. And there certainly are plenty of pictures for them to see. I'm not smiling in most of them, but I think I can explain that.

56.   The Colorama

Gone now, of course. And no one regrets it. Was it not the most visible and tawdry symbol of everything that had gone wrong with Grand Central? The epitome of all the creeping, commercializing gee-gaws and encrustations that over the years came to befoul the stately interior. The biggest disfigurement of them all. And with its destruction, its banishment, a wonderful shower of morning sunlight now flooded into the noble space. Now, an Apple store, of course — what else would be there? — occupies the eastern balcony of the concourse at Grand Central.

A few at least mourned the passing of the old arrival and destination boards. No one spoke up for the Colorama.

A few years ago, I was reading the New York Times one morning. I came to the obituary page.

"I read the obituaries first," my father used to say, "If I'm not in them I know I can get dressed and go to work."

That morning there was an obituary for a photographer. I wish I'd clipped it out. I wish I could remember his name because, I have to admit, over the years, I've never been able to find that obit again, though I've tried pretty hard.

He had been an employee of the Eastman Kodak company, a staff photographer, for almost his entire life.

The article described his career in some detail. As I read it, I felt a shock of recognition. Somehow, I always knew there had been someone, some one person, who had been responsible, and it was he.

The obituary described his promotional work for Kodak, the brochures, the books, the giveaways, the literature and the guides he had illustrated. The little paper slips, folded into long sixteenths that used to be included in every yellow box. The photographs exemplifying good technique, as well as bad technique, were all his. And, of course, the beautiful, huge, iconic images of the Colorama. That world ideal, vanished, if ever it was here. They were his too. So many of them.

And at the end of the article, just before listing his survivors, the reporter casually mentioned the fact that this photographer had lived almost all his adult life in a suburb of New York City, in Hartsdale, New York.

The newspaper fell to the floor. Now it all made sense.

This is why that world up there seemed to be just like mine.

That is why our world, the world I grew up in, had to be so typical.

It was because it *was* our world, my world, my Hartsdale, that he had chosen to make the Kodak world, to make typical, to present to the world as *us*.

And, indeed, it was us.

THE EMPIRE CITY

(1970s - 1980s)

1.   A Democratic People's Republic

I look down at the copy of *Howl* I hold in my hand and recall the spring
I bought it.

I was finishing my freshman year at Union College, the one full year
I spent there before decamping to Bennington. And one thing I knew
was that I didn't want to get drafted. Nixon was about to get rid of the
student deferment, or maybe he'd already done just that. I remember the
night earlier that year, the night of the first draft lottery, when they read
off the numbers and the birthdays. The first day of the year they picked,
picked at random, was number one. The second day, whatever month
and day it was, was number two. I would definitely have been called up
if I hadn't still been in school. If you had a student deferment, your 2-S,
that's what it was called, was good until graduation. My number, rather
the number for my birthday, June 29th, turned out to be in the low 100s,
a hundred-twenty-something, a hundred-thirty-something.

I was a dead man, without my deferment. I would have been snatched up
in a second by the Army if I hadn't been in school. They were taking guys
up into the one-fifties, or maybe two-hundred. I remember walking the
campus that night. Radios spilled it all out from open windows. General
Hershey that bastard, or whoever it, was reading out the numbers and
the birthdays. With every birthday, cries, of relief and terror and despond,
coursed from the dormitories. Young men hearing their fate.

I didn't want to go but I wasn't sure what to do. One weekend in New
York I went down to the War Resisters League on Lafayette, desultorily
studied their literature and listened to some overweight guy with a
straggly beard lay out my options. I was already intimately familiar with
every single one. And I had done my share of marching, or so I thought,
marches in New York, a few others. Then down to Washington for a
Mobilization, where I was thrilled to be able to throw a rock or two in
the general direction of the DC police and get tear gassed in Dupont
Circle at a ragtag, underpopulated SDS demo.

And, the following spring, we occupied the ROTC building on the Union
campus, a perfectly charming old Greek Revival house we proceeded to

treat rather shabbily. That earned us, all of us there at Union, the greatest sobriquet of all. For, the next day, during a press conference, Nixon was asked what he thought of the various student malefactors around the country, referencing us by example, since we'd also just happened to have burned him in effigy the previous evening — it did seem like the least we could do at the time — along with the demonstrators at Kent State, where there hadn't yet been any shooting. In response Nixon famously called us all "bums." That was beautiful, that was wondrous, but it helped me not at all.

So, late that term I found myself meeting with the wan college chaplain discussing the various options I might explore if I wished to be classified as a conscientious objector, none of them particularly promising. At the time it seemed altogether unlikely that a draft board would accept anyone's heartfelt asseverations of committed non-violence unless one was the product of four generations of the Society of Friends.

Nevertheless, I was resolved to do what I could. Something, anything. Maybe I could build a case, somehow, to convince a board in three or four years that I really could be a true and decent C.O. The good parson told me about a program sponsored by the American Friends Service Committee, an old and honorable Quaker group, we would call it an NGO nowadays, that had, in its day, supplied the ambulances that Hemingway and Stein had driven during World War I.

These days, among its other activities it participated in a so-called international student work camp program. They sponsored and sent American college students overseas for a few weeks each summer. The students lent a hand with a variety of public service projects in Africa or Asia or Latin America or Europe. The work consisted of Peace Corps-esque well-digging, education programs and the like. Of course, sponsorship didn't extend to paying the way. So, the students in question, or more often, the student-in-question's parents, were obliged to cough up a few thousand dollars. The brochure described adventure and altruism-driven satisfaction on five, or perhaps it was four, continents. Among those continents, Europe looked the most interesting to me. After all, if I was going to be doing good, I might as well be doing it somewhere where I might have a good time.

It ended up being a glorious summer. I hitchhiked across Europe, through France and Britain, hung out in Paris a couple of times, haunted London, ate amazing food and drank wonderful wine in France; and terrific beer and ale in Czechoslovakia and England. I met lots of fascinating and exotic Swiss and Danes and Frenchmen and hashish-dealing-Belgians, along with terrifyingly professional, middle-aged East German 'students,' unctuous British steam ship stewards, and sharp toed skin heads and softhearted Parisian flics. Best of all, I was fortunate enough, as the saying goes, to encounter all manner of wonderful English and French and Finnish and Swedish and Czech young women — and I owed it all to the Vietnam War and the Selective Sevice System and the American Friends Service Committee.

It was customary to participate in two camps each summer, and I ended up attending one in France and another in Czechoslovakia. I had a terrific time at both, met lots people, got a nicely in-depth picture of each country and engaged in some honest, if pointless, physical labor. The camp in France was located in the Bas Pyrenees and the twenty-odd of us were tasked with extending, by hand, a water line from the national highway that ran along the nearby ridge, down to a village which had no running water at all. In three weeks of digging, we managed to extend the line a few dozen yards, a distance that a back hoe could have dug up in a matter of an hour or two. But that wasn't the point. The point was that we had all gathered there from the four corners of the globe to help those folks. I remember we also helped them out with their haying. They seemed more appreciative for that assistance. After each day of stacking bales up into their hay ricks they'd stuff us full of sausage and red wine. They'd clearly long ago figured out how to live well enough without running water.

In Czechoslovakia the situation was different. The national organizing committee, the country-level entity that was the local equivalent of the AFSC, an innocuously dubbed peace and friendship committee, a product of the Dubcek-era — we were given to understand, now, two summers after the Red Army had rolled into the country, stifled the so-called Prague Spring, and reinstalled the local Stalinists — was itself going to be eliminated. This was the last summer this program would be run. I guess I was surprised that it hadn't been shut down earlier. While one might have assumed that the anti-war, pacifist leanings of the various organizations that had sent us there should have seemed useful to the new Brezhnevite rulers of the country, no doubt the headache of having to deal with all these demanding, free-thinking western college kids, and the damage they could do, with their rock and roll music, their blue jeans and so on, had clearly been deemed more trouble than it was worth.

At our camp we were building, or extending rather, a stout wooden stockade fence around the perimeter of the grounds of a hospital for children with severe learning disabilities. It was housed in a former aristocratic hunting lodge in a wood about sixty miles from Prague. We slept in an empty house in an oddly deserted agricultural collective, all bare whitewashed walls and empty lanes, about two miles away. We walked to the hospital along a country road, across the open fields, back and forth every day.

The girls slept in one room, the boys in another. We shared the single bathroom. There was a rude tavern in the ground floor of another home in the collective, where after work we would buy beer and cigarettes, Partizankas they were called, named after the anti-Nazi guerillas, from a stolid barkeep. Otherwise, we had no contact with any Czechs, except for the kids in the hospital, and the nuns who watched over them, with the exception of the four Czech students who led the camp. They were two medical students. And then there were their two girlfriends. It didn't occur to me for some time to wonder what kind of risks they might be taking by associating themselves with this sort of enterprise. They were smart and sweet and seemed tough and eloquent and, it also seemed to me then, entirely alive to the grimness of their situation, and what they, individually and collectively, had for a moment possessed: that heady freedom and sense of possibility. But there, in their country, it was expressed, denominated, so qualitatively differently. There, behind the Iron Curtain in 1968, the change that had been tantalizingly close, during the so-called Prague Spring that was now just a memory, had no theoretical utopian or millenarian dimension to it, at least compared to the slogans that had been shouted in the streets of Paris. It represented a specific alteration in governance. It was a real revolution. But they knew that was all over and gone. And what they had in store for themselves was a long, cold winter.

We talked long into the night and we shared the poetry I'd brought with me. Although, I am ashamed to say, it didn't occur to me to leave any of those City Lights editions with them, like this copy of *Howl*. When the camp was over, we vowed to stay in touch, and exchanged addresses. In fact, for a couple of years we did write to each other; but I grew increasingly concerned that I would be compromising them by maintaining a correspondence. I gradually slowed and then stopped writing back. Although, again, it didn't occur to me that they could have cut it off at any time if they felt it dangerous. And so, what did I do? Cut them off from one last avenue to the West? Or am I overestimating my impact on their lives?

In any event, there was a night, back in our rooms, when I fell into conversation with one of the young Czechs and the talk ventured, as it did surprisingly rarely, into the realm of politics. I'm not sure how we got onto the topic, though it shouldn't have been hard, since it was a topic on our minds all the time. The war. For some reason I ended up telling him where I stood. Maybe I was asked; perhaps for some reason I felt obliged to unburden myself. And it all came out: how the South Vietnamese were the puppets of American imperialism, how the US was committing war crimes upon a poor defenseless country, how the NLF and the North Vietnamese were the authentic embodiment of the eternal, unquenchable spirit of the Vietnamese people and how, to support their heroic struggle against Yankee hegemony, all right-thinking people should do whatever they could to hasten the NLF's, or maybe by then it was the PRG's, victory. I trotted it all out and maybe I even believed it.

"You, my friend, you are very smart and you are very nice, but you simply don't know what you are talking about," is what my Czech friend said, in a not unkindly tone.

"We, and all of our friends, and everyone we know, want you Americans to win that war. You have to win the war. You must. You don't know what these people are like. We do." And that is all he said. And that, really, was the end of the conversation. For some reason I didn't have the presence of mind to offer up the proper line, that is, to argue that the Soviet and the American regimes were two sides of the same coin which,

163

I knew, was a position that many of those who I would have called my peers had taken. For some reason I just couldn't think of anything to say. I think perhaps one reason I stayed silent was that I realized he might just be right. Perhaps I really didn't know what I was talking about. And so, the conversation ended. I had nothing else to say. What could any of us say to him? None of us were facing what he was facing. And then the camp ended and I left.

Eventually, in due time, after some requisite jaunts across France and England, the summer came to a close. I packed my rucksack for the last time, boarded another Icelandic Air 707 and returned to New York. And, although the big marches had ended, there was still plenty of action going on if one was looking to keep busy. I did go off to art school at the end of that year. One way or another, I didn't do any more marching. I'm not sure why. My politics, my professed politics, at least consciously, hadn't changed a whit. Eventually it became clear that the war was indeed winding down. By the time I graduated, three years later, they weren't drafting anyone with a number higher than thirty or fifty.

I, for one, was safe and I didn't have to think too often about that summer's conversations.

2.   *Back*

Three years later, after I finished college, I hitchhiked around the West for a while, from New Mexico on up to British Columbia. I was out there for about a year, most of the time in California. I did a lot of camping. I spent several months in the Bay Area. I thought perhaps I'd stay out there, but I guess it didn't take. The same day I left, flying out of LAX, on the way back to New York, the Symbionese Liberation Army got caught in that shootout in Los Angeles, the one that ended in an inferno. It was the end of something there and the beginning of something, for me, back here.

3.   *We Had to Destroy the Village to Save It*

I started writing again. It had been a good three years, at least. At times I had convinced myself that it would never come again.

College was over and what I had gone through, or been put through, or allowed myself to be put through, in finishing my senior thesis, a manuscript of poems, had so wrung me out that I hadn't wanted or needed or been able to write a line since. The odd thing was that I had been a witting participant in that rather ruthless rewriting and slashing, that editing, executed by my tutor at Bennington, Alvin Feinman.

This was Bennington not long after it had gone co-ed and a good decade before those kids who later became famous novelists showed up. It was the middle of the school year when I transferred in. The first boys had been admitted that fall. There were about fifty of us. While discussion of the male — female ratio inevitably elicited knowing leers from friends during vacation, on campus a lot of women weren't exactly thrilled with all these men, men-boys actually, suddenly in their midst, commandeering desks in the front row of class, dominating discussion, and had ways of making their feelings clear.

A charismatic figure on campus, an extraordinarily accomplished and connected poet — Harold Bloom was a friend and wrote about him, Alvin brooked little foolishness. And his definition of foolishness proved surprisingly expansive, though not in an unkindly way, for he was essentially a gentle as well as a thoughtful man. Nora Ephron captured that particular rigor of his, if that's the right term, in an article about the school in Esquire a few years later. Those two years I studied with him I remained entirely overawed. For a time, he lived on campus in a house known as the Robert Frost cottage. The apartment he kept in New York was upstairs from Max's Kansas City. That, actually, seemed to me even more impressive.

But the work we did together in my senior year, or, rather, the work he did while I sat, mostly mute, knocking the manuscript into shape, was perhaps the most powerful gift he could give me. In the same way that the final, residual effect of all the literature classes I took with him was to teach me how to read, the cumulative effect of working on that pallid collection was, in a very real way, to teach me how to edit. The larger lesson was that if you were intent on becoming a writer, and in this, I guess, he was consonant with the rest of the writers and teachers with whom I came into contact at that place, Ben Belitt, Stephen Sandy, Michael Dennis Browne, Barbara Herrnstein, Camille Paglia, Claude Fredericks, in writing workshops and conventional classes both, you had to know how to edit yourself.

The thing was that Alvin, along with the rest of them, did their job so well, that by the time that manuscript was finished, while I may have been fairly adept at smoking out unnecessary words and weak constructions, I felt that there was very little of me left in any of those poems. Not that there was much of me to put into them, or what there was would have been of much interest to anyone, I was just another college poet. The poems that I thought were acceptable, decent, presentable, ones that had already been through dozens of drafts, each had been picked up, transmogrified by him and sliced a few new ways. This process had, I see now, taken me even further from that vague scribbling, those hesitant word lists, that nascent inclination to look at words, at language, at poetry itself, in a way that had been stirring in me for years. It seemed hopeless.

Once in a class that had otherwise been devoted to some Stevens poem or another, Alvin had posited a theoretical question: was there any language that wasn't suitable for inclusion in a poem? What about an engineering chart, he asked.

I was the only one who replied. Yes of course, I argued, that could be poetry too. And I guess I said it with enough force, or vehemence that he didn't argue with me at all. He just gave me a look and went on. But I never followed that up, not while I was there. And by the time college was finished with me, such possibilities seemed remoter than ever. The whole project, doing writing at all, seemed pointless.

I couldn't continue turning out those small, neatly turned, precisely observed lyrics. That wasn't me. I stopped writing for several years, me, the person who'd conceived the notion that he was going to be a writer by the time he was ten or eleven, the one who'd been turning out poems weekly since high school. I didn't know how to write anymore. Nor could I guess that there were people out there who felt the same way as me, who were grappling with the same set of issues, and were on the way to shaping a whole new way of writing. When I met up with them, everything changed for me.

4. The Gotham Book Mart

It was so perfect that the Gotham Book Mart was on 47th Street, in the heart of the Diamond District. You went from the glittering shop windows and the hectic sidewalks packed, always packed with people, standing, chattering, making deals in thirty different languages, and descended those few short steps into another world. This one wasn't particularly quiet either, and was packed just as tightly with jewels too, but it embraced you from the moment you walked in. The row of new magazines on the left, and the cashier just past that, and the shelves of poetry a little further on, on the right. And they seemed to have everything of course, a kind of physical representation of the literary universe, as we knew it. Frances Steloff was still there, white hair and frail. Then Andreas Brown showed up, though he seemed to be lurking always in that private office in the back.

But it was the salesmen, two guys in particular whose names I never learned and with whom I don't think I exchanged more than a dozen words over the years, despite frequenting that store weekly, much more than weekly, for years, who seemed to be, jointly, the moving force in the store. One fellow was a tall thin, fifty-ish bespectacled character, always suited in Brooks Brothers, looking like he'd just stepped out of a Cheever story. The other was a younger guy, maybe my age, built like a linebacker but with long Prince Valiant blonde hair, tanned, a sort of surfer look about him. The two of them seemed to run the shop. They were forever calling out to each other, while simultaneously conducting long, solemn telephone conversations with customers searching for some edition of some Faulkner novella which they didn't have in stock, which might not have ever really been published with that particular introduction or jacket art which the caller was looking for, but which, it was quite likely, one or the other of them might just be able to locate, with a little detective work, for the right price.

I was blissfully ignored as I stood by the poetry section and its tightly packed shelves, and made my way through the alphabet. No one ever spoke in to me, unless my friend, George Pitts, happened to be in the store. George and I had been at Bennington at the same time. He was one of what seems now like an incredibly small number of black kids who were there then, and we had the same two majors and minors, poetry and painting. A couple of years after graduation, when I came to New York, we quickly connected again. George was continuing to paint the big, big vaguely Frankenthaler-ish, Emmerich Gallery-inflected canvases which almost all of us were producing at that school back then. After one or two attempts I gave up trying to find a space big enough to allow me to continue painting and thereafter confined all visual art production to work that could be made in an apartment, collages and such. But George landed on his feet. I remember visiting him once in a loft on Prince Street he was subletting and then a place on the Bowery he had for some time.

There was something about George. He was a beautiful young man, and knew it, and an artful dresser, far more dapper than I ever could be, and certainly, compared to any of us at that age, quite accomplished as a poet and a painter. Somehow, he got a job at the Gotham. According to him it consisted largely of delivering packages of books to the apartments of people like Jackie Onassis, who, he informed me was a devoted customer. He read once at St. Marks, at a time when I knew not a soul there. After a while, I never saw him at the bookstore any more, or later, when I began to frequent St. Marks and other stations of the scene, anywhere at all.

As the years went by, I would occasionally run into him on the street. He'd gotten married, moved to Brooklyn, both of which amazed me, and I think he started a family, which I found absolutely astounding.

5.   The Back Room

The back room, of course, was the most important part of the Gotham. That's where the magazines were laid out, rows and rows of them, academic journals, periodicals, more literary magazines than I think I ever saw in one place, before or since. Here and there some gems: *Adventures in Poetry, Telephone, The World,* and in particular, *Z.* I bought everything I could afford. I can see them on my shelf now. They seemed then such perfect representations of an idealized New York poetry world, elegant, funny, wistful, full of art and artists. Maybe it was a world still extant even then. By the time I got to know some of the people who appeared there so many others were dead, or had left New York, or others, like Kenward Elmslie, you just never saw around anymore.

But there were two magazines I came across there, almost simultaneously, which changed my life. One was Barry Watten's *This,* the other was Alan Davies's *Oculist Witnesses.*

The sixth issue of *This* was the first I came across. There were no biographical notes whatsoever in that issue, nor, I think, in any of the others in that magazine's run. Who was this Clark Coolidge? For that matter, who were any of them? Creeley, Hollo, those were names I knew, but Andrews, Palmer, Silliman, Davidson, Robinson, Perelman?

This 6 had a long brilliant, shining piece by Clark Coolidge. There didn't seem to be a title. I had no idea who he was, but on the copyright page of the magazine was a little note, "This Press has recently published *The Maintains,* by Clark Coolidge. Price: $3.00..." I ran up to the front room of the Gotham, and there, in with the other "C" poets was *The Maintains.* And it was beautiful. It was amazing.

It was clear to me from that moment on: you didn't need to tell stupid stories any more. A poem could be about what it was supposed to be about: the indigestible, irreducible, unredeemable words that flung themselves at us every day, the language that, in its infuriating, inexhaustible, immeasurable confusion, yet limitless precision, lived, teeming, out there, outside our door. There could be no other subject, or at least no subject greater than this. Let the words be themselves, don't try and yoke them into some tyranny of argument, they would tell you what they were about. And they did, they eventually told me that all poems, all art, in our part of the world at least, for the last several hundred years at least, had circled around largely the same set of worries, hopes, fears. This was the way to follow Williams' dictum. To others, what we produced seemed or seems still to be ugly, meaningless. 'This is not art,' 'this stuff is not poetry,' And that's the way it was, and the way it should be.

Turning those pages, reading the poems that appeared in them was like being struck by lightning. At one glance I realized that all the impulses I had been stifling for years, everything I had been doodling, noodling around with, all of my attention to words, an attention I always assumed was pointless, irrelevant to making poems, all that scribbling I had been making in the margins of my drafts, going back to the beginning of college, all of that made sense, finally.

And there were people out there who thought just like me. There were poets, some of them seemed to be in San Francisco, some might even be in New York, who were doing amazing, wonderful, strange, breathtaking things. They were taking poems, lines, sentences, words themselves, the world itself, taking all of it apart and putting it back together again on the page in an incredible new way that was so gorgeous that I had to sit down, right there in the back room of the Gotham, on one of the little stools that cluttered up the aisles, and catch my breath. Now I knew: I wasn't alone.

As I made my way home that day, I believe that, somehow, I realized this book, this simply produced book of Clark's, with its plain cover and unfussy type, was going to change my life.

6. Apartment Life

When I first came to New York not only did I have no work, but I had nowhere to live. I remained in that latter condition for quite some time. For the first year or so I slept on the sofa in a cousin's apartment in the West Village.

That cousin, and her friends, were my first introduction to New York. We all spent time together, hung out in the White Horse together, a few blocks north on Hudson. And they led me to my first real job. And then I got my first apartment, a sublet I held for a couple of months one summer in Little Italy. That apartment was in a big old tenement at the corner of Grand and Mulberry, in the very heart of that neighborhood, upstairs from Ferrara's. Actually, the apartment faced Mulberry, which put Ferrara's around the corner. Directly below the apartment was a now long-departed old Italian notions and souvenir shop, its signage all in Italian, its window full of washed-out maps of Emilia-Romagna and souvenir china celebrating Caruso and Valentino. There, hanging faded but unbowed in one corner, unbelievably, but there he was: a poster of Mussolini himself, scowling lustily through the dust.

The tenement, it was either an Old Law or a New Law tenement, it did have a sort of courtyard, which may have made it New Law, dated from the 1880's or so, and the tiling in the halls and the ironwork on the stairs and much of the cupboards and trim work in the apartment itself was astonishingly original. What was also original was the amazing paucity of space. This was the smallest apartment I had ever seen in my life, far smaller than anything I came across, before or since, say, in the East Village, generally a much younger neighborhood, or among the truncated studios of the Upper West Side or Yorkville. This apartment was tiny. You entered through the kitchen, dominated by the tub, which took half of its space. The so-called living room was far too small for a couch. The bedroom could contain a bed and precious else. The entire apartment could fit easily inside the mudroom of the house where I live today. But it was mine, at least for a few weeks, and that made it wonderful.

Little Italy back then had no boutiques or Japanese restaurants or French restaurants, and only two or three other people, like me, who weren't

Italian. Or Chinese, for Chinese people were already starting to surge up from Chinatown. The neighborhood was still full of old grandmothers, and idle guys hanging out in front of the social clubs. There were lots of tourists, and the restaurants there catered to them, but it was still a neighborhood, albeit one on the cusp of change. Cater-corner across the street, the Italian Food Center had just opened, an astonishingly big and bright salumeria. While the neighborhood was still full of bakeries and pasta shops and cheese stores and a few butchers, this emporium was a place where you could get everything under one roof. It wasn't for the people in the neighborhood, clearly. It was for their children and grandchildren who'd moved out to Elmsford or Merrick or Montclair. They could dash in and stock up, get all that good stuff the A&P in Great Neck would never carry, and scoot right back to the suburbs.

After my sublet was up, I left that neighborhood and ended up in Chelsea.

Shortly after I moved uptown an old roommate from school stayed with me for a while. Steve Keffer was an actor. He'd recently started the Mettawee Theater Company up in his parents' summer place north of Albany. He got connected with Ralph Lee, the puppeteer who lived in Westbeth. To publicize their first production, they wangled permission to stage a parade one Halloween afternoon. The puppets pranced and the musicians tootled. The parade started at Westbeth or Abingdon Square, ran down Bleecker and over to Washington Square. That was the genesis of the huge parades that now take over the Village and Chelsea every Halloween.

In return for crashing in my place for a month Steve offered to make me a desk. He sketched out a design and we went together to the Dyke's lumberyard on Eighth Avenue. I bought the wood and we carried it back to the apartment and in a few days, he had cut and sanded and assembled a wide, five-foot desk with big square legs attached with dowels and carriage bolts, easily broken down and so perfect for what looked to be an itinerant New York apartment life. I still have it. Until a few years ago it was the only table I ever wrote upon, or ate off for that matter, since it served as a dining table too.

As Steve cut, I swept the dust into piles. Some of it got caught in the gaps between the parquet. As he glued pieces of the top to the frame, we weighted it down with books. When he was done, he carefully brushed on a few coats of polyurethane. That drove us out of the apartment for a while. We went over to the corner of Eighth, to the Cuban Chinese diner across from the Elgin. There we sat and ate flan and marveled yet again at the sight of Chinese waiters shouting at each other in Spanish. We tried to imagine the politics of folks who we imagined had been driven out of China by Mao in 1949 only to be driven out of Cuba ten years later by Fidel.

But when it was done it was ideal, a pristine rectangle. It seemed as big as a Midwestern state, with room for neat piles of books or notebooks off to the side and acres of working space in the center. For some reason Steve brought home some flowers the last night he stayed. It was a kind of present for the desk. There it stood, clean and new, gleaming splendidly under the casement windows facing the street, graced with a bouquet of tulips.

Now, a quarter-century later — a few years after the turn of the millennium — the table sits in a corner of the family room, my wife does her work on it. A Macintosh sits on it. When I wander in, I'll see her or one of the kids checking their mail or doing their homework. It's kind of beat up now. The bolts don't come out anymore and the dowels, which a couple of generations of dogs have found irresistible, really need replacing. The surface has gotten a bit scarred over the years and it is not quite as rock-steady as it used to be. But it is just about the oldest thing I possess and I remember when it was new, when it just was coming to life, and my apartment was filled with the pointed perfume of sawn pine.

7.   *Jobs for Us*

When I first came to New York I also had no prospects. I barely knew anyone. There had been ample opportunities back in college to do something about that — to come to New York and do internships and temporary jobs in virtually any field. I had taken advantage of none of that. My parents offered to send me to graduate school. I got wait-listed at Iowa and was told I'd probably be accepted the next term, if I applied again. But my parents weren't going to pay for that. Law school they would pay for, business school too, but there was no way they'd bankroll me for an MFA in poetry. It didn't occur to me apply for financial aid and go it alone.

Eventually, of course, I came to the opinion that an MFA wouldn't likely have done any good. In terms of credential-collecting, yes. If I'd gone in that direction, tried to gain entry to that life, certainly it would have been a plus. And not just, as we said in the office, as a nice-to-have, but as an academic, obviously it would have been a must-have. However, as a poet, in terms of developing into a poet, when it came to what might or could or would make me a better poet, it became clear that it wouldn't have made much difference. There would be nothing I could glean about the writing life beyond what I'd been exposed to at Bennington. The first years there were chock full of writing workshops, exactly like MFA workshops, though they were, for me, succeeded by those inestimably more impactful tutorials.

Somehow, we believed — it wasn't just me thinking this sort of thing and this attitude wasn't just prevalent then — that degrees and jobs didn't matter. Writing was what mattered. Careers, all that stuff, you just put up with all that in order to be able to keep writing. So, it didn't matter. You could take one lousy job after another, just so you had enough time to keep writing. Was this left-over thinking from the Sixties? Some last gasp of Lower East Side New York School attitude? Or was it pulled from further back, a bequest from the Beats or some other batch of bohemians? Wherever it came from, it seemed ubiquitous among us. You worked at some sort of job. You wrote. You tried to get published and you published other people. You made enough money to make the rent and have beer in the house. Maybe a fifth of Jack Daniels. And cigarettes. And drugs, for some people.

A good number of years went by before it became clear that not everyone had taken things so casually. Some people had been thinking strategically all along.

My father found me my first job in New York, at a Camera Barn, part of a chain run by a friend of his. I stood behind a counter a few steps off 32nd Street and sold Kodak film all day, just as I had done through my summers in high school, in the stores my father managed. I lived on that sofa on Morton Street. I knew no one and, in fact, I was not writing. The money was terrible there, the work was stupefyingly boring. At the end of the day my feet ached from standing. And, I was simply not very good at it. Back then there were no barcodes and the cash registers were mechanical, not electronic. They didn't calculate change. Each salesman in the film and processing department had their own cash drawer in the register. At the end of the day the manager would pull the drawers, extract the tabulating tape from inside the machine and do his calculations. My drawer was always over, or under. I either had too much cash in the drawer, compared to the sales I'd rung up, or too little. At first, he thought I was a thief, then he realized I simply was incapable of accurately ringing up sales.

I couldn't do the math.

8.   Sending

Before everyone showed up, before I actually met anyone, I was corresponding with Alan. I was living on West 19th Street by then. After several years in New York, living on other people's sofas, I had a place of my own.

It was a ground floor studio in a Deco building. Every visitor had the same reaction: they thought they had arrived at their dentist's office. It was across the street from Dance Theater Workshop. Steve's table sat under the window. My recently acquired dinette set stood in what must have been the waiting room. Now I was all set.

I started writing again, this was actually a month or so before I had my Pauline moment at the Gotham Book Mart, and it was all so unsurprisingly discouraging at first. But at least I was writing again, and sending work around. I sent some work to Z where it was rejected in the nicest possible way. Elmslie sent me a beautiful Kodachrome postcard, some sort of heroic Hellenic sculpture, by its captioning clearly purchased in Greece, with a sweet and not entirely dismissive note penned in a carefree hand. I think I may have sent him a second bunch of poems, perhaps not. But the second person I sent anything to was Alan Davies, and that's when everything started.

Oculist Witnesses was a tall, simple, xeroxed, side-stapled magazine. The cover of the first issue I got my hands on bore the image of a kitchen grater, roughly photographed, near-life size, set against a plain white cover, not just plain but untitled, and breathtakingly elegant. As I write this, my copy sits in front of me now. As I recall, the first poems I sent to Alan were the same drivel that I'd sent to Z. But then something happened. Alan also replied promptly and kindly and also declined those poems. What they were, and where they are, I have no idea. But it couldn't have been more than a few weeks between my sending that first bunch of poems to Alan and the second, that the change occurred. That Coolidge had happened to me.

I had also been reading Burroughs, and with my girlfriend at the time, who was a dancer, was going to see a lot of Cunningham, which meant listening to a lot of Cage. We were also taking in a lot of the younger choreographers, like Trisha Brown, and Tharp. And I was looking at lots and lots of art, and reading *This* and *Oculist Witnesses*. And, I was reading Clark Coolidge, over and over. One day I found myself sitting down and just making lists. Not trying to make a poem, not trying to force some adolescent meaning into the words but just letting the words be.

I finally gave in to that impulse which had stirred first in me years ago back at Bennington. The words just arrived. They weren't just literary words, they came from all around, from The Daily News and the street and the radio and the TV and the flyers blowing down the sidewalk. Just being attentive to the words was enough.

I made the lists, then I sat back and looked at them. It was a Saturday. By now, I had just moved again, to my second apartment, on Morton Street, and I was sitting at that new big desk I had brought with me. Turning to one side I could look out onto the gray courtyard that provided the only natural light. Each list had some interest as one read down them but there was still a bit too much residual narrativism present, that mitigated against, it seemed to me, whatever innate discrete power or gnomic identity — what had impelled me to jot each one down in the first place — that the individual words possessed. Also, the lists looked much too skinny to me.

Then I looked over at the Burroughs I was reading. It was *The Ticket That Exploded*. I thought about the Cunningham performance that I had gone to the previous weekend. And for some reason I thought about my old, yellow-backed Bollingen edition of the I Ching, which I hadn't opened for years. I wasn't even sure where it was anymore and it occurred to me, and not for the first time, that I wasn't sure that I had ever thrown the sticks for it properly in the first place.

Then I looked back at the lists lined up on the several pieces of paper lying in front of me and it occurred to me to put them all together. If I took the first word from the first list and the first word from the second list and the first word from the third list, and the fourth, the fifth, the sixth and the seventh, I would have a line. And if I took the second word from each list, I would have line two, and so on. I got down to work and for a time tried not to think of what was forming itself on the page. I just worked, putting the lines together. When I was done, I had fourteen lines. 'But not a sonnet. No way,' I thought to myself.

I sat back and looked at it and read it out loud and I realized that for the first time I had made something that reached back down and tapped that sense I'd had years ago, that to the extent the world is made up of words, and that there is contained a world in every word, it is the poet's job to take the world apart and give it back to us in a way that we've never seen it before.

For the first time in my life, I had succeeded in making a real poem. It made sense, its own sense. Each individual, original list had some consanguinity, in terms of contextual focus or part of speech, that residual narrativism that had bothered me when I'd studied them in the first place. But when fitted into these lines they referred back to each other, in a vertical sense, as it were and, it seemed to me at the time, bound the poem together.

And while it might not be worth much to anyone else, that remained to be seen, I had accomplished something on my own terms. I pulled two words out of the poem for the title "Blunts Everlast." Of course, this was years before 'blunt' gained its current meaning. And once I had done one poem, they started pouring out. The words, for their part, were everywhere. And quickly, in a matter of days, I had four or five of these short, wide, dense poems. But there was no one to show them to, except Alan.

9. Alan Writes Back

When I first wrote to Alan Davies he was still in Boston, where he'd gone to college and gotten involved in the poetry scene. By the time he wrote back he was already on the road. His itinerary took him out to California and then, via that Great Circle route that so many other poets followed back then, he ended up in Boulder, and Naropa. He quietly and sensibly got a job as the night clerk at the Hotel Boulderado. There he came to know Burroughs, a resident guest. From the second or third piece of correspondence on, every letter from Alan was written on Hotel Boulderado stationery, and in them I eagerly read his mentions of Burroughs. Burroughs himself! The image of a young poet as a night clerk in a seedy old hotel out West seemed itself a trope out of Burroughs.

I sent "Blunts Everlast" and the rest of those short poems, all fourteen lines, to Alan. He wrote back very quickly. He really liked them. He wanted to publish them. I stood there in the apartment house lobby, my keys hanging from the opened mail box, the long Hotel Boulderado envelope lying on the grimy tiled floor, staring at the neatly typed letter. I thought, 'what were the odds?' What were the odds that these poems, made up of words which I had pulled up out of a place that I was sure no one else was interested in, and shuffled together in a way that, at the time, seemed almost idly chosen, in itself a chance operation, what were the chances that anyone else could possibly be interested in them? But someone was. I did a little dance there, a shambling poet's victory jig, there by the front doors.

Alan was starting a new magazine, it was going to be called *A Hundred Posters*, and it was going to be different than *Oculist Witnesses*. This magazine would come out every few weeks and be only a few pages long. Only one or two or three poets' work would be featured in each issue. Alan had the first few numbers set and filled up, but my poems would appear immediately thereafter. I went upstairs and read the letter a few more times. I'm not sure where it is now. But I can still feel the crackling stationery between my fingers, the odd, old-fashioned litho letterhead of the Hotel Boulderado, the page puckered a little at the top, where the press's platen had pushed the paper a bit. I'm not sure what I did next, who I called.

I know I wrote back excitedly to Alan and I know I sat down soon thereafter and wrote some more poems. The next series was similarly organized, but the lines were longer and the rhythms, as it were, more complicated, and I also sent those off to Alan, who was still out in Boulder, who I still hadn't met. I had no idea what he looked like, or anything.

10. *Some Other Furniture*

Besides my table there wasn't really much other furniture I could claim to own back then. There was the dinette set that sat outside the kitchen in my apartment in Chelsea, in the former dentist's office waiting room. It was a high Fifties piece, the table done up in flecked Formica, set upon highly-worked, black, cast-iron legs. Its four chairs had similarly intricate cast-iron work with pleated and tufted Naugahyde cushions. It was in pristine condition and remained so for as long as I owned it, since it never got much use. It was terrifically inappropriate and wildly out of keeping with every other stick of furniture that I possessed.

When it came to furnishing that apartment on 19th Street, straitened circumstances dictated very economical measures. I paid next to nothing, as in the case of the desk built for me, or nothing at all, which is how the dinette set, and a pile of silverware came to me. I had an aunt, Rae, one of my mother's many sisters. Her husband was Al. When I was growing up, they lived just a few minutes away, and so we saw them constantly. They had a business down in Soho. It was a body and fender shop on the corner of Mercer and Houston. They also ran an adjoining parking lot that ran along the south side of the street, all the way to Greene.

The parking lot was one of a long strip of empty lots along Houston, that stretched all the way to Sixth, leveled back in the Twenties, when the IND subway line had been dug. The big playground at Avenue of the Americas is where the trains turn the corner and head up to West Fourth Street, their next stop. Sitting in the office of my aunt and uncle's shop you could hear and feel the trains shudder by every few minutes. There had never been enough economic activity in that part of town to make it worth building on those narrow lots, and so there were parking lots from the East Side to the West, with a few gas stations near Broadway that catered to cabbies. One of them had a carwash that came to play a starring role in a poem I later wrote. All along Houston you could still see the naked sides of buildings, ones that faced the side streets, Mercer, Greene, Wooster, Thompson, Macdougal. They weren't meant to be seen. All of their neighbors to the north had been torn down decades ago. The city had condemned all this land by eminent domain and owned it still.

My parents having already retired down to Florida, during my first years in New York I spent many an odd hour lounging in Rae and Al's office, watching and listening to the neighborhood characters who drifted in and out. The tired old manufacturers reps and salesmen with their stained ties, wheezy Dodges, and ancient jokes. The sleek new artists in their knit pullovers and shiny Saabs, their tight smiles and impatient glances.

If I appeared particularly peckish, Rae would take me over to Food. She liked it there. The trays reminded me of a school cafeteria but I was in no position to complain. It meant I was sure to get at least one decent meal that day. Now and then, when it came time to close up shop, Rae and Al would treat me to dinner and take me to Ratner's, back then there were two Ratner's, or the Rifle Club, that Italian restaurant on Macdougal.

By the 1980s, the body and fender shop had shut down and the modest, one story building it had been housed in became, for a short time, a very hot disco. My aunt and uncle ran the next-door parking lot for a few more years, out of a trailer they parked by the sidewalk.

But back when I got that first apartment on 19th Street Rae took me in hand. Clearly, I needed help. One afternoon we got in her Cadillac and drove up to the Bronx. Two of her old friends were retiring, to Florida of course, and were getting rid of stuff. There might be something of interest for me. I vaguely knew this couple. He was a cop, one of those Jewish New York City policemen of which there used to be more than a few. In fact, all his brothers were cops too. He was the star among them, a big, strapping handsome man, he'd been picked for dignitary protection assignments as a young man. The department always wanted good looking faces accompanying visiting potentates and politicians when their pictures appeared in the papers. Eventually he rose in the ranks and commanded the motorcycle precinct located along lower reaches of the Bronx River Parkway, then served at the Police Academy and retired as a captain.

We pulled up to a trim house in Riverdale and his wife greeted us. A dark-haired young girl, a daughter, was introduced. She couldn't have been more than fifteen. She had a friend over and I have a memory of the two of them scampering, giggling, up the stairs. A lot of stuff was headed to the curb, but all I really wanted, or needed, was that dinette set. I don't remember how we got it downtown, it couldn't have fit in the back of my aunt's Seville. I took some silverware too. It was everyday stuff, stainless steel flatware, nothing special, but I was grateful for it. I was loaded down with as much of it as I could take, spoons, forks, knives, scooped into a paper bag and shoved in my arms.

Three or four years later I ran into that girl again, at Rae and Al's trailer. She was in college now, down in Florida, and visiting New York to see that girlfriend that she'd run upstairs with. I took her out and bought her a glass of wine on West Broadway, at the Ballroom. She told me about her plans. She and her friend were headed to California for the summer. A few years later I ran into her again. By now she had graduated from college and was in New York looking for a job in the movie business. Since I was working at Warner's at the time, my aunt thought I could be of assistance to her. She arranged for us all to go to Ratner's one evening. This girl had turned into a woman. Naturally I volunteered to help her in any way that I could. I asked her out a week or two later.

Then the time came for her to come to my apartment. By then I was living in Little Italy again, on Kenmare Street. That apartment on 19th Street was way in the past, as was the one after that. I was making her some dinner, and she volunteered to set the table. The dinette set was long gone by then. The only table that could fit in that shoebox of an apartment was the old desk that Steve had made for me. As she picked the first fork out of the drawer Robin gave out a little cry, and let forth with another with each additional spoon and knife.

This was the silverware from her childhood, which she hadn't seen in years, had entirely forgotten about, and now here it lay, in her hand. To me the seven or eight years since I had been to her old house passed quickly — one or two jobs, one or two apartments — but to her it represented a vast expanse of time that she had journeyed across, from childhood to adulthood. And here it was, all brought back to her in the form of some battered flatware.

I haven't looked recently but I don't think that silver is around anymore. I should ask her. It's been almost thirty years. A few other sets have been picked up along the way. We're married, you see. Some of what now sits in our drawers is surely laden with as much emotional freight, at least I think so. I want to believe our children will react similarly should they eventually, in turn, in their own time, happen to come across those forks and spoons at some point, years from now.

11.   James

My girlfriend back when I'd just moved to 19th Street had gotten a
job waiting tables at Fanelli's. At the time it was a bar that — like the
Spring Lounge, before that place became known as the Shark Bar and
not long after it provided an interior for *Mean Streets* — you had only
recently felt safe walking into. Before then it was clear that your type, our
type, was not welcome there. At least half of Fanelli's patrons were still
tough guys, guys of the sort that you never see anywhere around there
anymore, because they have no business anywhere near there. There
were no college students yet. Just some beat up artists, in addition to
the traditional beat-up working guys. And Mike Fanelli was still around,
he probably had another ten years to live, though he kind of looked like
the taxidermist had already had his way with him. Tiny, spare, white
shirt and black tie and slicked back hair. The place was said to possess
one of the oldest liquor licenses in the city. The pressed tin walls and
ceiling seemed even more ancient back then, and the walls were still
festooned with photos and posters of Mike as a young bantamweight, or
featherweight.

There was also a waitress station at the rear of the first room, near the
bathrooms where my girlfriend, Shannon, used to lean on her elbow and
write orders or catch her breath and chat with the other woman on duty.
It seems to me that when we first started hanging out there, there was no
back room, that they only expanded into there when the hipsters starting
frequenting the place. One of the other waitresses was a painter named
Jean, a bit older than us, cheerful, busy, with whom Shannon struck up a
friendship. She lived down near Chambers Street, the first person I knew
who lived that far south, in a loft building.

After a few months Jean invited us to a dinner party she was throwing
at her place. There were a good twenty people ranged along a long table
that evening. I remember getting into a pointless argument with a young
woman, who described herself as a labor lawyer, as to the true nature
of the CPUSA. Across from me sat a thin, balding young man, perhaps
a few years older than me, reserved, with cool thin lips. Occasionally
the lips curved into a thin smile, more often than not with one or both

corners turned down. His wife was a painter and a friend of Jean's, that accounted for his attendance, and they had recently moved to New York from Colorado. His name was James Sherry. He published a magazine and he was a poet.

"But I'm a poet too!"

The words just bubbled out of me. And as they escaped, I saw the corner of this fellow James's mouth turn down further. It was a slight reaction but unmistakable, and obviously meant to be so. A demure moue of disdain. However much distance he'd displayed before immediately doubled. He must be heartily sick, it occurred to me, of being pestered by every tea-swilling, watercress-sandwich-nibbling old lady who fancied herself a poet, or the feckless young-man-iteration thereof, a category he had clearly just relegated me to, who, as soon as he mentioned that he had a magazine, was busily importuning him to be published in it. That look by itself was enough to shut me up. I was ready to move on, try another dinner companion out for size, even to re-engage the labor lawyer. We hadn't addressed the Molotov-Ribbentrop Pact yet. But then James asked me a question.

"Have you been published anywhere?"

That was the first time, and almost last, anyone said that to me. I never heard it again — not for a good twenty-five years, that is. When I first left the city, years later, and came across some poets who had never heard of Language writing, or even St. Mark's for that matter, at not-dissimilar dinner parties, the question came back to me. By then I had a different answer.

When James asked me that question I hadn't in fact been published anywhere yet, not since college. But Alan had just written me with his news. I began to tell this story to James, artlessly, unaffectedly, in a hesitant attempt to establish my bona fides, entirely unsure if this would mean anything to him, make me seem any more real. But no sooner had I mentioned Alan's name than James's demeanor was utterly transformed.

"Alan Davies? Alan Davies knows your work? You've been in touch with him? He's going to publish your stuff?"

188

He not only knew of Alan, he knew him, from back in Colorado, from Boulder. They'd both been hanging around Naropa. And both, I came to believe, had gotten a similar cold, or cool shoulder from members of the transplanted St. Mark's scene who held sway there. Now James was in New York, sitting across from me. And I was not just another importuning scribbler but, apparently, someone who had standing, of some sort, in his world. Now we talked easily, of other poets and other magazines, of Coolidge and *This,* of art and New York, where we lived, he was in a loft on the Bowery, and what we were doing with ourselves. He didn't seem to be doing much aside from putting out his magazine, and writing, with some stock picking on the side. He was the only poet I knew, back then, who read the *Wall Street Journal* every day. We were off to a famous start.

12.   *Everyone Showing Up*

Over the next few months, everyone eventually showed up, or surfaced, or collected themselves, and by some sort of imperceptible action, a kind of literary-social Brownian motion, there now was a group, where before there was nothing, only some atomized individuals scattered across the landscape. Some people had been in New York all their lives, some for years already, some like myself, some had drifted here over the last couple of years, and a few showed up right then, within a few months of each other. On its own, without any individual's apparent volition, a scene was born. Just as, about ten years later, many of the same people, some of whom weren't talking to each other anymore, moved away, while a simultaneous dissolution was occurring out in California, and that New York scene, that original scene, dissolved. It was a wonder it lasted as long as it did. But over that summer, into that fall, no one was thinking like that. It was a heady time.

First there was James, whose big rackety place on the Bowery was divided in two parts, as it remains today, and his first wife, Lee, was painting in the front half. Ray DiPalma arrived in New York around that time too, having decided that the life of an academic in Ohio wasn't for him. Or perhaps Ohio decided he wasn't for it. Bruce Andrews had taken a tenure track job at Fordham and was living with his wife in the apartment he remains in today, just off Central Park West. Bruce and Charles Bernstein had recently met at a St. Mark's workshop that Bernadette Mayer ran. I only learned this a few years ago. I don't recall who mentioned that to me, it might have been Bruce or Nick Piombino, it might have been a third party. What I do recall is how we were treated for so long by the powers that be at St. Mark's. The Language poets were a tolerated, barely tolerated minority. They didn't like what we did. Our poems weren't funny, they didn't make sense and they were too easy. Anyone could write crap like that.

Nick was another who had been in New York all along but all of a sudden, as it were, was there among us, like Jackson Mac Low. There were others too, like Michael Lally, who was around, to some degree, then wasn't. And others, who were less frequently seen at first, like Ted Greenwald, who eventually was certainly around, as it were, though he was a New Yorker. Or others who rallied at the assembly point a bit later. Like Peter Seaton or Diane Ward, and then there was Hannah Weiner.

But those seven — Bruce Andrews, Charles Bernstein, James Sherry, Ray DiPalma, Nick Piombino, and me — comprised the original cell, as it were. Along with Alan.

Alan arrived from Boulder around the same time.

I really didn't know what to expect.

And it just seemed natural. Everyone was coming to New York. I'm not sure I had a picture in mind of what he would look like. His written communications, by now we had a fairly busy correspondence going, were direct, forceful, and unadorned. Big, small, fair, swarthy, whatever I had in mind it was vague, unclear and unformed.

Alan and I were the youngest of this group. We were between four and ten, twelve years younger than the rest of them. It was nearly a generational thing. I believe that we were the only ones that really listened to rock and roll. Diane Ward came along to CBGB's once or twice but that was about it. No one else went with us to the Mudd Club or Hurrah, and it wasn't because they had jobs they had to get up in the morning for. Half of them seemed to be listening to opera.

Everyone was older, everyone looked older, and when I met Alan for the first time, even I felt older than him too, and we are precisely the same age. Nothing prepared me for that first meeting, when he came to my apartment on Morton Street. I opened the door and here was a child-man. A slight — my size, but that seemed decidedly slight — fair, tousled-hair blonde kid. Slim, with a sweet, innocent, more than innocent, a prelapsarian, angelic mien about him. Of course, he smoked and drank to beat the band. But we were all drinking then, and I was smoking too. But he looked like a boy, and not just any boy: a choir boy out of some English prewar movie set in some dewy corner of Hampshire or the Cotswalds, with a weathered Norman church and an ancient High Street. But here he was, knocking back my Jack Daniels, thumbing through my Penguin Balzac, admiring the view from my living room window of the forbidding courtyard and its collection of sad garbage cans, all the while wryly recounting tales of nefarious goings-on at Naropa, and late-night dalliances among the denizens of the Hotel Boulderado. Each tale was recounted with a remarkable dose of empathy that seemed to build upon, or have at its core, some sort of forgiveness or acceptance, Christian or Buddhist — I didn't know enough about Alan yet to tell or know the difference — and all drawled out in that high, unassuming, quiet, sweetly uninflected Canadian accent.

There he was.

13.   *Learning to Read Through the Arts*

After a few months I'd lucked into my second job in New York, though it really wasn't anything to write home about, at Learning to Read Through the Arts, a program for kids co-sponsored by the Board of Education and the Guggenheim Museum. I worked in the office, counting the subway tokens we handed out to the kids, working on registration, making out attendance sheets. Everyone else was an artist. When I started it was housed in Westbeth, where Merce was dancing away up on the top floor.

The job often sent me to Brooklyn, to 110 Livingston Street and 65 Court Street, the once-legendary headquarters of the Board, where I got to see first-hand how bureaucracy really worked: floors full of accountants who really couldn't care less about your funding balance, paneled offices full of dignified factotums to whom, it was drilled into me, due obeisance was always to be offered. I also ended up taking the train to the far reaches of the city, during recruiting season, to parts of town where white boys in the mid-Seventies were rarely sighted.

Nothing untoward ever befell me of course, but I was continually struck during those jaunts by the vastness of this city and how, to my untrained, naïve eye, so much of it seemed to be in advanced decay. So very imposing, echoing, empty. But not empty actually. Those distant reaches were full of people, people of color.

So many, so very many places and parkways in distant desmenses of Brooklyn, squares and concourses in the Bronx, tumbledown, it seemed to me then, tattered, but which had been laid out, it was clear, not really that long ago, fifty, seventy, less than a hundred years ago for sure, for a robust and rising bourgeoisie that had peopled this city, had built it. Where'd they go? I was certainly familiar with Soho's grandeur, those cast-iron retail palaces now rusting and ramshackle, but this was different. And all these subway stations. Who knew there were so many express stops? Vast, clearly underused, half-abandoned but magnificent still, the tile gleaming through the grime. This was 1975.

I wasn't in the habit of buying the Daily News, but one morning I did, and I saw that everyone else in the project's office had too. The headline blared: "Ford to New York: Drop Dead." By some lights, that day marked the absolute low point in the city's fortunes, and not just in recent times, but going all the way back, back to 1664, when the Dutch woke one August morning to see the entire Upper Harbor filled with British men-of-war. Of course, truly, one had to admit than an even lower point had been marked not that many decades earlier, the day the Lenapes caught sight of Henry Hudson's caravel tacking towards them, coming through the Narrows. For them indubitably it had been downhill ever since.

This job only offered one meaningful perquisite: you got laid off every summer and you filed for unemployment. Then you were rehired next fall. How perfect was that? That first summer, I'd moved into 19th Street not long past, I idly picked up the copy of Swann's Way I'd owned for years and to my surprise consumed it in one big gulp. I did nothing else that day, maybe it took two days. By the time I was done I realized I had to read the rest, and right away. As soon as I finished that first volume, I marched down to the Eighth Street Bookstore and bought Within a Budding Grove, and then went back for the next and the next and within a week or so I had read them all. Granted, this was something I could do because I was ready for him — I'd already read Jean Santeuil and Contra Sainte-Beuve in college — but, more to the point, I wasn't doing anything else. I could spend all day reading Proust.

A perfect job, no? I had to have some sort of job. Everyone had to have a job of some sort, and this was one step up from working in a copy shop, but it was the kind of job people were still getting. It paid enough, and gave you enough free time, enough to let you do your real work. And if it paid just barely enough, well, that was okay. That's the way everyone, every painter, every poet, was living back then, or so it seemed. The Sixties weren't all that long in the past and that time, and its thinking — about money, ambition, the straight world and the cool, hip world, as well as what we could want, should want — had shaped us all. Career? We had careers, we were artists one and all. Wasn't that enough?

And to be able to do all this in this city — a city which didn't drop dead. Our pay got delayed for a month or two but that was about it — amidst all this glorious ruin of empire, how lucky were we?

14. *Noired*

And so, I read more Burroughs. He was someone who was always
around, as it were. You knew about him in college. He was another figure
from that generation. It seemed like they were from another age, a golden
age, even though they were really only about twenty years older than us.
I remember the first time I saw Ginsberg, way before I came to New York
and went to St. Mark's, in my first year of college. He sat cross-legged
in a common room and played the drums and sang, and I thought, 'he's
not that old at all.' And he wasn't then. Younger than we are now. He
must still have been in his forties. Of course, Burroughs was somewhat
older than the rest of them. He always acted and dressed older. The drugs
aided the aging process too, surely.

When I picked up *Nova Express* from someone's book shelf one day, I
found I could not put it down. The cutting and pasting had a decidedly
vertiginous effect, but I couldn't stop. I ended up buying everything of
his that Eli Wilentz had on his shelves on Eighth Street. There was that
feeling, that sensation, neither-here-nor-there, which his cut-up regime
conferred. It seemed to be a combination of not-knowing, of drift, of
things and people and words and sentences entirely unmoored from their
proper places and allowed to meander at will all over the page, across
the range of perception, in and out of the author's contract with reality,
to butt up against each other, to wander off. There was that. But it was
married up with such a very tightly written set of describers.

A noired, hardboiled, stripped-down, deadpan, detached, unsentimental
and dryly detailed style. This combination had the effect of
simultaneously rooting one and sending one flying. While it meant at
first that I couldn't read more than five or six pages at a time, the innate
force of this format, which Burroughs had struck upon, was undeniable.
It had the capability of picking the reader up and putting him down some
place that he had never been before, a place he could never get to any
other way, a place entirely foreign to anything he'd ever known but, at
the same time, so linked and caught up in, so connected to the world, the
life, the fears that he lived with every day, or dreamt about each night,
that he at once recognized this new place as one where he was obliged to
tarry awhile. And it was a place he needed to return to again and again.

There was something hypnotically charged there. There were things to be learned there, things to be carried back to our old, flat, uninflected world. In fact, the everyday world was never, could never be the same. Burroughs cut up more than just his language. He did more than just take those projectors, and throw narratives and scenes against the walls of his stories and the bodies of his characters. He didn't just send boys on roller skates through the ruins of desert cities. After Burroughs it became clear that the world was made up of broken pieces. Studied properly it was revealed as an ill-fitting pottage of shards, no more than that, sometimes slapped together to present a simulacrum of order; more often lying there unsorted, disconnected, reasonless, with terrible, dark lacunae gleaming dangerously between.

15. *The Late Imperial Precincts*

One day towards the end of 1976 or the beginning of 1977 Alan said to me, "I'd like to do a book of yours."

By now I was writing longer poems, pieces made up often of several sections, and producing collage illustrations for their covers, xeroxing them and sending them around to my pals. Eventually I realized that no one else was sharing their poems before they were published.

But it was easy to plan this book. Like the rest of the work that followed for years, the two poems in this book had a subtext grounded in New York City itself and so, at Alan's suggestion, with his encouragement, I went around the city taking photographs — the Morton Street apartment hadn't been robbed yet, I still had the cameras my father had given me as a kid — and also assembled new collages from stuff I found on the street, coming up with enough eventually so that each of the sections of the two works had an illustration facing it.

The city back then, so mysterious, impermeable. An impenetrable locus of hidden doings, serene, awesome in its ability to ignore. Its decay seemed regnant. And inevitable. There was no doubt that New York's great days were behind it. There was security in the knowledge that we were living among faded grandeur, that the theme was decline, that so much of this might be rubble soon. Some empire's capital, after it's been sacked. Matta-Clark was showing us, wasn't he?

When it came to this too, we were so wrong. And the swelling, apparently unstoppable revival — though *revival* is not the word that those who have been priced out of those neighborhoods use — that has long since spread to Brooklyn and the Bronx, makes those early days seem even further off, impossibly long ago.

The myriad worlds within the metropolis back then, each existed in parallel, independent of the other. Coterminous yet never touching, except at that one surface point: the street. There they deigned to let you peer at them. The world city, a new Paris. When, a few years later, in Superman II or Ill, Warner Bros. decided to place Lex Luthor's hideout in a hitherto-unknown concourse below Grand Central, it seemed obvious and easy. Of course, there were huge, abandoned train stations beneath our feet all over Manhattan. There had to be. This place was an endlessly arresting scrim. And all manner of dramas, from rewritings of Nadja to revivals of Fantomas, were surely being played out across it, beneath it, above it. If only it was possible to penetrate into those other worlds.

After I assembled all the illustrations, Alan and I went to work. The transformation of the rough typed pages along with the photos and pasted-together collages into a bound work seemed, as it surely does for everyone working on a first book, nothing less than miraculous. We worked with a pair of cheerily knowing lesbian typesetters. One of them adorned herself with radically sculpted eyebrows, a neat pageboy å la Louise Brooks, and extremely original makeup including large pastel-hued discs of pancake on either cheek. They were ensconced in a vast, dingy, echoing loft on Lafayette Street. Taking up a full corner of their space was a gigantic typesetting computer. The most advanced, the latest, the most up-to-date, we were assured. No doubt it had less computing power — as they say now about the Apollo space capsules — than today's cheapest phone. It spit out thin strips of damp copy, reeking toxically, like enlargements fresh from the darkroom, one laborious page after another.

I'm not sure how many other perfect-bound books Alan had published by that time. Certainly, he had done magazines. *A Hundred Posters* was still getting turned out with an estimable consistency. It would continue issue after issue, for several more years. Nevertheless, he guided the process with a confident hand, as if he had been doing this for decades.

This is the way it went with Alan: he asked me if I had any ideas for the cover. In fact, I had. A couple of years earlier, I had spent a lot time at the Queens Museum, a rather sad building back then that had been used for both of the World's Fairs. It was one of the sites to which Learning to Read Through the Arts had expanded. In a half-abandoned storage room there, I came across piles of glossy brochures Robert Moses had printed up to promote the 1964 fair's New York State pavilion. Across the front and back cover was a wonderful photo of the Verrazano-Narrows Bridge, under construction. In the foreground the Brooklyn approach ramps were already laid in and paved. The towers and the cables were already in place. Just one section of deck had been installed so far, though, in the center of the span, like a gigantic hyphen in the sky. It seemed to go so well with the photographs of the aerial walkways in the book itself.

My conscience was fairly clear when it comes to the means by which I had acquired my three or four copies of this brochure. I had essentially stolen them, certainly, but there had been piles and piles of them, stacked haphazardly in a sad, neglected corner of a sad, neglected museum. A museum so reduced in ignominy that it had to share its building with a skating rink. A museum whose principal attraction back then was a sprawling scale model of the city which hadn't been updated since the Fair opened, years earlier. These brochures were just waiting for the day when they'd be consigned to the dumpster.

My concern back then was that we were going to use that cover without permission. As I recall there was no copyright page in that brochure, and no credits listed either, of any sort. I want to say that Robert Moses's name or likeness appeared on almost every page. While I think he was good and dead by then, my then-hazy understanding of intellectual property law told me that what we were doing could conceivably get us in some sort of trouble. What kind of trouble, I wasn't sure but it seemed dicey. Part of me said that this was just poetry, just a poetry book that only a few people, a few hundred tops, would ever see. And no one cared about poetry anyway. But part of me was worried.

Alan took care of that problem in the same way that he dealt with every other issue, each of the inevitable glitches or apparent crises that arose while we worked on this book. He radiated calmness. He told me not to worry. So, I didn't. It was that unshakeable, imperturbable confidence, combined with his unfailing solicitude, continually seeking to ensure that my wishes when it came to the book were fulfilled, even more than the fact that this was my first book, which made this particular experience so wonderful. Each stage of the book's production thus turned into an occasion for pleasure: proofing the first set-up bits of copy the typesetters handed to us, reviewing the pasted-up boards, checking the blues. Because this was years and years before any of us acquired a personal computer, and anyone could produce justified text in any leading or font imaginable, that transformation, from smudgy typescript, itself just one step away from the handwritten sheet, to the bound book, was nothing less than amazing, a miracle in its way. And because Alan had everything so well in hand, this became, as it always should be for a first-time author, an adventure of unalloyed joy.

16.   *At the Far End of Spring Street*

Hanging behind the bar at the Ear Inn was an old illuminated Budweiser advertisement in the form of a light-box, from the Fifties. It showed two guys sitting chatting by the opened tailgate of an old, two-door, '53 or '54 Ford station wagon, just like the model Jack Carson drove in Star Is Born, pulling up with a screech of brakes on the back lot, scattering a flock of extras, to threaten James Mason or Judy Garland. The colors were not faded yet. It was often a great pleasure during readings to sit at the bar, if there was no room at the tables up front or if it seemed the greater part of discretion to sit further back, where one wasn't obliged to be particularly demonstrative, and study that picture. Alan preferred to sit at the bar, and Ted Greenwald too. An old station wagon, some dogs bounding about, a field bordered by a stone fence. It looked like one of those Kodak Colorama promotional pictures at Grand Central. Could it have been the same photographer? Who knows. Were they really holding shotguns? I don't remember. A clean, orderly, tidy, image out of some monied Northern Westchester of twenty, thirty years earlier. A place that may or may not have ever really existed but was all the more comforting for the contrast it provided to the poetry that got recited there, weekend after weekend.

Across the street stood a magnificent, then seemingly abandoned, Art Moderne Port Authority truck terminal, one of my favorite buildings in all of New York. UPS took it over years ago. All those years I'd walked around that building — and I had discovered it at least ten years before the readings started — taking in the wonderful diminishing three-point perspective offered by the many-block-long ranks of serried truck bays, I'd never noticed the bar. There was no reason to, until they changed the sign out front. It had been just one more workingman's dive, of which there were still dozens downtown. Paco Underhill was still there when the series started. He lived upstairs, if memory serves. The bar in the front of the place was populated with drinkers, loud drinkers, who had nothing to do with the readings, and who got louder as the afternoon wore on.

The sound system cracked and sizzled and dropped out from the very beginning. And despite infusions of cash from James's Segue Foundation, it never quite seemed to ever get any better. The cook in the side kitchen would start banging pots and pans halfway through the first reader. The first time I walked in, I noted the old style, smoke-darkened, wooden phone booth near the front door. It didn't seem particularly unusual. There must have been a fair number of them around still. At the beginning the series was run by Ted and Charles, as I recall. It would be decades before anyone used the term 'curator' to describe the people in charge of readings.

As I also recall, there was a conscious desire to create an ecumenical spirit, as it were, to encourage the St. Mark's people to come on over; to mollify them perhaps, to serve them up some of the harsher, tougher, Language stuff in digestible pieces. After all, there were still so many more of them, they were in charge of virtually everything and every day in every way they made it clear that they really didn't like us, approve of us, think what we were doing amounted to much. I don't have a copy of that first season's schedule in front of me but I believe each Language poet that first year was paired with someone more acceptable. I read with someone roughly my age, from 'over there' — Gary Lenhart perhaps, or maybe Bob Rosenthal. We hit it off fine, not that we ever hung out together thereafter. But we did chat cordially whenever we ran into each other, at a reading say, which wasn't particularly often.

I'm not sure what I expected for my first time. I expected to be nervous, which I wasn't, not after the first moment or two. I didn't expect the audience to be quiet while I read or display any especial appreciation afterwards, which to my utter surprise they did appear to do. And I certainly did not expect to enjoy myself up there, at the end of the narrow white room with the skylight, talking into the scratchy microphone, the other poets just a foot away, sitting around the little butcher-paper covered tables, smoking, doodling with the laid-on crayons, scribbling in their little notebooks.

I also discovered right there in the middle of that reading that if I slowed my pace it seemed to have a noticable effect. I could control the spaces between the words and between the lines and between the stanzas and that could add weight, distribute emphasis, and focus attention in a way that simply had never occurred to me before. The power of the pause came over me. It seemed to have a measurable impact on the crowd. I liked that. In years to come I think I came to like it too much. For some time now I've been trying to read faster, trying to avoid the appearance of having fallen in love with the sound of my own voice.

It came to a head, in a way, one day in the Nineties when Michael Gizzi came up to me after a reading in Great Barrington and said, "Man, that was great. But you read so, so slow."

I looked at him and a vicious thought appeared in my mind. It just appeared — from where, I don't know. Fully formed, some sort of incubus, it manifested and wrapped its malevolent fingers about my brain — 'This third generation-removed bebop wannabe scat poet who's been trying vainly to channel Kerouac's voice since he was fifteen, who reads so fast that every poem sounds like one long sentence strung together, has the gall to criticize me? And, on top of it, the long poem I've just finished reading is in fact dedicated to him, of all people' — that's what the incubus said to me. I, of course, never said any of that out loud. And as soon as the words formed in my head, I abjured them. That wasn't how I felt about Michael. No way. But where did that spurt of spite, that involuntary ugliness, come from? From where inside of me? Some reptile reservoir of vanity that had been breached? God, that was horrible to contemplate. I felt like I had thrown up in my mouth. And then, a moment later, I realized, of course, he had a point. Michael Gizzi was right..

But, back then, after the first reading at the Ear Inn, we all went up to Bleecker Street — not all of us, exactly. Gary and his friends, or Bob and his friends — whoever it was — they went off somewhere else, somewhere like Dojo's on St. Mark's for ramen and Genesee, I suppose. We piled into that restaurant that Alfred Leslie used to own, near where Bleecker starts, up by Hudson. It is long gone. I haven't even heard anyone talk about Alfred Leslie much at all the last few years, though his name was uttered back then in the same breath as Alex Katz and, say,

Leon Golub. It was full of those big flower paintings of his, and the food was great, and of course, I wasn't allowed to pay.

The next morning, best of all, the Sunday morning after the reading, the phone started ringing. It was my friends, Alan and James and Ray and Bruce and Charles and a few more, calling to say nice things again about the reading, and that was great. That was the icing.

17.   Morton St.

The best apartment I ever had in New York was the one on Morton Street, and I lost it because of poetry.

Before I lived in Little Italy the first time, I was living on Morton Street, sharing it with a cousin. I was sleeping on the sofa. Then I moved to for a month or two to Little Italy, to that tiny place upstairs from Ferrara, and then to Chelsea. From Chelsea I moved back to that same apartment on Morton Street, and I had it all to myself for a few years. And from there I moved to Little Italy a second time, to Kenmare St.

The apartment on Morton Street really belonged to another cousin, Rima. That is, the lease was in her name, but she had left for California years earlier. In fact, I had been imposing myself upon Rima's hospitality in Portola Valley, above Palo Alto, for months and months, on and off, before finally deciding to come back East.

Back then it was hard to find a cabbie who'd even heard of Morton Street. It was at the far, nether end of the Village. A few short blocks further over the elevated West Side Highway still blocked the sky. The Board of Education's old Liberty ship still rusted away at the pier, a faded example of some sort of ideal or boondoggle — typically New York — of vocational education. And all manner of nocturnal, and even diurnal goings-on transpired in the abandoned piers and the truck trailers parked beneath the highway. Morton itself was an archetypal Village street, though, with townhouses and tenements and a little curve in it. Belushi lived across the street, though you never saw him. Frank Serpico used to live down the block, but that was before my time.

My cousin Jessica, who was then in occupancy, and Henry, her boyfriend and eventual husband, had recently graduated from City College, as had all their friends. Jessica, a card-carrying member of the matriarchy of aunts and cousins that ruled my extended family, had recently gotten a job with the Social Security Administration. Henry was driving a cab at the time — along with several of the male members of a clutch of their college friends they pulled me into. There were three four of these guys, and they all went on to considerably more remunerative and professional careers, but at this point they were all satisfied to be hacking. While I never joined them in the driver's seat, I was happy and eager to hear their stories and share their bemused enthusiasm for the odd and bizarre, the ineffably-New York, which came their way every day.

The thing was, as they were the first to admit, they weren't very good taxi drivers. Among other shortcomings, they were lazy. They much preferred to hang out and drink coffee and shoot the breeze with each other rather than push their cabs to make that extra dollar. Their biggest problem, according to them, was finding a place where they could hang out, not just so they could use the bathroom, but where they could keep a booth occupied for several hours without getting the bum's rush. It took some doing, but eventually, according to them, they found the perfect location. A hole-in-the-wall pizzeria on the Upper East Side whose owner, a phlegmatic guy named Ray, didn't seem to care a whit how long they hung out there.

They hung out there so long, and so often, according to them, that the sight of all of their cabs parked outside eventually had the same sort of impact upon the neighborhood as the sight of rows of long-haul tractor trailers do when it comes to truck stops. People noticed all those cabs, and came to decide that if all these cabs were parked outside this pizzeria at all hours the pizza must be pretty good. Ray's started getting busy. It wasn't just a sleepy neighborhood pizzeria anymore. Business got so good that Ray eventually opened up another location, on Sixth Avenue and 11th Street and then another and then another. He got very successful and famous. In fact, he became Famous Ray, with locations around New York. Unfortunately, he apparently didn't get good enough legal advice when it came to trademarking the name of his business, so that very soon after he became successful so did several other Rays, or others who decided to name themselves so, to cash in on his, or, perhaps, my friends' coat-tails, and there was not a thing that he could do about it.

But that was another story, and didn't have much to do with Morton Street per se. Back at the apartment, Henry and I would meet up after work. For a while we go together for a swim at the municipal pool at Carmine Street. From there we'd repair to the Martins Bar on Houston, almost directly across the street from where the Film Forum is now, just east of Seventh Avenue South. Martins was a chain of workingmen's bars. There was a steam table, though since I was still a vegetarian, there wasn't much there for me to eat aside from the cheese sandwiches. It was cheese sandwiches and Heaven Hill on the rocks with a cheap beer chaser. Heaven Hill was the cheapest bourbon they stocked, and that was saying a lot.

I don't remember what Henry ate. He wasn't a vegetarian. They had boiled beef and cabbage and things like that. He ordered the Heaven Hill too. We went along like that, with an occasional night off, during which we'd hit the White Horse instead, for several months. The whiskey wasn't as cheap there but the atmosphere was marginally more elevated. By mid-winter, however, the inadequacies of an American cheese sandwich diet, combined with a steady nightly infusion of bottom-drawer rotgut, along with the two packs a day of cigarettes which surely didn't help, all lying on top of what now seems to have been a decidedly unadvisable exercise regime — you don't sweat when you are swimming but after an hour or so, you do know that you have given yourself a workout — combined to have a certain impact upon me.

All of that, however, might still have proven insufficient to overwhelm whatever worn and frayed resistance my body could have summoned up against the ravages of a more than usually harsh New York winter if not for the fell, evil, at the time well-known and widely reviled, landlord who held title to 67 Morton Street back then.

For, right at the nadir of that dreadful winter, the likes of which, naturally we haven't seen since — there were no winters like the winters when Nixon was president, that's just the way it was — somehow it made sense that he could make it colder for us than anyone else; after all, hadn't they tried to modify the weather over in Vietnam? — the heat went off in that building and it was weeks, weeks, long terrible weeks before it came back on again. Weaselly, vaguely worded handwritten notes appeared in the lobby for the first few days. A part had been ordered for the furnace. Everything possible was being done. Patience was counseled. And then nothing. We froze, I got sick, and stayed sick.

A cold turned into the flu and the flu turned into pneumonia. I tried everything: smoking Kools, bourbon hot toddies, nothing worked. I was sick for weeks. I blamed the landlord, along with Nixon. I was sure he was trying to drive out the old, rent-controlled tenants, the poor old Italian and Irish ladies. They probably survived that winter just fine, but it almost killed me.

Then there was that sublet above Ferrara's for a few months. Then, I found the studio in Chelsea and got my own place, in my own name. That was a decent-ish place. Of course, it was twice the size and its rent was a tenth of that of the studio where, a few blocks away, decades later, I write this tonight. But that is yet another story. I could have been happy there, or no more unhappy there, or rather, decidedly less unhappy there than in any other apartment I lived in in New York, but it was not to be. A few months after I moved to Chelsea, cousin Jessica and Henry decided to leave the West Village for Park Slope. The Morton Street apartment was now available. It was a one bedroom and it was cheaper. Of course, it was still an illegal sublet but that apartment had been passed from cousin to cousin for years now. There didn't seem much danger on that front. So, I moved in.

About ten years later, long after moving out of Morton Street for the last time, my wife and I were walking up Hudson one weekend morning, not so long before we left New York altogether. There were flags outside my old building. It was being converted into a co-op. We decided to take a look. It just so happened — what were the chances? — that the show apartment was my old apartment, that one bedroom on the third floor. My old place, my cousins' old place, now all tarted up with a granite counter in the kitchen and mirrors everywhere in the bathroom. Revisiting that apartment was just like returning to one's childhood home after years away. Everything was impossibly small, the walls close, the ceiling closer.

But for those few years when I lived there on my own, it seemed roomy and elegant. I had big black bookcases and that long blue rug and a nice new sofa. That's where I was living when I started corresponding with Alan and where I was living when I started to read and everything else started, including working with James on *Roof* magazine. I was there when I started a press of my own. I originally called it Casement Books and then eventually shortened it to Case Books.

The books were printed on a xerox machine. When it came to binding, I splurged on a heavy-duty stapler. I made up collages for most of the covers and had them printed on card stock. Over the years I brought out less than two dozen titles. It was long enough ago that it was only when I got to the latter part of the list were the authors able to supply me with their copy on floppy disks, No one had a computer before then.

One of those books, though, was commercially printed. It was a book of Ray DiPalma's, *Planh*. It was on 8.5 x 11 pages but we had it laid out by Brita Bergland, who also arranged to have it printed for us. Ray's wife, Betsi, did the cover. It didn't occur to me, though, to make any special arrangements with Brita, who was up in New Hampshire, regarding the delivery of the copies. The building's super, it turned out, accepted the cartons. I forget how he let me know that he had them. I had never said a word to him over the years. The book came out great. I was happy, Ray was happy, Betsi was happy. Everyone thought it was a terrific book.

A week or two later the eviction notice was fixed to my door.

All the evil landlord had needed was proof that I wasn't my cousin, the lawful tenant, and I had served it up to him with Ray's book, addressed to me, c/o Casement Books, apartment 3-A, 67 Morton Street, New York, NY 10014.

I got a lawyer and fought him halfheartedly for a few months but the jig was up. To save the apartment my cousin Rima would have had to return from California and she was not interested in doing that. The landlord did offer to let me have a lease of my own. Instead of the $160 I was paying, he proposed a new rent of $500 or $600. That was out of the question. I was insulted. I took a walk, and headed off to Little Italy again for an apartment half the size of the one I'd just lost, for only about double my old rent. That I could afford. But, if it hadn't been for that book, if it hadn't been for poetry, I would have been in that apartment still, coughing up each month in rent, unless I'd bought it when the building went co-op, less than what my son pays, when I am not looking, for a pair of sneakers.

18.   At the White Horse

There was so much to learn.

One of my first lessons, soon after I arrived in the city, came when I was living on Morton St. the first time, when I was sleeping on the sofa in the living room, hanging out with Henry.

We were going up the street to the White Horse almost every night.

We'd always see a drowsily tipsy, blowsy older woman tottering in, halfway through the night. Her dyed blonde flappers' cap and inexpertly applied lipstick in keeping with what came to seem a not entirely uncalculatedly sloppy approach, brushing up against the men, not all of the men, some of them, as she made her way around the room. "A rose for your sweetheart," she would drawl in a charming Irish-Hells Kitchen brogue, holding up a tired, cellophane wrapped, long stemmed. Not unlike her, no-longer-a-real-beauty.

You could hear the rise and fall of vaudeville, burlesque and Broadway itself in her voice. She must have been a charming chorine in her day. Minsky and Winchell and Rothafel and Runyon himself had doubtless dandled her on their knees. Now she was reduced to this. Thirty, forty years later, when she should have been regaling salons in Palm Springs or Palm Beach with tales of her youthful misadventures, instead she struggled across an unforgiving Manhattan, limping from bar to bar, cadging a dollar or two for a tired rose. What a life. What mistake had she made? What mobster had she spurned? Lansky? Siegel? Costello? Or, was it some wrong guy she'd hitched her star to? Had she pined away her best years for some worthless palooka sent up to Sing Sing for life? Why, how, had she ended up like this?

And then one evening I happened to be outside as she made her way from the bar. I know I wasn't out there having a cigarette, because you were welcome to smoke in bars then, and would be for thirty more years. And there were no railing or picnic benches outside the White Horse back then. No holding pens for benighted NYU students. It was still by-and-large a neighborhood bar, or at least we wanted to think so. Having said that, there was already a considerable amount of necrophiliac Dylan Thomas ephemera hanging on the walls. Even though he hadn't really drunk himself to death there. Henry and I had probably simply run out of cash to keep drinking and were pausing there at the doorway while we were trying, vainly no doubt, to conjure up something else to do rather than return to the apartment, and its stink of cat pee and the dim TV.

And while we stood there, I assume Henry was there with me, I can't remember a time I went to that bar without him, out she came, our ancient Roxy-girl flower lady, but there was something different about her gait. She was walking with more assurance, her spine straighter, her head more erect, her mien more alert, less gauzy and bleary. She was walking with purpose and, right before our dumbfounded eyes, we saw that she was heading directly towards a long, black Cadillac, a late model Cadillac, pulled up at the curb in front of the bar.

A man stood beside the opened rear door. He wasn't dressed in chauffeur's livery, but he might just as well have been. He nodded to her as she gracefully took her seat in the rear, closed the door politely and took his place behind the wheel. He pulled the car into the Hudson Street traffic, heading uptown towards — we suddenly realized, as all became clear to us, watching the limo's tail lights as it passed Bleecker, not a doubt left in our mind — her next destination, another watering spot, then another, and another. Just as, we were equally certain, she in fact was pulling far more money out of those bars, with the aid of those sad, drooping roses, than any of the bartenders who toiled there, even the crooked ones, perhaps even more than the owners themselves. It was a lesson.

19.   *In the Story Department*

Now we were closing in on the Eighties. The charm of Learning to Read Through the Arts had worn off. I was looking for a job. I landed a try-out for the Story Department at Warner Bros. in New York. 'This is a freelance reader slot. Got that? Now, read this 450-page novel tonight, write a synopsis, use this cover sheet. Tell us if you think it should be made into a movie and turn it in tomorrow morning.' I could do all that, standing on my head, though it was hard to believe that they could be interested in my opinion about anything.

Those days I was staying up late anyway. Around midnight I'd head up to Smilers in Sheridan Square and get a bottle of grapefruit juice and a bag of cashews to tide me over, or maybe wander over to Grove Street and the Pink Teacup, and let one of those motherly Black ladies ply me with grits and eggs. Then I'd head back to the apartment on Morton Street. They started giving me potential properties, as they were described, to read every few days. This work was even more uncertain — precarious, we'd say now — than what I'd been doing, but it was considerably more congenial.

After a couple of months, another position opened up there, working in the office. It wasn't much, it was likely the lowest paying job in all of Warner Communications, but I took it. Between that and the reading I now was making almost what I'd taken home at Learning to Read Through the Arts. Look at the college my parents had sent me to, look at what they'd shelled out, I know they said this to themselves, all so I could end up as the staff messenger and file clerk for the East Coast Production Department.

The job actually proved to be a great pleasure. I took the E or the F up to Rockefeller Center every morning, then got sent to fancy publishers' office to pick up manuscripts that were getting sneaked to the studio, to producers' hotel suites to deliver gift baskets, to a young director's apartment on Central Park West to hand him a Rolex. It was a present from the head of production, a trifle, a token of everyone's esteem, in recognition of the strong opening numbers his new feature had racked up the previous weekend. He didn't know how to work the clasp. It worked just like my Seiko. I got a warm thanks when I showed him. Was he actually impressed or just being polite?

I also took lots of cabs. Crosstown, uptown, downtown. I took more taxis in my first week at Warner Bros. than I had in all the years since I'd come to New York. Back then, by law, every cab had to have the name of the company that owned it painted on its passenger door. These were all holding companies or shell companies and a typical fleet slapped a different name on each of their cabs. But the names were wonderful. I started writing them down: *Sit In My Cab Corp., Nachis Cab Corp. Fighting Sixty-Ninth Service Corp.* I ended up writing a poem made up of those names, along with some of the cabbie monologue I was treated to during those trips. There was a taxi car wash around the corner from James's loft. I found one of their flyers on the sidewalk one day and used it as it the coversheet when I xeroxed up some copies of the typescript and sent it to my friends.

Another aspect of the job: I was delegated to stay in the office until 7:00 pm. Someone had to be there in case the studio called. I'd pass the time doing my reading — it was called coverage — or leafing through the Hollywood Reporter until it was time to lock up. The phone never rang but not infrequently the evening silence was shattered by shouting, screaming, cursing, impressively imaginative cursing, all emanating down the hall, from the largest office on the 13th floor, occupied by someone I came to know well. Sidney was the company's senior business affairs executive. He handled the biggest deals, like the ones with Clint Eastwood, the TV networks. Superman too. Hurling these wild imprecations at his negotiating partners was how he did business. It was immensely entrancing. Old Hollywood lived still, three doors down.

A few months later there was an opening for a junior role in Business Affairs. It paid a bit more than I was making, I took it. I wasn't a lawyer like most people in that department, so my long-term prospects now weren't the brightest, but I could use the money. Funny, when I started that job, I was still looking for that kind of easy gig that would just pay the rent. Just few years later — and this, as I look back now, is just how, and when, the Seventies truly turned into the Eighties — I found myself involved with some entrepreneurs who were deep into innovative financing and we were trying to start a business.

That's how things had changed for me, and when, and not just for me, I'd aver.

Sidney put me in charge of the filing system for the company's contracts — there were a couple of women who actually did that work — as well as various reporting programs, they were all done on paper then, that kept track of the company's properties, its features and tv shows and cartoons. He also taught me how to write a picture digest, the internal analysis issued for every feature the company released, summarizing its rights and obligations, from advertising to financing. Why anyone thought I was competent to decipher the profit participation composition and recapitulate the gross receipt calculations for these movies was beyond me. As I tried to get the hang of it, when I asked what I thought were perfectly reasonable questions, like how the studio could grant, to the stars of a given movie, a total of 150% of the net profits, I mean how could there ever be more than 100% of the net profits, I learned the limits of Sidney's patience. I also learned how sturdy were the old-fashioned manilla folders that the contracts I'd been poring over were bound into, since they could be hurled across an extremely large office and still maintain their integrity. Lucky for me, Sidney's aim wasn't great.

Each of those contract folders had a mate in the storeroom, another folder containing the correspondence, notes and deal memos and drafts, that had been created preparatory to the contracts themselves. Often, I had to refer to those too. Telexes too were often bound into that paperwork. They looked like old-style telegrams. The one that's stayed with me forever, from Sidney to Lord Lew Grade, a British film tycoon several of whose films Warner's distributed, read simply:

"Dear Lew. Stop. Fuck you. Stop. Rude letter follows. Stop. Best Regards, Sid."

Eventually, a few years later, a new regime took control at the studio in Burbank and Sidney's style of doing business came to be seen as a bit passé. He was retired — 'you've done enough,' as they say — and given his production deal, the sort that provided a small suite, but in a different building in Rockefeller Center, away from the action. Our office in New York was dismantled and I was out of work.

The start-up guys I'd tried my luck with, they struck out. Now what? The thing was, while I'd had to look for work before, something was different this time. I wasn't a kid anymore. I was with the woman who I was going to marry. And now it was clear that to get by in New York — we were deep into the Eighties. the Seventies were gone and forgot — you had to have a real job.

20.   *On Kenmare*

I was lucky to get this new apartment, and I had to remind myself of that every day. It wasn't like living on Morton Street. The apartment, though it had recently been updated, was still a dump, there was no getting around it. You walked straight into the kitchen. The kitchen sink was the only one in the apartment, the toilet was off the kitchen, the shower was around the corner on the other side. This was a decided step down. But the lease was in my name, and it was mine. And it was safe — that was the line on that neighborhood back then. The mob made sure there was no crime, other than theirs, in that part of town. The landlord of this building was a capo in the Gambinos. A few years later he got knocked off by John Gotti on his climb to control of that family.

Alan and I decided to do a collaboration together. We ended up working on it for, I would guess, more than a year. He'd just come over and we'd have a few drinks and have at it. We each have a copy now. It is more than 80 pages long. We certainly had a good time with it.

I haven't looked at it since we stopped. We never finished, we just stopped. The two of us managed to make sure, over the years, that we had copies stored away, safe, somewhere. But the thing I remember most was how little we cared, how little we cared for what the poem looked like. And, in this way, the experience was similar to every other collaboration I have been a part of. The pleasure of working with another, the novelty, the piquant sensation of having another to bounce off of, to serve as an emotional and intellectual springboard to keep one motivated, involved, was so rewarding, so fruitful, so engaging that I came not to care at all what the piece looked like on the page. I needed to say what I needed to say, and so did he, and so we wrote.

Eventually, Alan would leave, sometime during the evening or the night or the middle of the night. I would stumble off to bed. The alarm would go off in the morning. I would shower, shave, throw on some clothes, eat some breakfast or stumble over to the plain Greek diner by the Spring Street stop — the same one which I believe plays an important role in

Rachel Kushner's *The Flamethrowers* — where despite my intentions to the contrary, I always ordered the same thing: two eggs over easy with rye toast. And then I'd cross the street, go downstairs and get on the 6. I was working uptown now.

But, going out in the morning — not every morning but, it seems, every morning that followed one of our evenings — I would look down and there, neatly deposited on the floor beside my front door would be a little card, maybe it was a mass card, maybe it was just a little devotional card for a particular saint. Someone, one of my neighbors, had left it there during the night. Sometimes it was clear that candles and maybe incense too, if I am remembering correctly, had been burned there as well.

Someone had been looking out for us, or themselves, or someone. There had been something about what we had been doing the night before, some noise we had been making, some smell or scent or smoke that had escaped the apartment, which had clearly alerted, disturbed, distressed one or more of my more observant neighbors. And this is how they reacted. Were they threatened? Were they seeking to save me? Protect themselves from an evil eye? A little shrine to my, to our, misbehavior, our excess, our license, our requirement to go a little too far in the service of our own saints? At least that is what I thought at the time.

21.   *Bulk Rate Permit*

There were many less-than-scintillating tasks which James, displaying not inconsiderable skills in management and persuasion, got others to execute on his behalf. Among those skills, in a way that was increasingly impressive as time went by, was his ability to pass along, at least to some extent, onto others, the drudgery that was part and parcel of mounting the annual, or maybe they were biannual, mass mailings to libraries and other potential subscribers, extolling the unique virtues of *Roof* magazine. These weren't the biggest campaigns in the history of direct marketing, five thousand pieces, ten thousand pieces, they couldn't have been much more than that. How many college libraries are there in the United States? But there was a fair amount of work getting one out the door.

Getting anything out the door meant getting it down to the post office on Prince Street, that broad dignified pile with the loading docks on the side. But back then, on its second floor, where Macintosh evangelists now extol the virtues of software applications that will enable you, nay, empower you, to lay out the equivalent of a typical ninety page issue of *Roof* in about as much time as it took James to write a check to the typesetter, and for less out-of-pocket than he paid said typesetter for a single page, back then there was a warren of second-floor offices into the depths of which we would lug our huge, filthy, hopefully-correctly-labeled mailbags. There we would present our paperwork, with all the proper obsequies and demonstrations of humility, to a petulant, distracted, unshaven assistant postal supervisor who, assuming he wasn't too close to his coffee break, or wasn't busily engaged in cleaning his Mossberg over-and-under preparatory to mowing down a few dozen of his coworkers, would scribble his signature on the appropriate forms, attack them viciously with a stamper and send us back downstairs, around the corner to the loading docks, where the whole process would be repeated and then, finally, we would be relieved of our burden. Sweating and oddly enervated, the way one always is by the sudden relief of a great weight, we would make our way back to the Bowery, and James's loft.

But when it came to one of what we then called mass mailings, James called up the reserves. The job I remember in particular involved a

218

number of tedious steps: there was a letter, or appeal, which had to be folded, and perhaps an envelope, and maybe there was a return envelope and an order slip too. All of the collated pieces had to be labeled and arranged, that is rubber banded, sorted, and bagged by ascending order of zip code so that the four or five mail bags that all of these dozens of man-hours, actually poet-hours, which stand against man-hours in the way that dog-years stand against people-years, so that each of them could be sent to a different quadrant of the country, to some super-mail sorting facility. There they would be broken down and thence sent to the various states and locales to which they had been addressed.

The help consisted of the usual suspects: Bruce and Charles and Nick and Alan, maybe Ray showed up, but I doubt it, not Hannah, maybe Peter Seaton, or Diane Ward, though it might have been too soon for her to be around. As usual James had created a passing version of a workforce schedule and made it clear to all and sundry what was expected of them. And everyone pitched in, with the requisite amount of grumbling and slacking off, and trips to the bathroom and semi-surreptitious sips from bottles or cans masked in paper bags. But the work was getting done, though exceedingly slowly to be sure. Everyone had shown up and at least was going through the motions. Almost everyone, that is.

The work was being done over a weekend, and everyone was expected to make an appearance for at least part of both Saturday and Sunday. Charles never showed up on Saturday, which excited a certain amount of comment. By the time he did stroll in on Sunday, half of the work day, however that had been defined, was over already, and when he sat down and joined the work circle it quickly became clear that he had no intention whatsoever of actually making much physical contribution to this effort. He was treating it as a social event, making barely a sketch at the sorting or folding or collating or stuffing that the rest of us were busily in, more or less; all the while chatting away a mile a minute, giving every appearance of being simply delighted to be in this company and having the opportunity to see all of us at once. In short, he was negotiating the situation no differently than, say, an after-reading dinner.

I found that blithe disdain, that glad-handing refusal to pitch in, simply infuriating. And for the hour or two that Charles deigned to sit in with us, he simply would not take the hint. He managed to collate, if that was the work-step we were up to, the same number of pieces in twenty minutes as I did in two. I'm not sure what was making me angrier, the fact that he appeared to be so insensitive to our — at least what I thought was our — common project, or that he so clearly was of the opinion that he was above this kind of donkey's work. This wasn't right. We were all supposed to pitch in, help each other, publish each other, support each other. What was he thinking?

I did a slow burn. I had been working, it seemed to me, like a dog, for days now. The thing was, this kind of menial, thoughtless, rote production work was right up my alley. I had always, if not exactly enjoyed it, found it congenial. I suppose I must admit that I do still. It allowed me, I suppose, to believe that I was being productive while at the same time taking up so little of my attention, such as it is, thus allowing it to freely range over whatever topic, fantasy, possibility for a decent line or phrase, or compulsive anxiety that struck my fancy. I was also sporting the bureaucrat's eyeshade. That mid-level manager's officiousness was a pose I fell prey to often in those days. And perhaps do still. I was taking this mailing very seriously. It offended me no end that Charles clearly, obviously, blatantly, was not. It didn't seem to bother James, or anyone else, the way it bothered me, or at least no one else cared to show their annoyance. I must have made my feelings clear in one way or another, though I have no specific recollection of how I managed to do that, for a few days later I got a phone call from Charles asking if we could get together for a cup of coffee.

We met at the Chock Full o' Nuts on 57th Street, by Carnegie Hall, now long vanished. Why there? I must have been working in midtown already. Maybe we rendezvoused there because it was halfway between his apartment and my office. After sharing with him the famous Chock Full o' Nuts story — about the consultant who saved Chock Full o' Nuts millions of dollars simply by removing a quarter inch of padding from their stools' upholstery, thus making their seating sufficiently uncomfortable to move their lingering customers out the door with dispatch, freeing them up for new customers — we settled down to business.

Charles graciously opened by expressing chagrin that there had been something that he had said or done which had so clearly discomfited me. I accepted his acknowledgement. It clearly wasn't an apology, but it was, as they say in the world of diplomacy, an expression of regret. I went on to explicate, in what I thought were unprovocative but unambiguous terms, what I thought was wrong about what he had done, or, more to the point, not done, over the previous weekend. And now the interesting part of the conversation began. Charles did not accept my criticism. He just would not acknowledge that there had been anything inappropriate or insensitive about his actions, no matter how many times I tried to circle the conversation back to what I thought was a clear and simple issue of personal responsibility, the way so many issues for me, even back then, came down to simple matters of individual roles and requirements. But I could not pin him down. Gradually, we must have sat there for almost an hour, I came to realize that I never would. Charles had a facility which I could never hope to match, an ability to shape and focus a dialogue, to frame his responses to deflect or diffuse, to adorn and ornament, or perhaps to camouflage his verbs and modifiers to give every appearance of genial agreement, even light-hearted frolic, while never giving even an inch, all the while driving home whatever cold, hard point he deemed it necessary to deliver. I could make absolutely no headway. My verbal skills were no match for his, they never would be. And in this conversation the point he was making was that he would simply never agree to be held to the same sort of standard that we — the rest of us — apparently had to measure ourselves by. And that was that.

A few days later, as I walking home from James's place, an episode from the life of Pablo Picasso came to mind, and would not depart. There was a point in Picasso's career when his work was just starting to sell. He was still living in drafty digs in Montmartre, still part of the motley gang, along with Apollinaire and Braque, Gris too, all still considering themselves poor, bohemians, outsiders, revolutionaries perhaps. One evening they were all invited to a fancy dress party.

They proceeded to create costumes for themselves with whatever came to hand in their tumbledown studios. That evening at the party, as they admired or denigrated each other's odd, off-kilter handiwork, in strode Picasso dressed as a bullfighter. His costume was not just meant to resemble or recall to mind a bullfighter's. It was a bullfighter's outfit, an incredibly expensive, fitted, brocaded, silk and sateen ensemble, which as we all know, if we can recall from reading Hemingway, was so dear that it no doubt represented a financial outlay likely greater than all of the other assembled painters of the group had garnered from selling their work — not individually but as a group — so far in their careers.

22.   *The Book Fair*

For three or four years we did the New York Small Press Book Fair —
maybe that wasn't its name back then. Whatever it was called, it has,
I believe, long been subsumed into that New York Is Book Country
extravaganza. Maybe it even ran concurrently with it back then. Every
small press and magazine one could think of, and not just the ones from
New York, along with many that one couldn't think of, or didn't want
to think of, or about, showed up there. It was a trade show, pure and
simple, and the first one that I had ever worked, albeit unwittingly. James
had a table for *Roof* magazine, and then Roof Books. He and I shared it
with L=A=N=G=U=A=G=E magazine after it got going, which meant
Bruce Andrews and Charles.

The first couple of years we worked it the fair was located in one or
another venue at NYU, and then it moved, but I don't recall where.
The table we would rent would have all the latest copies of *Roof* laid
out artfully, or all the latest Roof Books. I don't remember any signage
though. No banner or flyers. Certainly, no hats or polo shirts with
the *Roof* logo, in fact there was no *Roof* logo. No giveaway pens or cup
holders or refrigerator magnets, none of the sorts of things you expect
at a trade show. Of course, nobody else had such things. Maybe they do
now. Just a long folding table, with the typical cheap cloth cover and felt
front hiding the cardboard boxes shoved underneath, and a few folding
chairs. The show was always crowded and there were always people
passing by who you knew, or wanted to get to know, or who you had
somehow avoided seeing for a year and now, behind our little table, you
were trapped into talking to. The hours were long. It went on for several
days. It would have been impossible for James and I to staff that table
for the duration of the show, so James dragooned everyone else to pitch
in: Bruce, Charles, Nick, Alan, even Ray. There was a schedule and you
were expected to show up on time, learn how to handle cash and make
out receipts, where to hide the cash box, and what to say about the
latest issue of *Roof.*

The work wasn't particularly onerous, you sat behind the table and when
some poor soul wandered over, tried to interest them in our wares, or
just let them browse, or tried to avoid meeting their eye, which seemed

the easiest course of action by far, and seemed to be the one pursued by most of the forced volunteers who worked the *Roof* stand. Except for Bruce. Bruce was different.

Bruce had none of the fear, or compunction, or, when it came to selling, none of the reserve, misplaced or not, that make such situations uncomfortable for any but those born to or disciplined in the ways of selling. He revealed a part of himself in those three- or four- or five-hour shifts that was amazing to behold. He had a hook, a line, a proposition for every item on the desk and every wayward prospect — because, clearly, he saw every hapless attendee as a prospect — who passed within earshot of our location. And not conversational earshot either. This was often barker-level, broadcast, view-hallo earshot. And he was good. He drew people in, he got them to pick up the titles, he got them to fork over their dirty, torn, bent and spindled fives and tens.

It came naturally to him. This was a side to him hitherto unguessed at. I had been selling since I was in high school, working in my father's camera stores, but Bruce was far beyond me. He had it, that charm, that effervescent momentum, that effortless confidence, it was a wonder to behold. This poet, this academic, this unreconstructed Marxist, had it. Somehow it had been bred into him, for clearly Bruce was operating on a level of assurance, of sweeping command, that was far beyond anything that could be taught. I sat in amazement. The investment banking world's loss was the poetry world's gain. The zero coupon and the municipal bond markets, the spot-oil pit, the gold futures exchange, they never knew they were missing. Bruce Andrews was a born salesman.

23.   *Ephebes at Phebe's*

It's still there, on the corner of the Bowery, Phebe's. Why we were all there for dinner I can't for the life of me remember. It must have been after an event, a reading. But why there? Nothing was going out on the Bowery back then. If there had been some sort of event at James's no doubt we would have stayed there. There was James's loft, there was CBGB's, there were the missions, there was Phebe's and then you had to head all the way up to Cooper Union before there was anything else going on.

The sidewalks on the Bowery always seemed wider than any other avenue. Was it that the buildings were so much lower than on Second or Lafayette or Third? Or was it the horizontal human forms, there were so many of them back then, stretched out hither and thither, pushing out the various vanishing points? Or was it that those sidewalks were always so uniformly empty? No one ever walked there. Staggered there, but didn't walk. During the day, outside the restaurant supply houses, the sidewalks were crowded with greasy, repossessed, eighteen-burner ranges undergoing what passed for reconditioning, the filthy spray from the high pressure hoses slicking the cement, rushing down the gutters, but at night the sidewalks were altogether deserted.

Hannah's apartment was right around the corner. Maybe we were hanging out after an event at La MaMa where the Last Tuesday evenings were held, but I don't think so.

There were six, eight, ten of us at the table and we were engaging in the usual, desultory after-reading, after-event conversation. Hannah was sitting directly across from me. She sported her typical expression, one we talked ourselves into believing was a discanted, introspective, observational, beatitude. After all, how else can one be suitably positioned, appropriately situated, to see words?

The talk would ebb and flow. Interjections would be inserted. Vaguely fashioned sallies, gibes, digs — all good-natured, of course — would be drawn up like odd, improbable, toy artillery pieces, their fuses ready to be lit. Like suspicious fireworks, smoldering away, towards which the crowd would edge closer in order to get a better look. More beers would be ordered, some would grow silent, recalculating their share of the inevitable, fought-over, that is to say disputed, check that would eventually land on the table.

The thing is, and I don't mean this in any self-serving way, but I always saw Hannah's default 'look,' that settled expression on her face, the kind we all have, when not animated by any particular emotion, the look that is perhaps the most revealing of any we display, in her case to be one of firmly-seated anger. Not dissatisfaction, not anxiety, not some somehow dissociated terror tamped down. No, real, righteous anger. Towards whom? For a long time, I could never make out.

That night was different. That night I must have said something, or turned to my dinner companion and said something. What it was I cannot possibly recollect. What I do remember is the kick in the shins. Now, this was back in the late Seventies or early Eighties, people were always brushing up against each other, after all, the Sixties were barely over. Brushing up against each other, by accident or on purpose. My friend turned to me and whispered something in my ear. Frankly, I didn't pay it much mind. Then she got kicked again, I saw her flinch and she turned to me. Then I looked across the table, and there was Hannah fixing me, not her, me, with a baleful glare.

It wasn't particularly hard to realize why she was attacking her. Hannah just didn't care for my girlfriend.

X and I had only been going out for a short time, and would only go out for a short time longer. She was a friend of a friend and we had originally crossed paths at a party. She was smart and sweet and not really married anymore and rather older. She had teen-aged sons, and this was at a time when I didn't feel much older than a teenager myself. A few times, after spending some part of a night in her apartment on the Upper West Side, we'd take her dog for a walk in Riverside Park. I'd borrow one of her sons' down jackets, which were big — and that is what always floored me — too big for me. I don't remember why we stopped seeing each other. Eventually, it just ended. I don't remember a scene, nor one or the other of us breaking it off. Maybe, though, my memory is just being kind to me. Of course, she was considerably younger then than I am now.

I do remember that I was working at Warner Bros. back then. And, as happened occasionally, I was the recipient of a spare set of house seats to Broadway previews. I would call her in the afternoon and we would meet later that evening, at the box office. One time, as I recall, she was wearing a fur and I had on a pair of jeans. The seats, as usual, were in the second or third row. As we waited for the curtain to rise, Ed Koch, who was still mayor, came through our row on the way to his seat, obliging me to rise. He gave her an appraising look and then one, which I took to be of approbation, directed at me. "How'm I doing?" I asked, throwing his trademark line back at him. For some reason he didn't appear to find that remark very witty. As for my friend, she didn't raise her eyes from the Playbill, but I could tell she wasn't amused.

But my girlfriend certainly wasn't wearing a fur on the Bowery that night. Over the years Hannah met all of my girlfriends, but this was the only one who caused her to make her feelings known with some keen blows to the shin. For a long time, I assumed that even without the fur there was something about this woman — was she wearing cashmere that night, or pearls, or was there something about her scent or hair or something else, not to be crass about it, which only another woman typically would notice — which Hannah had picked up on, which caused her to deem her to have the stink of the bourgeois upon her? And therefore, had Hannah decided that she was all wrong for me, and I should have nothing whatsoever to do with her and, for one reason or another, she felt it best to make these feelings known with her foot?

But now, as I write this, it occurs to me that perhaps there was something else on her mind: her own age — Hannah's age. And my girlfriend's age too. Maybe Hannah looked at this woman and realized that they were the same age, or close to the same age. And then perhaps Hannah asked herself why, if I was so interested in going out with older women, I picked that one instead of her? And then, again, perhaps not liking the answer, she decided to let her boot do the talking. I have no particular reason to favor this theory. In fact, much argues against it. God knows, I was no prize then and Hannah never gave one cause to suspect that she harbored any feelings towards me, or anyone else that I was aware of. It just now suggests itself because as I look back it is clear how young and not-so-young we were back then, and how entirely ignorant I, for one, was to the particular pain, and potential pleasures, of living in a world where one's peers are often much younger, and older, than one. And, further, how for example such pain, in particular, could come to hold sway, and reign, exercising suzerainty over us. And it only took me, how many decades to learn that for myself?

24.   *Rose*

The first time I was in New York after graduation I stayed at my brother Richard's apartment while I decided what to do. I had just broken up with a girlfriend; she was in graduate school at Princeton. We'd been living together down there, in a sad apartment in Cranbury, a few feet from the railroad tracks. I had a job at the university library and was growing increasingly desperate. After we broke up, I ended up going out West. That trip to California. But for a month or so before leaving, I slept on my brother's sofa.

From his top floor window, one could see the Statue of Liberty and the World Trade Center to the south. I remember quite blithely telling people how well the towers would serve as the raw material for a Barnett Newman sculpture, the kind where there's a broken shaft next to a straight one. To the west you had a clear view of the upper floors of Westbeth. The top floor, of course, was occupied by Merce Cunningham's company, and even without the aid of Richard's binoculars, through the row of tall windows you could see the dancers leaping, thrusting and turning. I also came to notice a funny little guy walking down Bank Street every morning, heading west, against the flow of people on their way to work. A compact older man with curly gray hair, an odd springy step and a decidedly distracted air. It was Merce.

A year later, after I returned to New York, I got that job that took me to Westbeth every day. Westbeth was the old Bell Labs complex on West Street that Richard Meier had recently converted into artist housing.

While I am not sure how much good the Learning to Read Through the Arts program did for the kids, or the artist-teachers, for whom this wasn't much more than a minimum wage job, it did confer one indisputable benefit, on me: for a time, I was the proud possessor of a Guggenheim Museum employee identification card. It granted me free entrée into all the museums in the city. And at that time, things that were free were about all that I could afford.

There's not a lot that I recall being shown at the Guggenheim back then that made an impression on me, with one terrific exception. As part of some larger exhibition, down in the museum's basement auditorium, for a week or two, Joseph Cornell's film "Rose Hobart" ran continuously. I'd never thought much about Cornell before. He was just out there, another odd duck. I was reading a lot of surrealists back then though. Breton, for one. I had also just picked up *Hebdomeros*, that incredible de Chirico novel. I had bought it as an imported English hardcover, spending what seemed a fortune at the Gotham.

I had never seen anything like this movie. It immediately took me in, picked me up and carried me along in its heady, throbbingly passionate repetitions. There wasn't much of an audience. People drifted in, stayed for a few minutes, started talking and laughing distractedly among themselves as it dawned on them that this movie wasn't about more than those framed moments, appearing again and again. Then they drifted out again. I stayed. I couldn't think of leaving. I was entranced. Immediately, every Cornell box I had ever seen made perfect sense. The pain and purity, loss and hope, has, for me, shone out of every one ever since. The movie presented a perfect argument. The fact that there was no plot, that the same scenes repeated themselves over and over was part and parcel of its majesty. Here was Hollywood, second-rate, B Hollywood, and a starlet — one who, on the face of it, could have been picked at random — appearing in what to most moviegoers had been an entirely forgettable film. All that remained of it were mere snippets, cut, spliced and reprinted and rerun over and over. The source was base and common, just like the raw material for his boxes, not unlike what Rauschenberg and Lichtenstein and Warhol were drawing on. Of course, there was no irony here, no distance, no commentary. It was unadulterated, abject passion. But all that contrast and that cutting and that repetition was unutterably moving.

25.   *Agnes*

No one talked about Agnes Martin at Bennington. I took as many painting courses there as writing courses, more in fact, and I would have noticed.

I wasn't an art major though. That meant I had to scrounge around for space. I wasn't entitled to a studio of my own. I ended up in a basement of an off-campus house in North Bennington. I had friends who lived upstairs. It was Hill House, as in Shirley Jackson's 'The Haunting of Hill House.' She and Stanley Edgar Hyman had lived here.

The art department at Bennington was an extension of the New York scene, but one somewhat preserved in aspic, whose clock had stopped at some point in the Sixties: Larry Poons, Anthony Caro and Kenneth Noland, and Lyrical Abstractionism of course. The department's high-water point, in a twisted way, had probably been that night, not so many years earlier, when David Smith died, or rather killed himself, as was the accepted version on campus, in his pickup truck, driving home from a party at Kenneth Noland's. And he didn't even teach there; he was just hanging out.

There was also the cult of Clem Greenberg. The line was drawn fairly clearly and cleanly from abstract expressionists to their grandchildren, teaching us — the Pat Adamses, Phil Woffords and the like. Lyrical Abstractionism, that's what it was called. And they all seemed to be shown at André Emmerich. As for Helen Frankenthaler, herself a Bennington alum, there was no escaping her. There was no room for Minimalism, much less Pop art, in this tale. And the paintings I turned out fit the mold precisely. Or, rather, they fit the mold, but somewhat palely. They were large, 6' x 10', unstretched, monotone stain paintings. George Pitts's were so much better. I would lay the canvas out on the floor, pour the paint on and tip one corner up and then pull another down until it looked more or less like everyone else's. Until my senior year. Then I threw all that over and sat down and started anew, making small, thickly impastoed, intricate geometric designs, along the lines of the pattern painting that was showing up at Holly Solomon, which my teachers liked, but the other students scorned.

Not long after coming to New York, one day I wandered into Pace Gallery and saw something I had never seen before. To be fair, while there was no work like this being done at school, Sol LeWitt had been invited to do a wall in the new art building shortly after I left. Having said all that, the training I received there did prepare me for that moment. When I walked into those rooms on East 57th Street, my eye was prepared. It knew how to look at these modestly sumptuous paintings. What I saw was overwhelming. That so much power could be presented so simply. I had seen Flavins and I knew Judd's work. His building was right down Mercer St., a couple of blocks from my aunt and uncle's shop. You could look straight in the windows and see whatever it was he had just finished, along with that rolltop desk of his.

But Agnes Martin was new to me and I was dumbstruck. It seemed to me that at least part of what these paintings were about was humility, and respect. There was so much power gathered there inside the frame of the picture; it was the painter's job, in a way, to honor it. By stripping away layers of personality, vanity, desire, fear, by taking away everything else, the underlying gravity and splendor of the project would emerge and the very buttresses of reality would stand revealed. It was clear to me what I was viewing there: the fundament of the world, the terrible pinions upon which the universe depends. The lesson wasn't lost on me.

There was so much that I would come to realize did not belong in my poems. My job would become, when the time came and I was ready, to make work that was — not purged — but freed of them. Those base elements like clinging narrative and psychologistic grammar. And I couldn't have done it without her.

26.   *At Cunningham's*

I went to see a lot of dance with my girlfriend Shannon. She was a dancer. We went to the ballet and we went to Broadway but mostly we went to performances downtown. She got us into shows and recitals for free, somehow. Every weekend we went to churches and lofts, in odd spaces in what wasn't yet known as Tribeca. Wrecks of huge old men's clubs, old union hall reading rooms with broken windows and piles of plaster on the floor that I recognized twenty years later, while leafing through shelter magazines, transformed into billionaires' pieds à terre.

Douglas Dunn made a big enough impression on me that I wrote a piece about him in L=A=N=G=U=A=G=E. His work seemed to be made up of bits and remnants of everyday life which he had been able to disassemble, or reassemble, and present to us — ten or twenty people — sitting in an airless, noisy Broadway loft above a rag and remnant dealer. Those sorts of businesses were still to be found in Soho back then. He let us see through those mundane gestures, picking up lost items, doing housework, navigating the streets, and by doing so enabled us to understand something new about the world itself around us, about ourselves too. The congruencies became clear. The discrete elements and components of our daily round that we never bother to grasp, or don't spend enough time to try and take the measure of, but that are there, inside every day, every moment: all were laid bare.

But if Dunn, who appeared to be only a few years older than me, and whose new work and whose ongoing thinking we could see and watch evolve in the occasional events he organized from time to time, was the closest to an approach or attitude to art that I felt that I was fumbling towards, Cunningham himself was a towering presence, a hegemon of ideas and productivity with a big company and a huge body of work, and the most impressive physical plant, sitting up there in his fortified penthouse on top of Westbeth. Of course, he was also the father and teacher of all the people we were looking at, the Douglas Dunns, the Gordons, the Paxtons, the Browns and the Tharps.

We'd sit on the floor, leaning against the wall around the edges of the big space up there, and the pieces would unfold. He had the biggest company and they would take up the whole floor, swooping from corner to corner. Then he would come out. In the mid-Seventies Merce was still dancing. If he wasn't still capable of the kind of amazing leaps that his dancers routinely tossed off, there was something embodied more clearly in his every gesture, more wonderfully than I had seen in anyone else. It was that terrific, amazing 'difference' between Taught and Thought, between movement that was generated by a choreographer from inside himself, which he shows to us with his own body, and that same movement which his dancers have to be taught.

One could see it over and over in the performances of so many choreographers dancing their own work, and it was here again. His dancers were perhaps the best trained one ever saw downtown. They rehearsed together the most, toured together, and because of that, most probably could come closer to their choreographer's vision than any other company. But when Merce moved something happened that was unlike anything that I had ever seen. It wasn't so much a sense of history — that here, in this little man's aging body all of dance history was embodied, a hinge between its beginnings, as limned by Martha Graham, his own teacher, and the present, or future — in the Judson dancers and the even younger choreographers we went to see every weekend. One never thought of that while he danced. Nor was it the almost intimidating presence of Cage and the likes of Rauschenberg or Warhol or the other artists who collaborated with him, and all that their presence said about the centrality of this work in the contemporary aesthetic. Neither was it the uncannily moving way that he could generate meaning with any part of his body, and in the smallest gesture animate the audience's imagination, taking one to places simply unknown.

No, what stunned me over and over again as I sat there, my knees and back aching on the hard dance floor, the skyline of New York on display beyond one row of windows, the lights of New Jersey winking from another, was something quite else. It was his basic, organizational building block: chance. Chance operations, chance calculations, chance combinations. How chance shaped and focused his movement, how the organizing and distancing power of chance permitted, enabled and focused one's vision, in a way that wasn't otherwise possible. Now we could see into the heart, as it were, of those gestures, those steps, those movements and combinations, their essential meaning and value, stripped clean of any civilizing disguise, any distracting confessionist, narrativist camouflage, any voyeuristic athleticism.

The workings of chance seemed to allow Cunningham to incorporate into his dances all manner of movement, not only the mundane, workaday gestures which Dunn, for example, had transformed into incandescent vessels of revelation, but also vast and formally florid, compound organizations of massed dancers that could have come straight out of Graham, or Balanchine or even Pepita. But here one could finally see them for the first time, see them for what they really were, an artist's bedrock demonstration of inconsolable contradiction, of unutterable connection. It was soaring, defiant adumbration that refused to be taken on any terms but its own and, simultaneously, presented itself as the most transparent, even most gentle, of welcoming beguilements. And it was chance, the clear, ineluctable, unarguable operations of chance, it seemed clear to me, that freed Cunningham and allowed him to pack all of this into each and every work.

27.   The Book-Storage-Conundrum

Among the things I did not have early on were bookcases. I did some shopping around. Bookcases were expensive. Even buying cinder blocks and boards seemed pricey, not that I had any idea where I could find cinder blocks in New York. Then I remembered something I'd read in Wallace Stevens' letters: a self-satisfied aside to a friend, describing how he'd gone out to someplace like Sears and bought a whole passel of inexpensive steel shelving and now he had an attic filled with orderly rows of a lifetime's worth of books. The idea of Wallace Stevens assembling bookshelves himself seemed improbable enough. The thought of him pacing the aisles of a Sears was even more unlikely.

There was once a used office furniture dealer in Chelsea, on the east side of Seventh Avenue, just below 23rd. He had piles and piles of used steel shelving: green, dented, dirty and dusty, in all shapes and sizes. I picked out enough parts to make two skinny units. He lent me a handcart and I trundled them to the studio on 19th Street. I bought some black spray paint and, in a few hours, there in my little apartment, I had two serviceable, if oddly ominous looking bookcases. They stood proudly in the corners.

I didn't own a whole lot of books but the two bookcases were nearly filled up that first day. It didn't take much time for me to run out of space. In fact, as the years went by, like everyone else I knew, I never seemed to live in a big enough space to be able to keep more than a few of my books around. Eventually, when I moved back to Little Italy, I replaced those black towers with some wire shelving units from a restaurant supply house on the Bowery. But there I never had more than about two medium-sized bookcases worth of room. So, I was continually packing up boxes of books and sending them away. I had a repository, as it were, in the city for the first few years but that didn't last long.

Eventually my books were boxed up and sent off to the country, rusticated, like inconvenient clergymen. They lived quiet lives in friends' and relatives' closets and attics and I didn't see them for years. It was only after I moved to the country myself, almost twenty years after leaving college, that I came to gather in all of my books together under one roof. Even then, there were boxes that remained unopened for decades more. Almost forty years went by before I found the catalogue that I'd bought at the Agnes Martin show, with two announcements I'd swiped from Pace's front desk, stuck inside.

That in-town depository where I stashed my overflow of books for the first few years was down the street from Rae and Al's body and fender shop, in the basement of their friend Irving's place, a few doors down Mercer. His cellar was a long, narrow, fairly dry space, with the typical painted stonework walls. It hadn't been altered much in the last hundred years or so. In the front, beneath the street, were the coal cellars, now empty, where the coal had thundered down through the chutes in the glass sidewalk and piled up before being shoveled into the furnace. Irving was a sweet old guy, approaching sixty. He lived somewhere on Long Island. He parked his car in my uncle's lot and hung out in my aunt and uncle's office, trading antediluvian jokes. He ran the prototypical old-line Soho business, the kind that had settled there around the turn of the century as the district had eased into its long decline. It was the kind of business which has utterly vanished from this earth, never to be seen again, except perhaps somewhere in the back reaches of some straggling godforsaken special economic zone in Vietnam or Honduras.

As far as I could tell Irving had one employee, an ancient black guy who ran the huge, dark, yet more ancient printing presses that took up Irving's ground floor space. I have the feeling that it had been Irving's father's business, and it had been passed down to him. I was just as sure of that as I was sure that there was absolutely no chance that his children had the slightest interest in following him into that business, which surely was just what Irving devoutly wished.

Just as Irving's company had just one employee, he had just one product. Those ancient presses, though still active, printed no more. No more handbills or circulars or wedding invitations. Like a pair of proud carriage horses past their prime, fallen on hard times, now reduced to pulling a renderer's wagon, their plates had been replaced with a set of dies. Neck tie shaped dies. The ancient black guy's job was to feed thin sheets of gray cardboard into the press. That's all he did all day. Out the other

237

end would come tie-shaped cardboard cutouts. Irving sold them to tie manufacturers. The tie manufacturers inserted them into the wide part of their ties where they served as stiffeners, protecting the silk, or rayon or Dacron, as they made their way to the stores. This was the Mid-Seventies and ties were very, very wide indeed. That's all Irving did. His business consisted of just that one product. I always wondered if he had any competition. How many businesses like that did the tie industry need? However many there were, it was clear that this business threw off enough cash to provide Irving and his family with a middle class lifestyle, and the ancient black guy, whose name I never learned, with what was certainly something decidedly less.

It was also clear that when Irving retired that business was going to go out of business. Which it proceeded to do, not too many years later. And my boxes of books, which had lain undisturbed in his basement for almost ten years, found their way to the country. A number of years after that, long after my aunt and uncle had themselves retired, and their one story body and fender shop had been reincarnated yet again, its short life as a disco now largely forgot, into something more respectable, and Mercer Street, one of the last hold-outs in that neighborhood, had been converted into another undistinguished stretch of restaurants and boutiques, and virtually all the hoary, grimy brick facades, with their cast iron pediments, plinths, capitals and columns, had been repointed and sanded and scraped and steamed and prettily repainted, Robin and I went to an opening there.

Tony Shafrazi, who up till then had been chiefly known for going into the Museum of Modern Art, deciding that "Guernica" needed some touching up, then throwing some ink at it, was opening a gallery. It was a Keith Haring show. Haring was someone who's work one had seemingly always seen around, chiefly in the subways, at the furthest end of platforms, drawn on the unused, tall, black rectangles where advertising billboard placards otherwise were pasted. I don't think it was his first show. What I do remember was that the street-level gallery was packed. They were giving away posters, white on black, just like in the subways. We still have ours, hanging in our guest bathroom. Andy was there, which was not particularly surprising.

We fought our way through the gallery. I recall that there was a great glass-topped desk in the back, fashioned from the same wire shelving as the bookcases in my apartment. There was a sign indicating that there was more to see downstairs. There was indeed more work downstairs. I think there were Warhols hanging there. It wasn't quite as crowded. But what shocked me, made me grab Robin's arm, was the sudden realization that I had been down here before, several times, many years ago. The walls hadn't been clean and white then but the rough stonework was the same. The floor hadn't been finished and polished, but the layout was exactly the same. This was the basement where I had stored my books for a decade or so, all those years ago. This was Irving's basement, and Tony Shafrazi's gallery was Irving's old tie-insert factory.

28.   *Ted*

There was a great reading at Books & Co. one evening. This was a
bookstore that you just didn't go into that often, mostly due to its
location. Unless you were visiting the Whitney, there really wasn't
much call ever to find oneself in that neighborhood. And, as literary
and comprehensive as it was, and despite the presence of Burt, that
former Strand manager who had been installed to run the place, there
was something a bit over the top there. It was all that carpeting, and
burnished wood paneling and fittings. Now, I don't actually recall if the
paneling was burnished, or even what burnishing does to paneling, or
how much paneling there really was, but when it came to whatever there
was there, there was a bit too much of it.

This was one of those events that had the entire second floor of the store
packed, with people leaning on the shelves, sitting on the steps, lining
the stairwell all the way down to the first floor. There were three readers:
Michael Lally, Ted Greenwald and Ray DiPalma. It seemed entirely
appropriate that these three should appear together, in some historical
or literary-antecedental way. They appeared in this light as a sort a
triumvirate, representing an older, more accepted generation of Language
writers, though now I'm not sure they should have or would have cared
to be so characterized. A generation that already had some identity, had
already been published before the Language thing got a head of steam
up, and had now, latterly as it were, either identified themselves, or
were being identified by others as part of this movement. And it wasn't
so much that their work had altered over the years as it was becoming
clear to others, to the rest of us, that they had always been exemplifying
or incorporating those particular interests or concerns or approaches
in their work even before Language writing as a collective identity, as it
were, had developed.

And here they were, all three of them together. The problem was, of
course, that back then, just as now, most readings consisted of two
poets reading from their work, not three. Three is always such a difficult
number to fit easily into in readings, just as it is into, say, romance.
Three doesn't go easily into anything, especially, as anyone who has tried

to schedule such an event has discovered, into the roughly two hours that nature decrees to be the appropriate span for a reading, including introductions and break. Readings comprising three readers require a fairly extraordinary degree of cooperation and rectitude on the part of all participants. Readings with four or more poets are easier, those readers understand that they are up there in the limelight for just a few minutes, but with three it is all unclear. Is this a regular reading or not? How much do I read? With three poets whoever is doing the introducing the poets has to be careful not to end up spending more time in front of the crowd than the poets themselves.

That wasn't the problem at this reading. I think it was Jeanette who introduced the readers. Whoever it was, he or she offered up remarks that were sufficiently brief that they made no lasting impression on me. What did make an impression on me was the length of the entire reading itself. As I recall Michael read first, followed by Ray. Or, maybe, Ted read first.

Michael was offhandedly charming, wielding his affect in the way he seemed to do so effortlessly back then. Ray was sonorous and exact, inviting us, but not too effusively, into his world, the way he too always read back in the days when he was out and about giving readings as frequently as any of us. And then there was Ted. *You Bet* might have just come out, which is a pretty long book. Ted was writing long works back then. He still is. Whatever it was, he got up and read a lot of it. Maybe all of it. He read and read and read, all in that defiant, Runyonesque twang. I have always thought of it as a Queens accent, because I know he grew up in Queens. But I'm not sure, upon reflection, where it comes from. Perhaps it sprang fully formed from his brow. His parents, who I know, and his siblings, most of whom I've met, certainly don't talk like that.

When I first met Ted, he was with Joan, his first wife, and they were still doing books, those wonderful Full Court books. Shortly thereafter he was on his own, living in a perfectly charming, bare, loft down on Desbrosses Street or thereabouts. Soon after that, it seemed, he was getting married to Joan, his second wife. I was working in Midtown and he was too, running Holly Solomon Editions on East 57th Street.

We would get together in the middle of the week, during the day. But what I remember most is walking around downtown with him, walking the streets of Little Italy; sitting in Café Dante or one of the other espresso places he liked on Macdougal, watching him wave hello as Shel Silverstein came in, and listening to Ted talk.

Ted has turned out to be one of those men whose appearance changes remarkably little as they age. Perhaps it is what he is made of, perhaps it is what he has put in himself, but those thin, sharp features — the high cheekbones, the piercing eyes, wide restless mouth, swept hair, slim outline — you can see it in the early pictures of him taken when he was just, as some people still put it, coming up. For Ted too had been the youngest of his time. A veritable boy taken up by a set of older contemporaries.

I didn't quite understand why he paid any attention to me at the beginning, why he seemed to enjoy getting together with me. It couldn't have been the scintillating conversation. For quite some time I felt just a little intimidated, I must admit, daunted into a kind of half-silence, muted. I don't think he was just looking for an audience, and there were certainly plenty of other folks, my age or older, who lived or worked nearby. I want to think that he saw something in me that reminded him of himself. Maybe that's wishful thinking.

If so, though, perhaps that accounted for the stories he chose to recount during these sessions: St. Mark's in the olden days. Back before Ted Berrigan ruled. Back when St. Mark's was the central, unrivalled downtown scene, as opposed to a place where, it seemed at the time, none of my friends nor I were likely to be offered readings anytime soon. Back when people there took poetry seriously, and folks got hooted down if they couldn't cut the mustard. When no quarter was offered or given. When favors were offered or denied, and nothing was forgotten. It was a tough-eyed take on the poetry world, unblinking, unsentimental, unforgiving. It was a perspective that was new to me and while shocking in some of details, I told myself that the sooner I acquainted myself with it, the better off, or, at least, the better armed, I would be.

About twenty-five years later a bunch of poets and their spouses were visiting us up in Connecticut one weekend afternoon. We were sitting on the porch and the conversation turned to Ted with whom, it became clear, I remained in greater contact than any of the rest of the company. When I mentioned that Ted was someone who I continued to turn to for advice, whose counsel I honored, there was a moment of silence. Then one of the poet's wives replied saying, simply, "Ted?"

No one sitting there had the slightest doubt what she meant: why in the world would I feel it necessary to get advice from someone who had ended up driving a cab? What could I possibly learn from someone like that? Before I could reply her husband broke in and hurriedly offered up some placating remarks. Surely, he said, Ted had a worthy perspective on things. I didn't say anything, nor did anyone else. I wasn't sure if he wasn't actually just mouthing those words, to avoid embarrassing me or to avert some unpleasantness between his spouse and his host. In any event, the talk quickly moved on to another topic.

But right at that moment, that long-ago Books & Co. reading came to mind. I hadn't thought about it for years. Sometime afterwards I came to query Ted about it. Why, I asked him, had he read so long? And he had. He stood and delivered. He read and he read, longer than Michael and Ray put together. He read and read and read. In response to my question, he gave me that trademark quizzical Ted look: askance, squinty, his chin drawn down, a half-smile sneaking across his features. It was simple, he said.

The reading was originally just supposed to be Michael and him. And then, according to Ted, whose account I have absolutely no reason to doubt, but for which I have no other source, Ray found out about the reading and decided he wanted in on it too. And what was supposed to be a nice posh uptown reading for two stalwart downtown presences, allowing both of them to spread their wings in front of what quite probably would be a new, possibly quite receptive Upper East Side crowd, turned into a cramped three-person sampler, one whose time constraints wouldn't allow any of the three to do more than offer up a tidbit of his work.

So, Ted reacted the way folks down at St. Mark's used to react. You didn't get mad, you got even. He read and he made sure that when he was finished reading everyone, everyone who was involved in putting the reading together, and everyone else who counted, that is to say the other two readers, knew that what they had done, or what they had acquiesced to, was very wrong. And he did it in the most appropriate way possible: not only refusing to read for the fifteen minutes or so that he'd been asked to squeeze himself into, but for more, much more than he would have if it had been a regular, two-poet reading. The audience may not have gotten the point, though some of them did or eventually did, no doubt. But though it may seem harsh to say it, the audience was rather beside the point. There was a point to make, and Ted made it, without histrionics, simply and effectively, the way a poet brought up in the rough and ready early days at the Poetry Project would.

29.   *Invited to Help*

As I recall, there was no conversation whatsoever about this new magazine beforehand. Before, that is, people were asked to contribute pieces. Bruce and Charles were doing a magazine. Fine. James and I were already doing a magazine, how was this going to be different? It became very quickly obvious just how different it was going to be. Everyone I knew was asked to write and virtually everyone did, including me.

I remember being struck when I held the first issue of $L=A=N=G=U=A=G=E$ in my hands, how much indifference it seemed to evince towards its own appearance. The logo and mast offered up a clear, cleanly branded message, although how to assign responsibility for that look and feel seems to grow more contested as every year goes by. The rest of the magazine seemed utterly ignore the impression it made. I wondered, at the time, was that part of its proposition?

As I also recall, no one really called it Language magazine, it was just Language. In the same way that most everyone, back then at least, consciously eschewed attaching the word 'poetry' to the word 'Language.' You could always tell when someone didn't quite get it — say, when offering an introduction at a reading — and they'd say 'Language poetry' — they wanted to be hip, but couldn't quite grasp all the implications, or make the requisite commitment, like those weekend warriors from back in the Sixties who'd show up on the odd Friday night and get high with the real hippies, and then straggle back to their regular jobs on Monday. We were poets, sure, and we surely weren't writing fiction, but to call this poetry didn't seem like a clean enough break with what we thought we were consciously, deliberately, violently rejecting. What we were doing was Language writing, and that's what we all called it. As I recall, that distinction, which seems to flare up desultorily now and again, retained its force for four or five years. Then it largely lost its steam.

At first, Bruce and Charles didn't seem to have an entirely different proposition than anyone else's: everyone did a magazine back then. Our magazines did seem to come out more often than magazines do these days, but perhaps it only appears that way. It must be some foreshortening trick that time plays on us when we get old. But it became clear soon enough, I'm sure it was made clear to us from the get go, that this wasn't going to be another poetry magazine like the rest, like *Roof* for example, or any of the others any of us might be involved with. This was serious.

I recall being too taken aback to want, or to be able to, or to get it together to, contribute to the first issue, though like everyone else who was around those days, I believe I too was invited. Eventually, I summoned up the concentration to put together a few pieces: one was a review of *DOLCH STANZAS*, an early book, of course, all the books reviewed then were early books, of Kit Robinson's, which, apart from its intrinsic radiant transcendentality, was partly built upon an early-childhood reading philosophy, known as "Dolch Words." The bulk of my piece was intended to draw readers' attention to that connection, for I knew that every single reader, in all likelihood, would assume that the word "Dolch" referred to some street that Kit had lived on when he was an undergrad, or some boss he hated, or the brand name of some surfboard he'd lusted after but never was able to afford.

In any event, the first issue of the magazine came out. Shortly thereafter Alan and Nick and I were invited to Bruce's apartment one evening. When we turned up Charles was there too. Once we had been plied with beer, the two of them launched into the following offer: there was a great deal of work that the magazine was generating, more than the two of them cared to, or were able to, cope with. They were offering us the opportunity to get in on the ground floor and become part of the organization, as it were, though that wasn't the terminology that they employed. As I recall, the work that they indicated that they needed help with included fielding everything from uninvited submissions to dealing with the mailing list to getting the issues to the post office.

I, for one, was somewhat taken aback. This was a lot to digest. The fact was, I was already involved in what seemed like a fairly demanding publishing enterprise. The heart of the editorial process, picking and choosing what went into each quarterly issue, was one that James generously shared with me from the start. That work was essentially non-stop. Alan, for that matter was fully engaged as well. He was still churning out *A Hundred Posters*. And here we were, being offered a kind of junior-editor-in-charge-of-scutwork position, clearly subsidiary, clearly 'in-support-of.' As I recall, the three of us were silent for a moment.

We weren't being considered 'peers' anymore.

Finally, I said something. Well, I wondered out loud, if we are going to be contributing so much time and effort into the magazine does it not seem only fair that we should have a commensurate role in such things as editorial decisions? What gets in, who is rejected? I was totally rebuffed. Swiftly, in no uncertain terms, Bruce and Charles shot that down. That was the end of that. A moment of silence lingered in the room.

Alan and I had major time commitments already, perhaps we used them as our excuse. Nick did go on to contribute many, many pieces to the magazine. But none of us, it turned out, appeared to be interested in being Bruce's or Charles's assistant.

30.   *Bring Out Your Dead*

Ray showed up in New York around the same time as everyone else; that
is to say, the same time that everyone else pulled into town or surfaced,
if they had been in New York all along. He and his wife ensconced
themselves in a perfectly nice two-bedroom apartment in Chelsea, much
nicer than any digs the rest of us could boast of. The back bedroom was
where Betsi painted, did her design work. Ray had a big desk set up in
the living room, along with his books, which were stacked up all over the
apartment, but neatly, very neatly. The rest of his items, his ephemera,
his collected printed matter and rubber stamp art and found objects,
were, likewise, carefully positioned, served up for best viewing in little
tableaux scattered here and there around the place.

Ray's apartment was rather unlike any other poet's in New York, not
by virtue of his aesthetic attentions, which perhaps were not all that
unlike many others, nor because of what I read from the get-go as his
presentational impulses, for who among us didn't find himself or herself
propping up front of our own desks odd little toy boxes or cluelessly
charming postcards, or matchbooks from roadhouses in Arkansas or,
for example, fortune cookie fortunes bearing such stupendously poorly
worded prognostications that reached so beyond the realm of inartful
transliteration that they could be read, at least by us, as nothing less than
koan-like bolts of riveting revelation? Indeed, at least at one time our
aesthetics, such as they were, were similar enough, that he and I passed
a good number of pleasant evenings collaborating on a series of collages,
each of us contributing a share of our own inventory of found printed
matter. One of them, close to thirty years later, still graces my living
room wall. There was something different, though, going on with Ray.

It had to do with his insistence that, when paying a visit to him, you had
to get the tour. You had to be walked from crèche to crèche, expressing
requisite appreciation when presented with whatever new acquisition he
decided to draw your attention to. Only then, once due approbation, nay
acclamation, had been uttered, could the conventional business be gotten
down to: careerizing, backbiting, gossip, whatever. Should it have been
clear back then, from what can now be seen as an arguably unseemly

attention to outward form and formality, precedence and manners, that there were other, deeper currents flowing?

Years later, years after I'd left New York but still, as I recall, a few years before the L=A=N=G=U=A= G=E logo imbroglio, in which Ray staked a claim to authorship of that magazine's masthead, a claim rather vigorously disputed, about which enough has been written that there seems no need now to revisit its conflicting arguments, I happened to have had a little chapbook published. It consisted of one long poem, a piece that subsequently was incorporated into a book proper that was published in the mid 1990s. The chapbook's publishers were nice enough to provide me with, as I recall, a good two-dozen or so author's copies, a rather generous gesture on their part, all in all, considering the economics of the project. According to my habit, I made a list of friends and others whom I wanted to send this to, and proceeded to do a little mailing. Shortly after sending them out, I realized that, for one reason or another, I had inadvertently, entirely inadvertently, neglected to send a copy to Ray, someone who would as a matter of course absolutely receive one from me.

The problem was, I seemed to have no copies left, although I must have received a few more at one time or another, because now when I look in my shelves, I can see that I have three or four nestled there together, off in a corner by themselves. But at the time, and I know this with certainty, I was all out. I had been too free with my free copies. There was nothing left in the larder, except, it turned out, for one, not quite shop-worn but in no way clean-and-untouched copy that somehow had ended up at the bottom of the pile, beneath the extra padded envelopes and the unused sheets of mailing labels, the usual detritus of a typical half-hearted poetry mailing.

For one reason or another, I had signed this particular copy, at the upper edge of the flyleaf or the title or the half-title page, though, for the life of me I cannot remember why. Who could I ever have intended to send a signed copy to, with just my name inscribed there, and nothing else? No note, no address, no date, nothing? It baffled me then as it baffles me now. But, nevertheless, there it sat, looking up at me, all innocent and unassuming, foursquare, on my desk at work.

What to do? It was the work of a moment to pop it into a jiffy envelope and pull from the aforementioned pre-printed sheets of laser-printed Avery labels — because, while I can see myself, by some exigency of inattention neglecting to set aside a copy for Ray, the idea that I would not have included his address in the proper and duly file-named sub-list in my contact manager is inconceivable — the label bearing his name and address. Indeed, I am confident that it only came to my attention that I had neglected to put aside a copy for him because I must have been idly reviewing the unused labels still sticking to the ready-for-the-garbage sheets I had been using for the mailing itself, when I came across his, inexplicably still remaining there, among all those 'others,' others who I hadn't yet removed from the list but for one reason or another because we had finally and irrevocably lost touch, say, because they clearly hadn't expressed any interest in staying in touch with me, as evidenced by the fact that my mailbox hadn't been graced with their recent books, which I know several other of my friends had received, or any of a broad range of other insults and irrevocable runes not to mention slights which we use, for the lack of any more substantial stakes, to mark our place in this world of ours. And there Ray was, among them. And he certainly didn't belong among that company.

So I plucked him out, stuck the label on the envelope, shoved in that last remaining copy, ran off a postage meter, for back then I, or my company, rather, was in possession of a Pitney-Bowes device of its own, placed it in the pile of outgoing mail, for in those days my business, and I had a business of my own at the time, had mail going out the door every day, mail which I would myself drive over to the post office in the small town in Connecticut where we lived, timing my arrival just so to ensure that I got there no more than sixty or ninety seconds before the dreadlocked driver — there seemed to be a new driver every year or two but each and every one of them for some reason sported long, impressively robust and wondrously formed dreadlocks — arrived to take this poor rural post office's paltry outgoing mail off to some massive, monstrous handling center near the Hartford airport.

It did occur to me, as I slipped the book into its envelope, that I had in no way personalized the inscription. The problem was, my signature was at the very top of the page. I couldn't think of any way to add Ray's name or a comment or expression of fondness or any sort of note, because, in conventional terms, of course, all such other notations should naturally appear above, not below, the author's signature. Perhaps I just didn't give the matter sufficient thought, and so all that ensued should really be laid at my feet. It did not occur to me, for example, to dash off some sort of baroque, Raworth-esque congerie of commentary, salutation and personalization which could have taken up the entire sheet and easily encompassed what, when looked at alone, upon the bare printed page, appeared to be a misbegotten, misplaced, random, admittedly haphazard, brusque and impersonal signature. I could have, for example, easily placed a signature on every corner of the page, planted Ray's name in the center and populated the intervening space with all manner of florid decoration, curlicues, furbelows and flourishes, and it would have seemed, indeed, would have in fact been entirely apposite, appropriate, and, I am convinced, received with real pleasure. But I did not.

My thoughtlessness didn't redound back upon me for a week or so. Then, one afternoon, I happened to be passing by one of the printers in my office which did double duty and also received faxes, when I heard it begin to whir, indicating that it was about to spit out a communication from someone, somewhere. I am sure I was expecting one prospective client or another to be sending back a signed contract. When wasn't I? But that is not what slid out and deposited itself in the hopper. It was a note from Ray. Neatly laid out beneath a letterhead, one he had quite probably composed for this letter, an assessment I feel comfortable making since every single note I received from him bore a different letterhead, each one laid out in different font, with a different surmounting widget or graphic. But of all the notes and letters I'd received from Ray over the years, or which, for that matter, I'd been in receipt of from any writer, or anyone, just plain anyone, no one had ever written anything like this to me before, not in this lifetime at least.

Passing quickly over my inexcusable gaucherie with regard to the book's inscription, Ray proceeded to expiate at length upon the egregious misdeed that had really and truly gotten his goat. The single, long poem which the chapbook consisted of, entitled 'The Night Book,' was my attempt at a meditation upon the onset of mortality, occasioned by the brushes with death two poets close to me had just passed through.

It includes the line, "Bring out your dead." While I am not sure what precisely I was thinking of, if anything in particular, when I wrote that down, I tend to think I was just trying to summon up some general, medieval-Black-Death-related reference, though it is not inconceivable that there were some Monty Python echoes bouncing around back there somewhere. So, I am certain that I was not thinking of Ray or any of Ray's work, much less in particular one of his poems which, as he curtly informed me in this note, had been published in a magazine, a magazine published by Andrei Codrescu, someone I knew, but not well, which I had never, to my knowledge, laid eyes upon.

The thing is, not only did Ray accuse me of plagiarism, in just so many words — and over an innocuous phrase in such wide circulation as that — but he did so in such violent terms that, as I stood there over the fax machine, with people passing by me, people who worked for me, any one of whom just as easily could have caught this fax and taken a look at it as they brought it to my office, anyone could have seen this, absolutely anyone, my gorge rose. I actually felt it ascending, and that was a first. I felt a wave of nausea pass over me the likes of which no person, and no piece of writing, in fact nothing in this world short of a particularly violent descent in a clapped-out USAir 727 into an August-thunderstorm-wracked Philadelphia Airport, had ever induced in me.

That did it for me. Though we talked again, eventually, and not just civilly but warmly, from time to time, Ray and I never got together again, and now, I am confident we likely never will. But I can't say I was surprised. Those visits to his apartment years earlier, that very first visit, should have, indeed did, forewarn me. This is mine and this is mine and this too. So, when that brouhaha over the L=A=N=G=U=A=G=E logo blew up it was no surprise, no surprise at all.

31. The Brooklyn Bridge

We all drank a lot back then, at least it seems like we did, perhaps we weren't paying all that much attention. I know my head used to feel rather lousy in the morning fairly often, back then.

Several people had cars, back then. It seems rather remarkable now. Charles always had a little beat-up Toyota or a Nissan, or maybe it was a Datsun. He and Susan were forever dutifully shuttling it among the alternate side of the street parking spaces on the Upper West Side. Shannon and I had an AMC Hornet station wagon for a year or so, which we used to get away up to Vermont, then we broke up and it disappeared somewhere. And Alan had an International Scout.

At any rate back then, for a while, Alan had wheels. He was living in Brooklyn now, in Park Slope. We had been out. To a reading, or listening to music or just out drinking. I don't recall who else was there that night. Maybe it was just the two of us, maybe not. The next morning, I got up and went to work, with my head feeling like an overinflated, excessively prickly pincushion. So much of what my eyes cast their gaze upon seemed somehow soiled, which in Manhattan meant everything, including what I saw in the mirror when I shaved. In short, I was hung over. Later in the day, or perhaps the next day I got a call from Alan. He wasn't in jail but he'd gotten a ticket, or a summons, or something. The cops had not been amused. That night, on the way home from whatever we'd been doing Alan had gotten into a little accident. He hadn't hit anyone else or hurt himself, but the Scout was gone. He'd gotten into an accident on the Brooklyn Bridge. He had hit it.

This was amusing, at the time. People weren't supposed to drive drunk, but it happened, it happened to the best of people. And the Brooklyn Bridge, that was perfect for a poet. To be able to say that you crashed into the Brooklyn Bridge, how lyrical, how New York. And, in a way, it also perhaps expressed that unpronounced sense of mission, of superiority even, that we carried around in ourselves. Unacknowledged purposiveness, that the Poetry Project's day was done, that the New York School was finally dead and buried, and we were the ones with the shovels. We might admire the bridge, walk across it like so many generations before us. But we were not the sort to write poems about the Brooklyn Bridge. The way we expressed ourselves was by ramming our motor vehicles into it. That was fitting and proper.

That feeling, that sense of superiority and mission, how long ago did that disappear?

32. *African Art*

There were so many ways to make money, lose money, spend time wondering about money while not having any, or much. And yet, and still, somehow getting by those days, in the New York of those days. And what do you know, here we are, or some of us are, years later, to tell the tale.

And then there was Mr. King. He was one of the last survivors of a vanished New York. Back in the Twenties the car business, like the jewelry business and the novelty business and the garment business and the insurance business had its own district: the far West Side from the Forties, where remnants of it remain, up to Columbus Circle, where there were once grand showrooms, through the Sixties to 72nd Street. Lincoln Center had wiped out most of the northernmost dealerships and gas stations and repair shops, in the same way that it eradicated San Juan Hill, that neighborhood which came to be immortalized in West Side Story. In precisely the same way, a few decades later, the World Trade Center erased a venerable Middle Eastern neighborhood and the flourishing radio district west of Wall Street. But Mr. King, who'd been in the tire business, had somehow held on. And, somehow, improbably, he became, of all things, a dealer in African art. He was a tiny man, hunched over with arthritis, with an equally ancient tiny wife who never ventured out from the back of their miniscule shop. They were a part of New York that was over, and gone, and yet they'd survived.

I first visited them in the company of a colleague from Learning to Read Through the Arts, a painter who'd somehow fallen in love with African art. Eventually, I started collecting too. I came to haunt what were then called welfare hotels on Amsterdam and Columbus, where the dealers, known then as runners, from Mali and Liberia would hole up for weeks or months at a stretch, while they sold down the contents of the shipping containers they'd brought with them from Paris or Brussels if they'd made intermediate stops, or directly from West Africa. Their rooms would be stacked to the ceiling with art, redolent with the smells of Africa too, the dirt and blood and mud encrusting the work, and the smell of the food they cooked for themselves there.

Bargaining with them in my college French consisted of circling the room, picking some pieces out of their stacks and piling them up in the middle. Then the dealer would pull on his chin and quote a ridiculous price. At that point it was time to make a show of outrage and leave the room and then, from the hallway, counter with an offer. always precisely half of what he'd just mentioned. Eventually, with much expostulation and drama, a price right in the midpoint between the first two numbers would finally be arrived at.

But Mr. King was different. First of all, he never went to the Africans. They must have come to him. He certainly wasn't mobile enough to make it over to the Hotel Lucerne. Second, Mr. King was not particularly interested in bargaining. I came to spend a good amount of time just sitting with him and his wife in his shop. The office for the arts program had moved to the Upper West Side, to a school in the Eighties, and it was a simple matter to walk down to his place, look over his new wares, sit with him and listen to him talk, and keep him company for an hour or so after work, before heading back downtown.

It was also an education to watch Mr. King and his customers. All manner of New Yorkers dropped in every evening. They knew their stuff. Mr. King had a lot of junk but he also came across, not infrequently, very decent work. He recognized it and so did his customers. He would quote them a price and, by and large, that was the price they had to pay. They knew that they were still getting a bargain, compared with the galleries on 57th Street. The price was the price, and they had to respect that, or at least accept it. There was a little world of these men, and they were all men, white, older, in their fifties or older yet, lots of doctors and lawyers, who would drop by on their way back to their apartments and their wives after their days in the office. Well dressed, urbane, appreciative, eager, somewhat suspicious, and avid, like all collectors.

Shortly after I began to hang out at Mr. King's shop, I started dealing myself. I'd buy a few hundred dollars-worth of pieces and sell most of them, mostly to friends, and make a few dollars. In addition to the few dollars in profit, the pieces I'd decided to keep wouldn't end up costing me anything. I was on my way to becoming a dealer. I sold to friends and friends of friends. Some artists, friends of my brother, a guy or two in the recording industry, people like that. My parents, of all people, were remarkably enthusiastic. I think they could see this turning into a real business. That appealed to them, or the idea of it did.

But it didn't take, and I am not sure why. My taste started to change, that was part of it. I started getting interested in more modern, non-traditional work, like those wild, moving, Ghanaian fantasy car-and plane-and-rocket-shaped coffins. Then there were those wonderful, eerie, Yoruba twin photos, commemorating dead twins, the ones created by making double exposures of the surviving child. I grew less interested in the traditional masks and ritual objects that had enthralled me earlier, which represented what most people were then collecting. And perhaps I was just not ready to commit to all this, like my parents wished.

But sometimes I wonder if Mr. King had a bigger effect on me than I realized. I assumed for years that I just lost interest in the art, and fell into other things. And I really liked Mr. King, and I respected him and his life and his choices, and, most of all, his resiliency, his ability to adapt, his combative, Irish, old-New York, knowing, worldly take on the world. An attitude, that could take in the likes of me, as well as the rapacious landlord, as well as the art film cinema next door as well as the occasional black mail carrier from the huge post office across the street who would wander in looking for some bronzes or a nice string of beads, all with equanimity. And when he or his wife would show me pictures of themselves, and their stores, for they once had a chain, run by him and his brothers, and they looked so young, and strong, and prosperous and confident, what did I see?

Did I see an alive-to-the-end engagement with the world that was inspiring, even if perhaps I didn't realize it, or did I see the white hairs of age and care bringing them in sorrow to their infirm ends, brought low from their proud youth, having outlived their families, their children too perhaps? Or, did I just walk away, did the prospect of it all, whether realized or not, realistic or not, seem just too daunting, just too much to try to accommodate?

Mr. King is long dead. His shop is gone. The movie house is gone, the giant Ansonia post office, a post-war behemoth in its own right, that too is long gone. The welfare hotels were converted to condos decades ago. The ground floor of the Lucerne became a Charivari store, a ridiculously expensive boutique chain, itself shuttered for good decades ago. And who remembers any of it? It is all gone, or nearly gone, or soon gone.

33.   *What We Did to Pay the Rent*

I'd left my job with the Guggenheim and the Board of Education years ago. I'd left Warner Bros. by now too. I had begun working for a private detective. In four years or so it would be time to leave the city, but for now I was working for a company that sent me into restaurants and clubs and hotels. This company had as its clients the fanciest places in Manhattan: the Russian Tea Room, the Four Seasons, the Pierre, the Regency. There, we would act like typical customers and have a meal or a drink or two or spend the night, all the while assessing the quality of service we received from the employees of the establishment under examination. Back in the office we'd write reports which were forwarded to the management of these businesses. Actually, measuring the quality of service was often secondary to another mission. Usually we were there, wasting away perfectly lovely afternoons sitting in some godforsaken midtown hotel bar for one reason only: to try to catch out the bartender — who we knew, I knew and my boss knew and the bartender often knew we knew — was clipping the place blind.

It seemed innocent enough at first. I heard about a job. Someone paid you to go to restaurants and eat, and write about it. I can do that, I thought. And at first it was quite easy. Then, they started teaching me about what was called the 'integrity' component of the job. The basic premise was that everyone in New York who worked behind a cash register, everyone who handles cash for a living, quite simply is a liar and a thief and they are stealing from their bosses. It was our job to catch them. I needed a job badly right about then and, at first, the moral dimensions of the work weren't discomfiting at all. That only came towards the end. Every morning I'd put on a suit and a tie and drag myself to a suite of tired old offices on lower Park Avenue. The place featured gum cracking secretaries from the outer boroughs and an elderly bookkeeper wheezing over an equally ancient Burroughs adding machine.

In the morning I'd receive my schedule for the day. It might start off with coffee at the Ritz Carlton, then lunch at one of the restaurants overlooking the ice-skating rink at Rockefeller Plaza, followed by a light shopping foray among the boutiques on Madison Avenue, then drinks at

Maxwell's Plum, a nice long dinner at the Regency and then more drinks at a disco, someplace like Regine's.

After a while, after a few months, it stopped seeming so innocent. While I never managed to summon up any sympathy for people who were stealing from their employers, it gradually dawned on me that I wasn't exactly cut out to bring them to the straight and narrow. There was an element of social justice, as it were. The Helmsley Hotel chain was one of the firm's biggest clients. And then Leona Helmsley went to jail for cheating the IRS out of millions, famously muttering under her breath that "only the little people pay taxes." At the very same time we were busy getting her bartenders fired for stealing fifty or sixty dollars a week. It all became rather macabre.

I also grew to rather despise the pretense of it all: the deception and underneath it, the base stakes, the low motivations, both on the part of my quarry and me. It was these guys' jobs that were at stake, and it was my job to catch them out, but it was only a lousy, few bucks we were fighting over.

Even worse was the deception I carried out every day, just getting dressed and walking out the door. I was wearing nice Italian suits, I carried a fancy briefcase. I looked like a moderately successful architect or advertising executive. I was pulling down more money than I ever had before, but that wasn't saying much, and I was doing it by getting room service waiters thrown out on their ears.

One day I was crossing Park Avenue, not far from the Helmsley Palace, on Fifty-first Street. There standing next to me waiting for the light to change was a kid from Warner's, He'd been hired a couple of years after me, straight out of Syracuse. He had been shoved into a broom closet office on the other end of the floor, in the TV sales department. An awkward, transparently thrusting jerk back then, we'd all patronized him relentlessly. Yes, me too. Standing there, I desperately hoped he wouldn't notice me.

He'd gotten on at the studio. He'd found a champion. He'd done well. There were other people in that unit who I'd known and admired. They'd been shunted off or forced into retirement, yet this bounder was blossoming. He was a vice president now. You could read about him in *Daily Variety*, not that I read that anymore. And as for me, in the intervening years my stock, as it were, had declined as precipitously as his had risen. And there he was, turning, recognizing me, calling me by name. I had no choice but to say hi. He seemed genuinely pleased to see me. He inquired pleasantly about my present activities, a question for which I always had an innocuous response, studded with words like 'consulting' and 'analysis' and 'assessment.'

As we chatted briefly, my opinion of him softened, despite my long-held feelings. I realized that he was looking upon me with some approval, taking in the Armani suit from last season, and the polished French loafers from Wallace Steiger, and the new round eyeglasses. I could see him running the numbers. I was doing okay, it seemed to him, and he found that comforting. Maybe there was a life after Warner's after all. Who knows what kind of fears he lived with? But maybe he was just happy that I seemed to be doing fairly well.

And that's what got to me. I wasn't doing well at all. I was making a few hundred dollars a week more than I had when I worked down the hall from him but my financial situation was still altogether precarious. I was still living paycheck to paycheck. He surely had a mortgage on a place in Amagansett and a lease on a BMW to get him there, not that I wanted those things. It was the sham that pained me.

And there was worse than that. One day we got a call from the New York Times. One of the firm's friends, a client who was an executive at Restaurant Associates, the huge company that operates restaurants all over New York, in places like Rockefeller Center, the Met Life Building, the Metropolitan Museum and the Metropolitan Opera, had told one of the paper's feature writers about us. The reporter was curious, he smelled a story. He wanted to get together. The boss was cautious, he wasn't sure he wanted this kind of publicity. I was delegated to meet the guy. We got together for drinks a few times. He was my age, and that was part of the rub. You'd recognize his name if I told you. His byline still appears regularly in the paper. He was of my generation and we looked alike, in a way. Same build, same complexion, same hair. While I was much better dressed, dark suits compared with his undistinguished blazers, he was garbed in an air of breezy, not unfriendly, effortless competence. Maybe it was arrogance or an ingrained sense of superiority, I know more about The Times now than I did then, though by then I had already been reading it every day, day in and day out, for twenty years. Maybe it was just plain confidence, along with a carefully calibrated, upbeat bonhomie, that he beamed across the table.

We talked about the business and I told him some war stories. Some were mine, some were ones that I knew the boss bandied about fairly freely. Then, eventually, as it always did, the question I dreaded reared up. How had I gotten into this line of work? I had different versions of reply to this question, which arose not infrequently, tailored for different audiences. They were all true, they all tracked the same narrative, some were just more detailed and dug back deeper than others. How much did I want to tell him? Should I start at Bennington? At Warner's? How much of my arc of descent should I reveal? He told me where he'd gone to college and what paper he'd started out at. Neither was particularly impressive. He just hadn't become a poet, and hadn't continued to make the kind of critical mistakes poets seem prone to, or did, at least back then, when it came to making a living. And here he was, "a gentlemen of The Times," and here I was, sitting opposite, a two-bit fake detective with no career and no prospects who had started off with just as many, in fact, possibly, more advantages. And look what I had done with my life.

"The Times will be happy to buy us a drink," was a line he used. It caught me up, for I had once or twice had the occasion to use it myself. "Warner Bros. will be happy to take care of this check," or, better yet, "The studio will cover this one."

Those days were long gone. I looked at him across the table. I didn't want to tell him my whole story. I answered his question by only going back a year or two, to my first days at the detective agency, for that is what that firm was. I decided I preferred to let him think that this was my life, and I had come up in it, and let him make his assessment about me based on that, rather than see what I was sure would be the pity in his eyes if I told him my whole story.

34. Getting One's Head Bitten Off at the Lions Head

One night I was hanging out with Peter Golub. We'd gone to college together and ended up living in the same neighborhood. He had been a music major. By now he was Charles Ludlum's in-house composer and music director. Ludlum and Everett Quinton lived down the block, on Morton Street. Ludlum's theater was in Sheridan Square, over by Seventh Avenue. Marlboro Books used to be upstairs, or maybe it was gone by then. Their theater was in the basement. Sometimes Peter got drafted into productions himself; always, for some reason, it seemed, cast as an innocent young girl about to be violated.

Across from Ludlum's Ridiculous Theatre Company, on the north side of Sheridan Square, sat the Lion's Head, the famous writers' bar where I found myself now and then, and where I never once espied a single writer. Save for this particular evening. Peter and I were having a drink with Stephen Sandy, a poet and a teacher from Bennington. I'd taken a course or two with him as had Peter, I guess. Peter must have been friendlier with him. I liked Sandy well enough and was impressed with his writing. I'd never taken any writing workshops with him, though. A few years had gone by. Both Peter and I had graduated. Peter's work was getting performed everywhere, I was just starting to get published. It was an exciting time for the two of us and here was one of our old teachers with whom we could share it all.

Perhaps they had had dinner there and I had dropped by for a drink. Maybe all three of us had dinner together. I forget how much we had been drinking but now, it seems to me, it must have been a fair amount. I forget, also, what we were talking about, at least at first. Peter must have been sharing tales of Ludlum. And then there was a lull, which I took as an implicit invitation to take the helm, as they say, and drive the conversation, at least for a while.

Now, I don't think I was bragging, at least not in comparison with the kind of auto-reportage typical in the part of the literary world I was entering, or trying to enter, much less according to the mores of the greater world of young New York strivers and what passed, or passes still I should think, for modest self-assessment in that world. I was simply talking about what I was doing, what I was looking forward to, what I expected, hoped for, was waiting for. Having said that, I am certain I was aware even then of the raging incongruities, the appalling lack of scale and pretty-much-entirely notional sense of value attendant upon any quote-unquote achievement in the poetry world, and the inescapable irony to which, of necessity, any reference to it would properly need to be firmly and unreservedly attached.

Whatever it was I said, whatever I said that I was up to, was, I am sure, framed in that way. But it didn't matter. Not that I had that much to share, or boast of, of that I am also sure. Maybe an upcoming reading at the Ear Inn, certainly not a location that would or should have elicited any particular jealousy in the heart of anyone at all particularly familiar, as it were, with the relative status of reading venues in New York. The 92nd Street Y it was not. Likely enough, I may have mentioned that there could be an appearance in a magazine in the offing. But, again, none of the magazines which I may have named would likely have been recognizable, much less carry any weight whatsoever with someone like Stephen. There is no way that it could not have been clear as day to him that whatever patch of ground that I was claiming, or had pitched myself upon, was doubtless at the farthest, sketchiest, least reputable reach of the poetry world.

But none of that seemed to matter. I think I understood even then, as his fury summoned itself, balled its fist and prepared to rain its blows upon my head, that this had nothing to do with me. I was just an excuse for him to vent. I was an innocent, or quite nearly so, hapless, caught in his sights.

And when he let loose it was with both barrels. I wish I could remember the terms of art he employed and the conditions and degrees of fecklessness, pretension, vacuity, fatuity, immaturity, self-delusion, and the lack of standards, morals, ethics, self-awareness, and pudeur, both aesthetic and personal, which he laid at my feet. All of it delivered with an unanswerable venom, an ire, a viciousness of which, until then, I had never been the recipient. Part of it was simply that no one had ever talked to me like that in my life; this was the first time but not the last. Subsequently, my experience has been that every once in a while, like a kind of hundred-year flood, a similar sort of extraordinary, almost act-of God-like event lands in my vicinity, sending various parts of my self-affect and import spinning off, like so many bits of Oklahoma double-wide when a tornado decides to set its sights on a trailer park. But now I know, or at least I want to believe, it has happened often enough, that it has nothing to do with me.

Stephen had me quivering in my seat. Peter would not meet my eye. That was an eloquent tell, all by itself. I shut up. That much I knew how to do.

The waves of insult and imprecation crested and broke upon me. It wasn't a conversation any longer, it wasn't any longer even an embarrassment. It was a wreck. One of those nightmare crashes on the interstate that you end up having to drive past. The state troopers haven't yet raised up the screens to shield you or the victims — which is it?

People all around us had put down their forks and were staring. It occurred to me that we might be asked to leave. But then I thought, hell, we're sitting in what is supposed to be a writers' bar. People pay good money to come here with the expectation or at least the hope of witnessing just this sort of scene. In fact, though, I was powerless. What could I do? I couldn't get a word in edgewise. There was no way I could even consider talking back to him. And it was not just because this was a former teacher, it was more because nothing in my life had, or had yet, prepared me for this sort of onslaught. I didn't know any better. But as the mockery and the slurs and the slurring went on and on, I found myself wondering, because there certainly was enough time for this kind idle consideration, since this peroration was showing no signs of running out of steam, just what sort of lesson I should consider taking away from this humiliation.

And the lesson was what? Was it watch who you drink with? I thought I had learned that lesson long ago but, it occurred to me, it might be one that it would be useful to recall from time to time, in just the way that this little moment was so obligingly doing for me now.

Or, was the lesson: be careful who you brag to? I pondered that for a while, but I didn't find myself able to draw any firm conclusions one way or the other. After all, bragging, puffery, self-promotion, 'thrusting' as they would say in Thackeray, in one form or another, whether in a manner blatant or bland, breathtakingly boorish or silkily self-deprecating, in fact was, is, surely will forever remain, dearly and indubitably, such an integral part of our lives, and not just as poets but as witting, sensate actors upon whatever stage we'd decided to play upon in New York, that to in any way consider abjuring it, as an activity, was obviously and simply risible. And, of course, I knew, I had enough self-awareness to be confident in my assessment that whatever such imposture I had just engaged in could not have been all that immodest, not inappropriate in the context of our conversation.

On the other hand, was the lesson as simple as don't forget the power of words, even when they are words about such powerless things as words, or the most powerless of any words, that is, the words that make up poems? I wasn't altogether sure that could be so, since it was abundantly clear, from the moment he called up his ire and began to deliver, that this had as little to do with his poems or my poems as it had to do with me. This was all about Stephen and whatever was possessing him, whatever couldn't, wouldn't let him go.

Should I, did I, resolve that evening to be more circumspect in my self-adumbration, in particular when exercising that especial vainglory in front of not-entirely-vetted audiences? No, I should say, not particularly. I was already well acquainted with my relative incompetence when it came to self-promotion, for varied and sundry reasons, none of them, I should hasten to say, in fact, reflecting in any way especially well upon my character. Without going into detail, the sharing of which would redound even more poorly upon me, suffice it to say that my lack of career-tending skills, when it came to poetry, was and remains, a habit I fell into for all the wrong reasons.

The more thought I gave to this, the more difficult it seemed that it could be possible to derive or glean any lesson, so it seemed to me at the time, from this verbal violence. One possible contributory factor: that this was in fact some kind of rage-of-age, not unlike Hannah's kicks beneath the table, occurred to me not at all. Why would anyone want to hurt me? Get angry at me? I was so nice, and cute, and harmless, and good? Wasn't I? And young — that seemed connected to the 'harmless' quality. How threatening could I be, as young as I was? It never occurred to me what foreboding and foreshadowing, what dread and, yes, rage, the mere presentation of youth could possibly engender. How its very fecklessness, its lack of awareness, could itself seem so dangerous, so threatening.

But what did I know? So little. Perhaps not much less than now, but certainly, it is altogether obvious now, how little I did understand of what getting old meant, or, if not old, then simply, what it meant to be no longer young. But those realizations were years away. All I could do was avert my eyes and repeat what I had often told myself over the years, starting when I was a boy: remember. Just remember. If you have one job it is to remember. You may not be able to sort it out. It may make no sense. Not now, not ever. But for now, just remember.

35.   Cap Toes from Brooks Brothers

I was on the B train, heading uptown. It was the middle of the day and the car was empty. I had just started at Warner Bros. so the suits and blazers which eventually comprised my wardrobe hadn't yet taken over my closet. I remember what I was wearing: a pair of button-fly Levis, a striped Brooks Brothers button-down shirt and one of the cast-off, vintage, that is to say, used sport jackets. which in most cases were in fact parts of old suits, which I'd picked up on lower Broadway. Plus, a pair of cap toe Brooks Brothers oxfords. I had two pairs of them, one black, one brown. Not wingtips, those were even more expensive. These were the restrained cap toes with that single, discreet band of decoration across the toe box. As the messenger for the Story Department at Warner's I could see, because I got around town quite a bit those days, that I certainly wasn't the best dressed messenger in the industry, but I was holding my own. These were the standard elements of my get-up and with one exception, they all comported with my station in life. That is, neither the jacket nor the pants nor the shirt by themselves, when it came to the pathetically paltry salary I took home every two weeks, broke the bank.

Then there were those shoes. They seemed astronomically expensive at the time, And not just then. Now, decades later, I wouldn't dream of walking into Brooks Brothers, or its equivalent, and plunking down for a pair of shoes a sum equal to, adjusted for inflation, what each of them had set me back. But I was single, and when it came to the sumptuary laws I deigned to recognize, I had definite and unwavering opinions. As a longtime subscriber to Interview magazine, I knew that Andy typically attired himself similarly, though I'm not sure that was a significant driver for me.

I'd spent more on those shoes than any other single purchase I'd ever made, save my rent, and there it was a very close call as to which called for a bigger check to be written, with the possible exception of the Borsalino fedora purchased around that time at Paul Stuart.

So, imagine my surprise when, in that nearly empty B train, on its way to its terminus at 57th Street and Sixth Avenue, out of the blue there appeared a well-dressed gent in his sixties sitting himself down on the same long longitudinal bench I was occupying. As I recall, he was wearing a very presentable suit, a gray pinstripe or a heather, along with a very richly complex silk tie, Hermès perhaps. And, to round it off, a suitably expensive-looking and appropriately battered Hartmann briefcase. Entirely in keeping, all of a piece. But what drew my attention were his shoes.

I could not take my eyes off them.

They were remarkable. They were magnificent. They were simply splendid. I had never seen anything like them in my life. Just looking at them, simply having the opportunity to clap eyes upon them was, I realized in a flash, a life lesson in itself. And, the amazing thing was, he was wearing precisely the same shoes as me.

All the while I was goggling at this man's footwear, I was thinking about the evening in front of me, for some reason. Those thoughts were uppermost in my mind and have remained, bound up with the rest of the memories of this moment. There was some reading scheduled for that night and it was going to be down in Soho. Or maybe it wasn't a reading, maybe it was a concert. We were all going to see a lot of John Zorn around then. Bruce had turned us on to him. In any event, we were all going to be down there that night and my thoughts were tending to which place, for certainly it was going to have to be decided among us, we'd end up having dinner at afterwards. And I remember remarking to myself, at the very same time as I took in that amazing pair of shoes, that in all likelihood we were all going to end up at the Prince Street Bar, a joint for which I had developed a particular detestation.

Someone did have an affinity for that place, maybe it was Bruce, maybe it was Charles, perhaps it was someone else entirely. In fact, the restaurant was, for our purposes, entirely serviceable: the beer was reasonable, the burgers were big. The source of my resentment at least for that night was that we were going to end up in such a patently gauche place the likes of which, if I had my druthers, I would never have been caught dead in. The fact is, of course, that the Prince Street Bar itself is long gone, replaced decades ago, first by a series of dismayingly expensive French shoe stores, then by a succession of progressively down-market designer jean emporia.

The Prince Street Bar disappeared off this earth so long ago that certainly there must be middle-aged, indeed, aging, veritably aging, New Yorkers who fondly look back upon their salad years, when they were young and thin and poor, for whom recollections of the Prince Street Bar forever evoke comforting and warm memories.

For me, there was One University, which I was frequenting around then. It certainly seemed like it was going to become a permanent New York fixture. But how many people now remember Mickey Ruskin, who owned it, and who for some unfathomable, inscrutable reason deigned to let me and Alan and others who I would show up with, past the bar into the dining room area, that exclusive, well-lit, roped-off dining room? Why us of all people?

Max's, which had been his place too, was long gone by then. In addition to its role as a Warhol hangout, and a downtown music venue, Max's Kansas City had served as a Bennington rally-point in New York. And then there was the Lower Manhattan Ocean Club on Chambers, which he seemed to have open for a few weeks only before he moved up to University Place. We made it there just a few times. It was expensive too. The last time: Talking Heads were playing, and Andy was at a table nearby, with Fran Lebowitz. But that was gone already as well. Long gone. Andy was someone you saw all over town. At openings, at parties, in espresso shops in Little Italy, at Ballato's on Houston St. So, there I was on the train, thinking those thoughts. I who had been in New York all of perhaps six or seven years, and had read my Proust, and thought I had that whole remembering-or-trying-to-remember-your-past-thing, that whole thing, well in hand.

Then I looked up from my neighbor's footwear, took a look at his face and realized that I was sitting by John Vliet Lindsay. It had only been ten years or so since he had been mayor, or so it seemed, since he had been done down by Mike Quill, the transit union boss who brought the city to its knees. Now an MTA garage uptown has been named after Quill and half the buses cruising the streets of Manhattan have decals plastered on them trumpeting his name. But John Lindsay, who some used to credit for keeping New York from going up in flames during those hot summers of rebellion in the Sixties, when almost every other American city was burning; who seemed, at least to several newspaper writers at the time, have the makings to be another Kennedy — young, aristocratic, an embodiment of the future, our future — there's nothing in this city bearing his name. He was just sitting there, unheralded, unacknowledged, unrecognized, on the uptown B train.

The sight of this man wearing the same dress shoes as I was wearing, as I'd seen Andy wearing too, as I gazed down at his oxfords, threw me for a loop. The thing was, Lindsay's shoes, though they were the same model, and looked actually to be the same size, and doubtlessly were bought in the same department in the same Brooks Brothers on Madison Avenue, were entirely different from mine or Andy's. His pair had never, and this was indubitably clear, had never once been shined or polished or come within fifty furlongs of a shoe brush. They were stupefying. They were fantastically cracked and dried out and peeling. They resembled nothing so much as some three-dimensional, magisterial apotheosis of desertification, an object lesson of some sort, demonstrating to some hapless audience the price of inattention or irresponsibility or the wastrel life or something similar. They were fantastically ruined. They looked like Auden's face, but, if possible, worse.

I had never seen anything like this. And, glancing back up at the immaculately groomed Wall Street lawyer, for that was the life Lindsay had assumed after retiring from public office, in his irreproachable suit, I realized this was, indeed, after all, just a studied indifference. He was making a point. He had probably been buying just these shoes since he was a sophomore at Harvard, unlike me, or Andy, who had come so late to them. In fact, his brothers and his father and all his uncles had no doubt been wearing them for time out of memory. And, indeed, his treatment of them was surely, to his mother or his sisters or his wife, not all that unusual. He no doubt went down to the store, bought several pairs, wore them to death and then, five or ten years later, when they were finally dead, dead, and dead, scooted back to the shoe department and picked up another half dozen pair.

At this point that I remembered that Lindsay was a twin. Wasn't his brother a Wall Street lawyer too? It didn't matter, I decided.

A passage from a biography of T.E. Lawrence just then flashed through my mind. I must have read it back in high school. When he wasn't flying across the desert on a camel, Lawrence of Arabia made use of a Rolls Royce, according to this book. At that time, at the dawn of the auto age, those vehicles weren't only luxury rides for the rich but also, apparently, were sturdy enough to serve as staff cars for generals and such. Apparently, Lawrence flogged his Rollses, or Rollers, mercilessly, until they were ready for the junk heap. Then he would have them driven off a cliff and simply order up another one. It all seemed of a piece.

And these were the same shoes. We all were wearing the same shoes. And Andy and I were wearing them because... because of chance? Because of some sort of shared susceptibility to some larger sensibility? There were the shirts and the 501s and, yes, the shoes. But with Lindsay, it was different. I was certainly a part of the world that Warhol inhabited, though certainly only a tiny, insignificant part, but John Lindsay, he inhabited an entirely different world, light years away.

If I fell into a conversation with Andy what ever would I have to say? 'I read Interview every month I have a tall pile on my shelf in the apartment. Bruce Andrews came by one day and tried to talk me into giving them all to him, but I said, 'No.''

Oh, that would go over really well.

And, of course, when it came to what Lindsay thought of Warhol, one can only conjecture. And yet, and yet, there we were: all dressed, at least from the ankles down, identically.

I wanted to believe, as I sat there on the B train, thinking of Andy, and all the places one ran into him, so many of them lost and gone already, and how it really wasn't so far-fetched after all, that I could run into this former mayor in the afternoon and maybe Andy this evening, though certainly not at the Prince Street Bar, didn't it say something about this violent and decayed and vicious, yet somehow leveling, open — in some bizarre way — city, that we would all be so similarly shod?

But then, on the other hand, there was Lindsay's indifference to his footwear. Perhaps a studied, Episcopalian affect. But an indifference, a disregard, nonetheless. I would never have dreamed of treating my shoes, my most expensive possessions, so. I am sure Andy wouldn't have either. Maybe Peter Beard, but not Andy. So, was there some sort of message in Lindsay's oxfords? Some end-stage aristo gesture, some sort of insulting fillip that in all likelihood only another old St. Paul's or Buckley boy could decode?

I wasn't sure. The train pulled into 57th Street. We rose and I followed him out, impossibly tall and composed, the features weather-beaten yet still entirely aquiline, pushing through the turnstile, up the stairs to Sixth Avenue, to a part of Manhattan where not only do the skyscrapers create their own weather, setting up vicious windstorms on corners of their own choosing, but where they manufacture their own light too, an alternating, chilling shadow and black disorienting glare, into which, once my eyes finished adjusting, I saw he had disappeared.

36.   The Empire City

And then suddenly one day it became time to leave New York.

Some of us had started families. Many of us had, somehow, sprouted careers. Not a few — notwithstanding how improbable, how impossible it seemed back at first, bearing in mind how much hostility we and our project had engendered, a hostility, naturally, we, or at least some of us, had reveled in, what better validation could we hope for — had found their way into academia, with all the expected, consequent implications which flow from the migration of an avant garde into the world of the university still, several decades later, being sorted out.

And so, fifteen years or so after that unsettlingly expectant season when everyone seemed to show up all at once, the tide turned and a good number of people packed up, got in their cars — they had cars, we had cars — us, how odd, owning cars, with insurance too, who would have thought, and simply left town. The same phenomena seemed to strike the Bay Area too. One after another, address book listings with Oakland and Berkeley and San Francisco zip codes got crossed out and replaced with entries in Detroit and Philadelphia and Maine and Washington, DC.

I left too. I had just started a family and just started a business. It seemed like time to leave. The baby and the business were both blooming and the latter would clearly, due to the cost of doing business and the vagaries of the labor market, fare better almost anywhere rather than New York.

The city we had known, the city that had drawn us in, the empty, deserted dark city, half-ruined with cracked and cratered sidewalks, grass luxuriantly rising from the fissured pavement, bowed hydrants and darkened traffic lights, a place encrusted with neglect and grime and graffiti, the city of night-time vistas of Federal restraint and Second Empire grandeur, of Beaux Art flora-abundance and City Beautiful exuberance, now all sagging, stained, placarded and spavined, and all the more alluring for all that; a vast, pulsing sibilant ruin, like a quattrocento Rome where sheep still grazed in the Forum and an arc of ramshackle shops leaned up against the Coliseum through which we had glided safely, invisibly, now seemed somehow, all gone.

No matter how dangerous the city had been back when we arrived, we had been, at least it appeared to us, armored against any danger by our innocence, perhaps by our ignorance, certainly by our youth. And now, years later, we had wives, husbands, partners, we had children, we had careers, or at least jobs. Now, we weren't young anymore. We were middle-aged. And for some of us it was time to leave.

So off we went and lived our lives. We upped house and lit out for Connecticut, for upstate New York, for Buffalo and Albany, for the aforementioned Washington and Maine and Philadelphia and Detroit and Pittsburgh and San Diego too, for Providence and Great Barrington and points further west, further astern, further adrift, further askew. We had our babies and we brought them up. We had our jobs, our careers. We taught, we consulted, we started businesses. We did this and that and we had lives, just the kind of lives that anyone else might have recognized. We got sick and our parents got sick and died. We divorced and stayed together. We went belly up and we got fat.

And some of us didn't make it. Some dried up and some stopped. Some should have stopped but didn't and just kept repeating themselves. Some died.

And, of course, there was no relation between who was the most wondrous of youths and who ended up prospering most; between those whose work, when we heard it back there in the Ear Inn so long ago, was the most shocking and enthralling, most breathtaking, most awe-inspiring and terrifying, and who, among us, has become the most anthologized now, now most widely taught. That is the way of the world. There are laws the world obeys. The poetry world too. That is just the way things are.

And then, almost two decades later we came back. Or, at least, or rather, some of us did. Or, at least I did. The vicissitudes and turns of the screw and jokes of fate that in 2005 deposited me back on the streets of New York, back in the very streets I had haunted thirty years earlier, in Chelsea and the West Village, are best reserved for another time, but here I was, walking the same avenues I had eagerly, fearfully explored in my youth.

And so, like Proust, in his last volume — not that I for one, nor we, any of us, can or should ever compare ourselves to him — I returned a few score years later, to a world I thought I had known, a world I once thought had been mine, a world from which I thought I'd been firmly exiled. In that volume Proust talks of relegating himself to a life of toil in a library for all those years of 'away' before, finally, he returns to his old world, the milieu and the parties of his youth, at the very end of his tale. It is a world populated now by the children and grandchildren of those characters who originally ransomed his imagination and who in turn, in the earlier books, enthralled and horrified us. Of course, it bears remark that to many it will seem no small degree an indice of how apparently, and wonderfully, out-of-touch was Proust with any economic realities of his day, that the epitome of drudgery for him was employment in a library, surrounded by books, of all things. But return he does.

And what does he learn upon his return? What does he see as he closes those final connections? What lesson does he learn, does he share with us as he sees himself, his friends, their children, their grandchildren, all teetering like uncertain carnival walkers upon the unsteady, uncertain, ridiculous stilts of the generations that came before them, wavering insecurely upon their forebears' shoulders? In a not dissimilar way, when it came to this city, the one I thought I knew, the one I thought I'd tried to capture and span and sum up in the poems and books of my youth, this metropolis now appeared to me, in these first days and weeks and months upon return, to have grown, evolved, launched itself into a future I was altogether unsure I understood.

I once thought that this was my city. At least, I had thought so for many years, even though I had written the line, years earlier: "This is not your city." However, just being able to articulate that fact, that is to say, being able to put a 'name' to the ungraspably, unutterably, polymorphously polyglot, vainglorious, variegated wonder of it, evinced some ownership. But in the final respect I was wrong. It truly was mine no longer, and it had indeed, apparently, changed out of all recognition.

Or, perhaps not quite entirely. All those lost, once gorgeously deserted neighborhoods and alluringly dangerous after-dark streets, those same neighborhoods now, thirty years later — their night-time avenues were thronged with people. With slim, attractive, well-dressed young things, focused, intent on their pleasure, and properly so, cruising, shopping, comparing, dining, drinking, wooing, declaiming, defending, deciding, declining in short, engaged in all those specious and vital and venal rites which our generations proceed through via the declensions of aging: this is what is appropriate for you in your twenties, your thirties and so on.

Fourth Avenue was supposed to be deserted after six o'clock. Why would there ever be any one there? That was the New York in which I had come of age. And Twenty-Third Street, or Sixth Avenue in the Twenties, why would anyone be there at night? No one ever was. It used to be dangerous to linger there, it was so desolate at that hour. Now the danger was that if one didn't walk swiftly enough down the sidewalk the press of shoppers, of pedestrians, of residents, of visitors, of whomever, surging in and out of the plethora of shops and cafes and restaurants would simply bowl one over.

It was all so distracting. How rich, how splendorous, how well-off this city had become. Streets were paved and smooth. And here, in my old stomping grounds, now there was landscaping, and tidy, well-tended perennials and conifers and weeping willows gracing the little traffic islands, along Hudson for example, or Fourteenth, or all around Union Square. Were these not the same little lozenges of raised curbing that to my mind would forever, and should forever, consist solely of some cracked asphalt along with a brace of weeds peeking up, entwined in the twisted stump of a Yield sign or a No Parking sign snapped off years ago, never to be replaced, its absence never even noticed by the powers-that-be?

Three decades later this had become an impossibly rich city, overrun by thousands, tens of thousands of rich and beautiful boys and girls. While every night, as I made my way through the streets, looking to pick up something for dinner, seeking one or another indelible, now lost, landmark — the taxi garage on Hudson replaced by condos, my aunt and uncle's body and fender shop replaced by a hotel, that taxi carwash on Houston replaced by an Adidas store — each and every one, along with so many others, gone without a trace, half-lost amidst all the stores and the restaurants and the black cars... somehow, it started to dawn on me: this didn't quite add up.

In the same way that, looking back at those years, at the 1970s, it didn't seem as if the city could have been possibly as doomed and decayed as it appeared, as perhaps we wanted it to be, as we flattered ourselves it was, elsewise our heroism might well have seemed somehow diminished, by the same token now, it occurred to me, could it be possible that this burnished and glossy place was not, could not in fact be as blessed and carefree, and released from the bonds of decay or the inexorable rules of boom-and-bust as it certainly appeared to be? Was there a rent in the lining? Was there not still some fugitive garbage collecting in the odd storm sewer? The occasional dented and bombed delivery step-van still making its way down Ninth? Certainly, there were still sad men, just as piteous and soiled as they used to be, filling sacks of bottles and cans and trundling them in those battered shopping carts, along with the rest of their worldly possessions, to the nearest Gristedes. So, perhaps this new city wasn't as different, wasn't as golden as it seemed at first blush.

But one thing was indeed different: we were different. In some ways it was hard enough to realize, back when we left the city years earlier, that when we departed, we were no longer young, no longer the youths full of fire and fear. We were burdened down with families and careers. We'd become middle aged.

But now upon returning to New York that earlier realization seemed mild and innocuous compared with the conclusion, the inescapable conclusion, that stared back in the mirror every morning: we are different now in yet another, just as particular way. We are not even middle-aged anymore. Now we are old. We're fortunate if we're not ailing. These kids running around the city, this is their city now. It seems as if it's not ours anymore, if it ever was. They are young enough to be our children. Some of them are our children. One wants to say that it's their time now. It's their hour. What we can do is watch.

And yet. We aren't dead yet. The fact that we remain, mobile, mensurative — we can still make observations — that must count for something. And if we are ignored, perhaps we should be, by now. There are worse fates. And so, it seems, we're still here, as we were, as we have been, as perhaps, if we are lucky, we will be for some time to come. Walking the streets and taking it all in.

But I am getting ahead of myself. First, I had to get married, and start a family, and start a business. Before returning I had to leave.

And after I left the city, a lot happened.

That's what comes next.

THE LIFE WE HAVE CHOSEN

(1990s - 2000s)

1.   *They're Pulling Cable*

There was the turn off, right where I remembered it, at the bottom of the big long hill. I slowed down and made a careful right, from Route 44 onto Housatonic River Road. Into the woods. After a few yards, the asphalt yielded to dirt. A cloudless August afternoon. We'd been in the car for two hours, there had barely been any traffic. Dust flew up behind us. The baby was still dozing.

Around the first turn, more woods, and then I stood on the brakes. Right before us, blocking most of the road, a long column of huge telephone company trucks, parked nose to tail, towering, white and gray, bucket trucks and long beds bearing giant spools. We passed more of them as we made our way down the road. Summoning up nothing so much as that allied invasion force, the Americans and the Brits and the Canadians and the French and the Poles and all their impedimenta of war, preparing to board their LSTs, the day before D-Day. It turned out these guys were here to pull cable today, as they say in the telecom business.

The movers were Israelis. All of the movers in the New York seemed to be Israeli back then. In my usual way, I'd prepared a map for them, unbidden, neatly noting with green hi liner their route up into deepest Connecticut incognita. When they showed up that morning, the crew's foreman waved me off. "Map? We don't need maps. We were all in the Israeli army." Back then that seemed funny.

There was only one phone line in our new house. That didn't seem like enough. What if there were two people working at once? And we had a fax machine now too. I didn't need a line for a modem though. I had a computer but I didn't have a modem. I wouldn't for a few years. I didn't know anyone who did.

Nevertheless, as the crew chief at the head of the convoy patiently explained, even though I'd ordered a measly three additional lines, there were no spare facilities — that was how he put it — on our road. Not one spare line. Clearly, the phone company had installed no additional service for residents on this road since telephones had been first put in people's homes around here, back in the Twenties or Thirties. So today, Southern

New England Telephone had linemen up on poles along the road, one after another, bringing a fat new cable from the state highway all the way down to our little house.

We had thinking about schools for a while now. Our daughter Isabel was about to turn two. It was 1991. Also, I'd started a business a year earlier and it was growing fast. I was going to have to start hiring people soon. There was no compelling business reason for this business to be in New York. And, maybe, possibly, were we getting tired of city life? It was dirty and dangerous. Although, it had always been so, hadn't it? Having said that, someone had just been murdered around the corner from our apartment. He was the son of a guy I'd worked with years earlier, at Warner's. In the final respect, was the city all that different, or was it us? I'm still not sure. Nevertheless, we'd decided to leave town.

Robin and I were married now. The wedding was at a restaurant in midtown, a client of the detective agency. There were ninety people there, a table full of poets.

We had a car now and we'd started taking rides to the suburbs. Why not? Back to Hartsdale a few times. It had really changed. Those tatty garden apartments down near Central Avenue and by the train station, they'd all been transformed. Condos now. They weren't half bad, but they were out of our reach. We quickly realized we couldn't afford to live anywhere near the city.

Summer arrived, a lovely summer. We were often spending weekends with my brother and his family, up in Litchfield County. We started looking at houses around there and came across an old clapboard house for rent sitting on the corner of a big farm spread out along the Housatonic, in the next town over. It had originally been built for someone who worked there, the farm manager maybe. There was a cow pasture next door and a pond out back. It had enough bedrooms for us, and a dining room too, and space for a home office. There was a washer and dryer, and a dishwasher in the kitchen. I'd never had those before. Most importantly, we could afford it. The place had been unoccupied for a few months. Its dirt driveway had turned back to grass. As bucolic as they come.

A good number of our friends were taken aback. Why were we leaving upon such short notice? Who were we to leave at all? Some people seemed to find it disloyal. 'What kind of New Yorkers are you, anyway?' A few weeks later, when we came to have visitors, aunts and uncles and friends, they seemed a bit shocked to see where we'd ended up. From the heart of the great metropolis to five miles down an unimproved road. At times like that Robin enjoyed donning her haughtiest Eva Gabor mien, looking down her nose at us all, and breaking into a few bars of the theme from Green Acres: "Dahling I love you, but give me Park Avenue." In fact, she missed the city not at all.

Within a few months, we also had a puppy, and a kitten, and a dining room table. Our daughter was in day care. Robin and I worked away at adjoining Ikea workstations in the back of the house. We were hiring people to help with the business. The first thing in the morning, I'd head into town, to the pharmacy in Salisbury, where a copy of the Times waited for me in a cubby labelled with my name. Every day at lunch time I'd take the dog for a walk, up Wildcat Hollow Road, through the forest and the glens, past the upper pond and its little dam and past the spring house that fed all of the homes on the farm. And I hardly thought about New York City at all.

2.   *The Pointed Perfume of Sawn Pine*

It was evening now. I sat in a house a hundred miles from the city, at this table, once again. This table where, now that I think about it, I've written everything I've ever written. Including *this,* now. That evening is now decades in the past. The table back then was barely twenty years old. Today, sitting here, I run my hand across its top, so many more scratches and nicks. All told, half century of wear.

A table where, for some reason, that evening, I felt like I hadn't sat for a long time. Of course, that wasn't so. I'd never stopped writing, never completely stopped with the poetry, but still. This was the table that Steve Keffer made for me back when I'd just moved into my first apartment, on 19th Street. Then, as the years rolled by, it moved with me to the apartment on Morton Street, then Kenmare, then Bank. Now it had been pressed into service as our kitchen table.

3. 'Pasadena?' That Means They're Passing

I sat down and started writing again. I hadn't been writing much, not much poetry that is. While I had been publishing here and there, Ray DiPalma did a special edition of a magazine for me back then, something had happened. It happened to a lot of people. All the folks leaving New York and the Bay Area, that was part of the same phenomenon. Quitting, people were starting to quit, to disappear. I've written about this elsewhere: the when and the why. As for me, some years earlier I'd gotten that bug and tried my hand at some fiction, when I was still at Warner Bros. I knocked out three chapters of a novel about the movie business, it was titled *Gross Receipts*. I thought that was funny. I read some of the novel at the Ear Inn once. There was a lot of laughter. Then Bruce Andrews came up to me afterwards. He'd been laughing along with the rest. 'Why would you ever want to do something like that?' he asked.

Bernie Shir-Cliff, who worked downstairs at 75 Rock, the editor in chief of Warner Books, found me an agent. It took him one call. He said, 'Where do you want your agent to work?' I said, 'I don't know. Either William Morris or ICM, I guess.' He said, 'Well, pick one.' The next thing I knew I had an agent at William Morris. Mel Berger. Robin had her own name for him: Marvelous Mel.

I remember the first time we met. William Morris was up the street, in a building on Sixth, MGM was in that building too. When we were done, I told Mel that I wanted to say hi to so-and-so. So-and-so, whose name I've long forgot, was in business affairs, like me, but older. We had done some business from time to time, but we'd never met. He was a vice president, I a glorified admin.

What did I think I was doing? On my way out I stopped by this guy's office, on a lower floor, just went right in. 'Hi, it's me. Just wanted to say hi. I'm here because...' And I saw something on his face. Uncomfortable? Something more uneasy than that?

His look should have said: 'What are you doing here, you jumped-up file clerk? I'm going to call your boss right away. Does Sidney even know you're away from your desk?' But that wasn't his look. Instead, it was: 'Am I trouble?' Was I someone who could make trouble for him? Who did he have watch out for now? The fact was, I had no business being there. I was just showing off. Making a grand gesture. But for who? This was the sort of move that execs from the studio would pull when they flew in from the coast. Walking the floor. Making an impression. Gladhanding. Who was I to pull something like this? A few seconds later I was in the elevator heading for the street, but I never forgot the look on his face.

Mel went to work and he worked very hard. This was back when agents sent around actual manuscripts. Paper copies of manuscripts, in those big tan padded envelopes. When I was the messenger for the Story Department, my first job at Warner's, I lugged envelopes just like those all over town. What did editors think when they got an envelope from William Morris and they opened it to find a manuscript that had been clearly read, passed around, handled and handled again? I can't imagine that he xeroxed a fresh copy for each editor. What did they say to themselves?

In any event, in the fullness of time Mel gave up. He'd fought the good fight. He was at it for more than a year. I liked him a lot. A good guy, and funny. When he was done, he sent me back the rejection letters and the manuscript. I probably still have it all in one of my boxes. It was a battered thing. Woebegone, a relic, a scarred shin bone from some saint. Except, not to be venerated. The opposite. It had been roundly rejected by the New York trade book business, jointly and severally, the industry entire.

That wasn't the last time Mel sought to sell work of mine, though he, and I, never had any better luck. So, I remained a poet those years, but not for the lack of trying.

4.   *The Myth of the Return*

I've often had trouble with titles. This time, Geoff Young saw it before me. The title was his idea.

It seemed odd. Funny. Ironic. I had to leave New York to realize that writing about New York was what I had been doing all along. And would forever.

Speech, signage, various and sundry found material snatched from the streets, all of it had long found its way into my work. But now it was clear, finally, even to me, that this place, not just its language but the place itself, was central to my writing. And yes, I was writing again. The title of the first poem in *New York,* the book Geoff Young came to publish shortly after we moved to the country, was 'The Great Pavement.' A nickname for Manhattan itself. It came to me just as we were piling everything into the car, leaving that morning, leaving the city perhaps forever.

Geoff had left California and moved to Great Barrington, Massachusetts, not far from us, a few years earlier. He was keeping on with his press, The Figures, and starting up a gallery too. While this would be the only book of mine that he published, he designed several others.

The title of the second long poem, 'The Ulterior Parkways,' came from my trips back and forth, because I couldn't quite, couldn't completely, stay away from the city. The Taconic State Parkway, the Saw Mill, the Sprain, the Bronx River, the Henry Hudson. Those limited-access byways from the Thirties and the Forties, their quaint Tudor service stations and faux-rusticated wooden guard rails, their semi-neglected copses and greenswards. What might traversing them as often as I did betoken?

5.   Defenestration, as Metaphor

As a poet I'd long been of the opinion that engaging in metaphor was a species of pandering. In fact, as part of our project, as Language writers, among all the old furniture we tossed out the window, along with formal structure, meter, rhyme, everything from subject matter to capitalization, all vestiges of metaphor were discarded or rather, first cuffed a bit, given a good beat down and then unceremoniously kicked to the curb. At least that's the way I want to remember it.

But New York, I realized as I came to work on these new poems, was my metaphor. The streets, the street names, the names of the businesses, the stores and restaurants, those still with us and those long gone. The refuse, the garbage in the street and the garbage that was talked in the street. I didn't need metaphors. I had this city. It was, it is, the world, the world in toto, the world in our hand, and just capturing pieces of it and serving them up, placing them on the page, that would be enough.

And when it came to 'list,' plain and simple: before this new work, I had never put that into a poem before, without any wrapping or upholstery. And then there was also some memoir — bits and pieces, some extended, like the story of Isabel's fire truck, her ride 'em, emblazoned with the great, golden Figure Five, just like in Williams's poem. And, along with the cops' spiels and taxi drivers' dirges, there were also purposely hopped-up lyrical bits, florid, full blown, fly-blown, literary language, some recondite, others as recursive as I could manage. And there were fictions too, several of them: snatches, pieces, capsules. I came to believe that all of this could belong, did belong, in a single poem. I welcomed them all. Come right in.

As mentioned elsewhere, what I didn't realize then was the degree to which those three poems, 'The Great Pavement,' 'The Ulterior Parkways' — along with *The River Road* which Peter Ganick would publish separately soon after — would serve as templates for so much of what I've written since. The lists. I came eventually to write poems, long poems, made up entirely of list. And found material too: two long poems all of found material, one about 9/11 and the city, the other about Covid and the city.

Again, New York. And from those bits of memoir that surfaced first in the book that Geoff published, I came eventually to write two memoirs, and now this third one, collected here in this volume. And fiction, that too.

But first I had to go into exile from New York.

6.   *What Else Was I Going to Do?*

I always needed a job.

Back at the beginning, when I fetched up in New York, it all came down to this. There were three possibilities: you could teach, you could work in a copy shop, you could get a real job. I couldn't teach. No way. And, in point of fact, there were no teaching jobs for poets like us, not back in the beginning. Everyone hated us. That was so exalting. Nor did I want to live the life that I called 'working in a copy shop,' shorthand for any one of a variety of lousy minimum wage jobs that, when we were young, poets naturally gravitated to. They just paid the rent. They allowed you as much time as possible to write, all else be damned. 'All else' included, back then, being able to afford modern conveniences of any sort grander than an impecunious undergrad could afford, like, for example, a toaster oven or a coffee mill, or, more to the point, eventually, the wherewithal to envision having a family.

But real jobs never came along all that easily either. That Guggenheim job never paid much more than a subsistence wage, nor did working at Warner Bros. lead to unimaginable riches. Eventually, I married. Robin and I started a family. I had to do something. We were still in New York and I hated it there at the detective agency.

7.   *Wait, You Don't Even Like these Guys*

Back when we were still in New York, at that last job, for a time I liked telling people I worked at a detective agency. It certainly didn't have the makings of a career, but I needed to make money. What were my options? Then it came to me.

I'd been there a couple of years and now handled the sales and marketing. I'd just pushed out a campaign to all the cruise lines, promoting the agency's mystery shopping services. We had been doing some resorts in the Caribbean and I figured cruise lines were just like resorts, except they moved around, big hotels steaming from port to port. One of the big lines responded to the mailing. The head of operations wanted us check all of their ships twice a year. 'In the winter they're in the Caribbean and Hawaii. In the summer, they go to Nova Scotia and Alaska,' he told me, 'Get a copy of our schedule and come up with a proposal.'

Monday morning, bright and early, I was at my desk, studying his full-page ad at the back of the travel section of the Sunday Times, as I dialed their 800 number. But I couldn't get through. I just wanted them to mail me a schedule. I was on hold, I was in the queue, I got lost in the VRU. After ten minutes I gave up. I thought to myself: 'If this guy knew how terrible his phone service is, he'd have a fit.'

Then I thought, 'Wait. That's a business right there. Instead of going out to these bars and restaurants and clubs at all hours, we could just sit in the office and call these 800 numbers and check on the service from here.' Then I thought, 'That's such a good idea, why give it to your bosses? You don't even like them. Go do it yourself.' So that's what I did.

I came up with a name, and a vague idea for a logo. I went to my friend Ronnie, a designer who had me meet him one evening at Push Pin Studios, where he was renting a desk. The design he showed me on the monitor was just perfect. When I asked to see it on paper, he directed me to the next office where it was being printed out. The thing was, I didn't hear any printer running. When I got there the page was already lying there in the tray, so sharp. The gray tones were so smooth and the black was so solid.

Only one thing kept me from dashing back to Ronnie's desk and gushing over his work: that printer. Not only had it pushed out this art incredibly quickly but it had done so virtually silently. It was a laser printer, an Apple LaserWriter. I had never seen one before. Laser, not dot-matrix. The sheets slid out silently, swiftly, emerging fully inked, cool and dry. I stood there gaping.

One of the other things I had to do right away when I started my business was to open a checking account. I went to the Chase branch on 34th Street. There were problems, of course. I didn't have the right paper work. I hadn't received the correct IRS forms. But eventually, after two or three visits, I got it all worked out. As I was finishing up, I commented to the manager, good naturedly I thought, that it all did seem like a lot of rigamarole. She was young black woman who I thought I had been getting along with well. She replied with not a small amount of asperity, or perhaps it was something else: "Well, what are you complaining about, you're going to have your own business."

'Well, you could have yours too, if you wanted. What's stopping you?' I thought to myself, at least at first. After a while, a few years later, because, you see, I never quite forgot her, I came to believe that maybe I shouldn't have assumed that it would have been as easy for her to start her own business as it was for me.

8. Back Then DM Stood for Direct Marketing

DM News was a trade newspaper, a fat weekly, targeted at people who worked in the direct mail and list and catalog and call center businesses, and companies with 800 numbers. I had just gotten my own 800 number. As soon as I did, I placed a small ad in DM News. Amazingly enough, prospects started calling. Within a few months, J. Crew and Jos. A. Bank Clothiers and Hanna Anderson were clients. Lots of catalog companies at first. It seemed like only a few weeks since I'd decided to leave my old job.

Back then, at the very beginning, I did all the work myself, in the bedroom of our apartment on Bank Street: making the calls, placing orders, pretending to be a bona fide customer, evaluating the service, listening to the recordings and transcribing them on the little Mac SE I'd just bought. That first winter I worked seven days a week. That was the year the Giants made it to the Super Bowl. As I typed, I'd watch Mark Bavaro, the shy, stolid, humble, unstoppable Mark Bavaro, tight end nonpareil, shouldering his way, Sunday after Sunday, into the end zone.

Then there were too many calls for me to handle myself, so my parents down in Florida pitched in. And then there was too much for them too, and Robin quit her job and started making calls as well. That's when we realized we didn't need to be in New York anymore. By the time we were settled in on Housatonic River Road, not much later, our client base was expanding beyond the catalogers. In short order, we were signing up banks and cable companies and credit card companies, like American Express.

Just a few months earlier I'd been spending a lot of time down at the World Trade Center. All of the restaurants and bars there were clients of the detective agency, including a sad little bar about halfway up one of the towers. Its entrance was right off the sky lobby, where you changed from one elevator bank to the another. A few stools, a couple of tables, grimy white walls, scuffed and stained tile. The only decoration: a few faded, mis-hung, black and white photos of the complex under construction.

The place was always empty. I had a soft spot for it. Something out of Blade Runner, unashamedly dystopian, except it was always sunny up there. Now, I was walking straight through the concourses downstairs, past the places where I used to try and catch crooked bartenders, and across the pedestrian bridge over West Street in the shadow of the towers, over to American Express's own building in the World Financial Center, where I was ushered into meetings with executives. I was using much bigger words now. Now I was sitting in a soft swivel chair in a carpeted conference room, with views of the Statue of Liberty and the Upper Harbor.

9. *All that Time. What to Show for It?*

As I started on the first of those poems that Geoff came to put into *New York*, it hit me.

'Oh no,' I said to myself, 'there's that feeling again.' I hadn't felt it in years. Weird sensation. Always was. I remembered it from college. Back then, it came over me all the time.

It was a feeling that arrived whenever I started up again, each time I resumed writing after stopping for a while. In college it might have been a matter of weeks, perhaps a month. I might have been travelling, or just not writing for one reason or another. And then after I graduated, I really did stop for a while, three years, partly because I was hitchhiking around the West, but mostly because I just couldn't write anymore the way they wanted me to.

'They' were Alvin Feinman my tutor, and the rest of the poets and the literature department at Bennington. They had successfully turned me into a young poet in their joint and several likenesses. A little Ammons, a mini-Merrill. I did owe Alvin so much, all of them really. They gave me a superb grounding in literature. They all taught me how to read. And Alvin taught me, in a way, the activity of writing. What working at this work meant. That is, he taught me how to edit myself. But this likeness, this simulacrum of a young poet, this was not me. I didn't know what else to do, so I stopped altogether.

When I did start again, I was in New York. It was still a few months before I had my moment at the Gotham Book Mart, where I discovered *This* magazine and Clark Coolidge, that moment when everything changed for me. But that first day, the day I started up again after school, several years after graduation, I did have *that* feeling — and I recognized it then, having encountered it many times before — and now I felt once more, years later, right after we left the city, sitting at my table, as I began work on these three long poems.

This was *that* feeling: every time I started writing again, no matter how long it had been since I'd last sat down, I felt, I knew, that in terms of what I was doing, what I was focused on, what my work looked like, it might just have been only few days since I had written last. All of that time, however much time had elapsed, was for naught. It didn't count. I hadn't learned anything. All of that life experience which I was so sure I'd accumulated since last putting pen to paper? It wasn't showing up on the page, that was for sure. My disquiets and distresses, my vocabulary, whatever formal topics I was working through, they were the exactly the same as I had been engaged with, or struggling with, when I'd last sat here, a month ago, a year ago, years ago.

I'd wasted all that time. I wasn't the better poet for it.

10. The Functional Equivalent of Young Communist League

What does she remember first? You'll have to ask her. Of course, I remember us coming home in a cab from St. Vincent's, the day after she was born. Now we were a family. And I remember walking the hall in the apartment on Bank St., night after night, trying to get her to sleep. And then standing over her crib watching, after finally putting her down, watching her purse her tiny lips, dreaming her infant dreams, Robin and I, amazed, awed, like every other pair of new parents.

When Isabel was still in the stroller, I remember having lunch at Café da Alfredo, on the corner of Hudson, across from the apartment, with my friend Peter. And I remember us walking down a street in the 20s, off Fifth, me and Robin and Isabel. She was walking by then. And there was Maria, Maria from Sesame Street, herself, coming out of a restaurant. Isabel just stared up at her. 'It's Maria!' we said. Maria was so nice about it. And Isabel just looked up, gape-mouthed. She couldn't believe it. And then of course, when it was time to leave New York, there was the fire truck.

We moved to the country two months before she turned two. One morning, not long after that birthday, we got in the car and drove to the other side of the state. We were on a mission. Robin and I reasoned that since there was a pond right behind the house, and there was, in theory, the possibility that she might fall in while we weren't looking, we should get a dog, and not just any dog, but one bred to save drowning people. The logic was impeccable. That day we purchased a Newfoundland puppy which Isabel named Daisy, who, while marvelously caring and protective of her in remarkable ways, proved to be vehemently allergic to water. Nevertheless, somehow, our daughter did not drown. Within a few months Daisy was larger than her.

The place we were renting was on a working farm. There were Black Angus cattle, two barns full of horses and a couple of farm hands. And chickens. And sheep too, way down the road, watched over by an aloof Italian sheepdog. Isabel liked to toddle down to the chicken coop across the way and take in the doings of the hens and the rooster.

One evening, as she was tucking into dinner, she asked Robin what was on her plate.

"Oh, it's chicken," came the reply.

"Chicken? Chicken? Like from the coop? Those chickens?" Isabel asked, staring in horror at the snap peas and the Annie's Mac 'N Cheese and the cut-up chicken breast on her plate, her lip quivering.

Silence fell upon our house.

"Oh no," Robin assured her, heroically maintaining her composure, "This is chicken meat. Not chicken. Entirely different thing." Our daughter considered this for moment or two, fixing piercing glances upon us both. Then after a few more beats, apparently assuaged, she resumed eating.

And of course, there were horses. She liked to visit them in their stalls down at the other side of the farm. We took a walk down there of an afternoon. I assumed this is what inspired an interest, a decidedly strong interest, in *My Little Pony*, a cartoon series we all, somehow, were dragooned into watching, and all of the attendant merchandising opportunities its creators thoughtfully served up for our, or rather, her delectation. These included an unending parade of bedizened and bedazzled toy horses, with sparkly manes, all pink and purple, which found their way to her room: Miss Sunset Diamond Dreamer, Miss Pearly Glow Blossom, and Miss Fantastic Golden Galloper, at the head of a herd of many, many others.

Several afternoons a week her friend Kara, who lived in another tenant house on the farm, would come over with her horses. They would sit on the floor of Isabel's room and play. Of course, these gals, the two little girls' horses that is, each had their own splendidly sparkly convertibles, and ranch houses, and accessorized outfits, special saddles and blankets and bridles and assorted tack.

Whenever I passed by her room the two girls invariably seemed deep in thoughtful, amicable, complex-compound discourse, focused on the game itself which their horses were going to play with each other. This talk always sounded kind of theoretical to me. It seemed to be about the rules of this game: which horses could be allowed to prance and preen, and in which order, and how many points would be awarded for which feat of dressage or jumping. But their horses never actually seemed to play that game, or any game. The girls never got past defining the game itself. Hypothecating, expanding, ratifying, amending the rules. That, in fact, it took a while but I finally figured it out, that was the game.

I should mention that when I have brought up this memory with at least one of the parties mentioned above, I have been informed that my recollections are entirely inaccurate. In fact, said interviewee, who bears the same last name as me, makes the rigorous argument that the rule-making conversations I describe above always gave way swiftly to actual play itself. Duly noted, I say. Nevertheless, I stoutly maintain that my version is a faithful recounting.

Of course, that didn't last long either. Real horses came along straight away, which meant lessons and eventually even more. That is, we came to lease a horse. Leasing a horse, a common arrangement, as we learned, in the riding world turned out to be very much like leasing a car. But not a cheap car. A BMW, not a Toyota. And not a bottom-of-the-line 3 Series BMW either. And along with the horse and the lessons, the new shoes for the horse every few weeks, and the regular visits from the veterinary dentist, who may in fact have driven a BMW, and certainly not a 3 Series, came Pony Club.

Pony Club was like Cub Scouts, but with horses instead of lanyards. Actually, it was less like scouting than, it seemed to me, Young Pioneers, or Komsomol. We're talking Young Communist League, in the Soviet Union. The same kerchiefs and pins and uniforms, or quite similar. The same informing on the parents. The only difference was that instead of tractors, everyone in Pony Club rode around in Range Rovers. Except us, of course. And then when she was older, after Pony Club, came eventing: two-day events, three-day events — cross country — and that was truly scary. People really got hurt doing events. She not only had to wear a helmet, but a Kevlar vest. But that was years in the future.

11.   *The Dish*

Of course, our daughter was only able to immerse herself in the mores and modalities of *My Little Pony* because we acquired a satellite dish shortly after taking up residence in the country. There was no cable service on our road. This was a few years before those ubiquitous small satellite dishes started sprouting on rooftops everywhere. Back then, the only dishes available were the original, white, two-meter monsters, the ones that seemed like they could double as NASA ground stations. When you installed one next to a home its visual impact was truly transformational. Any dwelling, regardless of architectural pedigree, even a Federal-era farmhouse like ours, seemed instantly to assume the froideur of a double-wide trailer. I kind of liked the look.

The dish was controlled by a wired remote attached to our TV, bristling with so many buttons it could have passed for a PC keyboard, and could be aimed to capture signals from a great swath of the northern hemisphere's sky, from any satellite fixed up there in the geostationary firmament, each satellite fitted out with a dozen transponders, each beaming a separate TV channel back to earth. Some of them were pay cable services to which we duly subscribed. Some were regular network broadcasts which we got for free, just as if we were regular suburbanites. There was also a lot of Canadian stuff, including some very odd children's shows which Canadian friends of ours recalled with great fondness. We told them it wouldn't change our opinion of them.

Other transponders were just as easily accessed but not meant for public viewing. They seemed to be used by the US networks to send programming from their headquarters in New York to their affiliates around the country. Some of the transponders were also used to send semi-edited, or even live, news footage back to New York. It turned out that Dan Rather, stuck on-location at one disaster or another, was capable of summoning up extraordinarily creative curses if he decided one of his CBS producers back at Black Rock wasn't paying him due deference.

Whenever we wanted to change channels, we'd have to push the correct buttons on the remote, in the proper order, and then wait, sometimes for several minutes, for the dish sitting out there next to the garage to angle itself in its newly assigned position and acquire the new signal, grinding and whirring all the way. You could hear it clanking from the living room, awkwardly, disarmingly robotic.

In the weeks before the first Gulf War broke out, all of the networks set up operations in Saudi Arabia, installing equipment on hotel roofs, arrogating satellite space for real-time feeds back to New York, letting their cameras run live, day in, day out. You could get onto one of their transponders and take in the Riyadh night sky: the tops of the palms waving back and forth, stars twinkling above. And every night, their night, a correspondent would shamble up, adjust the mic clipped to his safari jacket, glance down at his pad and do his stand up. After, of course, flubbing the intro three or four times. And every now and then, after hostilities commenced, if you waited long enough, you could catch, streaking across the night sky, an Iraqi Scud missile. Then the flash, first. A moment later, the boom as it impacted somewhere outside of the frame.

For my money though, nothing the dish offered up could beat NASA TV. NASA TV was great. It had clearly been programmed by some NYU dropout who'd majored in critical studies at Tisch with a concentration on Warhol's early, durational 16mm work. For the most part the offerings were eminently forgettable, press conferences and such. However, whenever there was a shuttle mission it became pure, priceless art. Live blast offs, of course. Space walks too, naturally. But when there wasn't anything special going on the astronauts would just take their camera and point it out the window, aiming straight down at Earth. You'd see sweeps of ocean, the Pacific perhaps, an atoll occasionally scudding by, then a fleecy floor of cloud, then more ocean, hour after hour after hour. I'd sit in the on the sofa with a book and watch. It drove Robin crazy, but it was wonderful.

Now and then, only rarely, in the evening, they'd switch to something even better: a camera positioned inside Mission Control. A vast, lofty chamber. All those consoles, high-backed swivel chairs, rows of them, curving into the dim reaches. Late at night, almost entirely deserted.

Eventually you'd make out three or four people, studying their screens, occasionally standing up, stretching, strolling over to another glowing monitor to chat with a colleague. It was so peaceful, reassuring. And then, once or twice, to make it absolutely perfect, a door opened way off at the far end, casting a long shaft of light across the serried ranks of workstations. The hallway beyond must have been brightly lit. A guy would be standing there. One of the three people on duty would get up and approach. There would be a handover. The door would shut, everyone would gather at one of the desks. The proffered box would be opened and everyone would lean over to take a look. Was there extra pepperoni? A pizza had just been delivered to NASA and everyone in Mission Control would take a slice.

And then, later, when it was time to turn off the TV, I would read to Isabel. We read *Goodnight Moon* so many times. We read Beatrix Potter over and over. And E.B. White of course. We read *Charlotte's Web* so many times we went through three copies and each time, when we got to the end, when Charlotte is mourned and memorialized, and remembered as 'a good friend and a good writer,' I wept so predictably that my little daughter would wait for it, roll her eyes, and if it didn't seem as if my voice was cracking sufficiently, she'd poke me in the ribs.

Both of my children did the same every Christmas when *It's a Wonderful Life* came on the TV. 'The one time a year when Daddy cries.' Of course, I cried. Not just at the end when everyone cries, but also when George Bailey tells himself all those lies at the beginning of the movie: that the world would be a better place, that his children would be better off without him. But I am getting ahead of myself.

12. Where'd Everyone Go?

Back before we left the city, well before, walking the West Village, you could tell, it was everywhere.

People were dying. Poets were dying. Jim Brodey, Tim Dlugos, others too. On the street, men with Kaposi's on their faces. Emaciated men waiting in line in front of you at the drug store. Guys in the bank, at the newsstand. Men in our building. I'd thought they were my age. Transformed, now ancient, frail. And then, I know, they were gone. And St. Vincent's, where Isabel was born, the hospital I walked past so often, whose emergency room I myself had frequented, where so many people in my family had been admitted — my Aunt Jennie, my father, others, because my cousin Ruthie had worked there for years — transformed into that disease's front line.

And other people, other poets, while they weren't dying, were giving us scares. Was there a lesson here? We weren't young anymore. We were now in our forties. And yet, here we were, some of us at least, still around far longer than some of us, many of us, ever expected.

After I started having kids, it occurred to me: it's children who make you old. They can only grow, thrive, by sucking the life-force out of you. They can only grow up by making you grow old, by draining you of your youth, your precious body fluids.

Other parents would laugh along as I proceeded through this logic exercise. 'But,' I would add, 'there is, of course, a glaring flaw in this argument. 'The fact is, as we know, those among us who don't have children get older too. How can that be? Don't worry. I have dealt with this apparent anomaly with the following corollary.' I'd continue, 'Our friends who don't have kids get older too because they get to keep doing all the things that we had to stop doing when we had kids. Hitting the clubs. Staying out til dawn. Drinking. Taking drugs. Having fun. All that. That makes you old too.' And that would get a bigger laugh. A salute to our dear departed former lives. An existence putatively dedicated to self and sensation, to abandon unto dissolution perhaps, a life from which, by embracing parenthood, we'd decisively exiled ourselves.

How true was that joke? It only became clearer as these years wore on, and we lost a number of people and we got very close to losing several others. I published a book at that time, *Gorgeous Plunge,* and when I look back at it, I see that the people who I dedicated poems to in it, are many of those same people who, if we didn't lose, it surely seemed like we were about to. There was Michael Gizzi, a lovely man and poet who we were lucky to keep for a good ten more years, and Alvin Feinman, who died a few years after the book was published. There was Alan Davies, who we didn't lose then, thankfully.

And, also, there was an extended quote from Ted Greenwald incorporated into one of the book's long poems. Ted was not someone who seemed at the time likely to leave us, but his quote was altogether apposite, for those times, for those situations, for us, at this time in our lives: "It's good to be the poet until you're around forty. Then, the thing to do is hang on until you get to your sixties."

And then, aside from the people who were gone, or who we feared would be gone soon, there were the people who decided to quit. This seemed a new phenomenon. Earlier, one or two people had just upped sticks and made for the territories, even though those territories might still be in Greater New York. Peter Seaton comes to mind. He just decided he'd had enough. He didn't want to have any more to do with us, with this scene, with this world. It was pretty disconcerting, and not just to me. You could still go see him, that was easy. He held down a shift at Coliseum Books, in Midtown. He worked there for a long time. He'd be friendly. He'd say hi, but he really didn't want to have anything to do with us. And you had to respect that, even if it didn't seem to make sense.

Then as the years wore on, more and more people dropped out. And it wasn't just poets our age, it was younger poets too. 'Why do I keep doing this?' I heard that not infrequently. Some folks finally just got sick of putting their all into a life that gave nothing back. That's how they put it. Others grew tired of what they described as the toxic social or, as it was frequently worded, political atmosphere of our world. There were those who bore grudges, festering resentments that eventually burst. We laughed at some. You've been carrying *that* anger around all these years?

You still think so-and-so did you the dirty back then? You're still angry about *that?* But they would take a walk anyway. And some people just plain disappeared.

Those first few years, back when we were young, when we were just discovering each other and just starting to get ourselves and our work out there, those years already seemed so long ago.

But, as for me, what was I, now? Now, sitting at this table, in my kitchen, in the country. I wanted to think I was the same poet I was before we left New York, but was I? There were a good number of poets who'd been the young 'uns just venturing onto the scene back then, who were now well established and ruling roosts of their own. Did my name even ring a bell anymore? I kept writing because, well, I had to. Didn't I? And James, sainted soul that he is, did keep publishing me, as did others. But one day he said something troubling.

"Hey, Michael, we'd like you to do a reading at Segue next season."

Where was the reading series located back then? It wasn't at the Ear Inn anymore, certainly. Was it already at Double Happiness, that subterranean bar on Mott, the location for several years? Or, before that move to Little Italy, there was that black box theater in Soho. Here Café, wasn't that the name?

"But we're going to have to pair you with a New York poet, a local person, to get people to come."

What? Could this be true? I wasn't a New York poet anymore?

13. Wildcat Hollow Road

Our house sat at the corner of Housatonic River Road, which parallels the river it's named for and which lent its name to *The River Road*, and Wildcat Hollow Road, which started there, another old dirt road which rises out of the valley we lived in. That byway, I was told, is a stretch of an early east-west route that wagon trains once followed, crossing Connecticut, traversing New York State and continuing further west. Before then, we learned, it had been a Native American foot path. The road curved up through slopes of a thick forest. Lots of maple, ash, pine, some cedar. Typical secondary growth.

Bordering the road, both sides, and, here and there, at right angles disappearing into the trees: tumbledown stone walls. All this had been farmed once, open country. These walls marked fields. The colonists who arrived here in the middle of the 1700s piled up those rocks as they tried to plow this stony land. But it was never that good for farming. That's why so many of them, shortly after the Revolution, followed this same road into Ohio where they settled an expanse known as the Western Reserve, after first treating the Indians they found there to the same how-do-you-do they'd rendered upon the ones who'd been living in these valleys and hollows. Native Americans became, for the most part, no more than a fading memory around here. A set of hard-to-spell place names. Though the Schaghticokes do have a reservation in Kent, two towns away.

Also, often quite near the road, you could make out the remains of charcoal pits. Circular depressions in the ground, about ten feet across and three feet deep. Here, in the eighteenth and nineteenth centuries, charcoal colliers would pile up freshly cut timber — the old growth forest is now all gone, and this is why — and burn it, slow and low, for days. Then they would load what was left, the charcoal, onto their wagons and trundle over to Mount Riga, on the other side of Salisbury, once a center of the iron industry in North America. There tools and armaments and cannonballs were forged, the furnaces fueled by the wood from these hills.

A stream ran along the road, sometimes on this side, sometimes on the other. It fed the pond behind our house before running down to the Housatonic. About halfway up, behind a small concrete dam maybe a hundred years old, there was another pond, edged by a small marsh. During out daily walks, Daisy and I liked to pause by that pond and watch the ducks, who studiously ignored us.

Near the pond there was a wide cut in the woods that crossed the road. It was AT&T property, marking the path of a transcontinental long-distance line. Warning signs were posted all about. You never saw anyone there, but the groundcover was always cropped. The guy who owned the farm said that one day he and his guys were digging with a front-end loader nearby and no sooner had they cranked up the machine than a helicopter arrived with angry officials telling them to back off. But as far as Daisy and I were concerned, it just afforded us the opportunity to see far up towards the top of the valley, and occasionally catch sight of a coyote loping along the crest, maybe a hawk loitering on an updraft. We walked there every day. And when we had weekend guests, we'd take them on walks there too. Quiet and peaceful. Towards the very top of the road, it ran right along the lip of a ravine. Close to the stream's source, you felt like you were looking straight into the heart of the hollow. Once I did see a bobcat down there, or maybe it was a wildcat.

14.   The Trouble with Neoliberalism Isn't in the Stars. It's in Us

As people were leaving New York, as people were leaving the Bay Area, it occurred to me, and not me alone, I know that, that perhaps the scenes we were part of, those social structures, were only meant to live for a time certain.

New people, younger people, were showing up, creating their own scenes. At first, we used to think them, rightly or wrongly, as second-generation Language poets. But after a number of years, they came up with new names for what they were doing, Flarf and Conceptualism, as they put their riveting, compelling writing out there.

Some of those who left town got jobs in academia. Those were careers that seemed absurdly, entirely out of reach to many of us, early on. Back in the Seventies, we'd ended up doing this kind of writing in no small part in reaction to the stultifying, dead hand of academia, hadn't we? And the rejection that we encountered at first, the hostility that rained down from those redoubts of right-thinking English departments and creative writing programs, as well as the incumbent power-centers — though it's always hard to write such a phrase with a straight face — of the poetry world in New York, both uptown and down, only confirmed our faith in our cause. So, it was a surprise to some of us when others among us, upon leaving New York and the Bay Area, ended up in tenured slots at universities, in endowed seats even.

The impact of that development upon the poetry world, our part of the poetry world, became the subject of debate that's continued ever since. At the end of the day, the arguments that arose seemed to focus on the following, separate but not unrelated, questions: what did this transformation of our world do to the *people,* and what, if anything, did it do to the *poetry?*

As the Nineties progressed, certain kinds of voices seemed to be left by the roadside. Was our kind of writing — Flarf and Conceptualism aside, along with the writing associated with Ecopoetics — growing more homogenized, more monolithic? If so, was it partly because so many voices had gone quiet, had trailed off, or perhaps been silenced? And if all that is so, is it because this kind of poetry now had a firm footing in the world of academia, and those who now live there quite naturally, quite properly one could say, took advantage of the courtesies, the perquisites, the power — yes, there's really no other word for it — that that world conferred on those who lived within its domain? What kind of power? The power to publish, to confer advantage and advancement. Language poetry, some would say, became what *they* defined it, what they wrote, what those who they favored wrote. And why not? This is how the world works, isn't it?

There was a lot going on that I didn't know about, that so many of us who were not part of that world, that now-academicized Language poetry world, simply were ignorant of. As the years went by relationships were forged, students became graduate students, graduate students became junior faculty here and there, and soon everywhere. And conferences were held, fellowships and grants awarded. People started travelling, to Europe, to China. This was now a credentialed world. And why not? People needed jobs. People needed dental plans. What's wrong that? People, poets, deserved to live decent lives, no? And was this not a way, the way, to make all that happen? For poets just like you and me?

For a good long while it was only the odd, left-out among us who thought there was something wrong. They were the ones who weren't getting invited to the conferences, who weren't getting invited to read on campus, who weren't included in, say, certain anthologies. "What about me?" you'd hear people say, "I was there, back then!"

The years rolled by. The second generation were admitted to the academic fold, and they prospered to the extent they were able. Then the third generation came along, the ones who really got to enjoy what life in academia had turned into. That is, adjunct life, with its divers pleasures, like being allowed to hold down three part-time gigs simultaneously, all the while living in one's car.

Questions started getting asked. Like, what responsibility do the poets of my generation have, the ones that trailblazed the way into academia for this kind of poetry, for all of this? When it comes to the *people,* does my generation have any responsibility when it comes to all the immersated, debt-ridden young poets who are struggling so?

And what about the *poetry?* What about the poems never written? How many poets are unknown to us because our world came to be dominated by an academicized version of this writing, a world that valued and prioritized and gave attention to certain poetry and certain poets who lived in that world?

And, what else was going on in the Nineties? Did we not see in other realms the rise of a set of similar, supposed consensuses? There arose allegedly agreed-upon definitions when it came to how we should organize ourselves, what the role of, say, government and the private sector should be. With the fall of the Soviet Union and the concomitant refutation of all politics or organizing principles smacking of socialism or Marxism, we grew increasingly aware of being in the grasp of that social-political regime eventually known as Neo-Liberalism. To the extent that Neo-Liberalism gained sway in country after country, as has been noted, it came to assume the attributes of a monoculture.

This is the way it is. The way it always was. Always will be. Is it a stretch to say we saw the same forces at work in the poetry world? As the Nineties progressed, and the academicization of this kind of poetry proceeded apace, did a monoculture arise? As, in the fields of the Midwest, with their endless acreage of corn and soybeans, those monstrous combines and harvesters, all those chemicals, so, in these precincts of poetry? And the same danger? Monotony, boredom, susceptibility to all sorts of pests. As this monoculture rose and rose, did dissenting or nonconforming voices grow fewer or fainter?

15. Lucas the Babyman

After a few years we bought a house and moved closer to town. There was cable service on that road, so the satellite dish stayed behind. The business continued to thrive, outgrowing the little rooms in the back of our first house. We moved it to a small commercial building in town, taking part of a floor, then a whole floor. Around then our family grew too. Lucas was born in 1993.

When he was a toddler he'd sit at the top of the stairs with his Legos, and push them gently off the top step, over the cliff, and down they'd fall. He wasn't doing it to be destructive or make a mess, that was clear. He just wanted to see how they fell. An engineer from the get-go.

And, just as naturally as now seems in retrospect that Isabel started riding, so, when it was his time, Lucas fell in love with hockey. Before his first season of youth hockey, he was so excited at the prospect that he'd go to his room after dinner and put on his uniform, then come down and proudly show off his dressing-prowess: sweater, shorts, socks, pads, he donned it all, and got it all right. With one minor exception: he kept putting his athletic supporter on last, on top, instead of first.

A month or two later, the memory of those evening fashion-shows prompted a comment I shared with him in the car on our way home, after one of his first practices. Half an hour earlier, as I sat in the stands, one of the other parents recounted to me a conversation she'd just had with him while kindly tightening his laces. Where had I been? Tying some other kid's laces? I can't remember.

'What do you want to be when you grow up, Lucas?' she'd asked him.

'I want to be the first Gottlieb to win the Stanley Cup,' he proudly announced to her.

As we drove home, we talked about that. I felt I had to set him straight. 'I heard about you winning the Stanley Cup. But I'm not sure you understand what kind of stock you spring from, son. You should know, Lucas, you're the first Gottlieb who's ever actually worn a cup."

16.   Only Two Hours Away

Maybe it was because we were only two hours away.

Despite James' declaration that I was now an out of towner, I still wanted to believe I was a New Yorker and a New York poet. And maybe by the same token, my relative cluelessness as to the evolution of the poetry world that I continued to believe I was a card-carrying member of, allowed me to keep identifying as a Language poet, even as that world was changing out of recognition. Ron Silliman, for example, argues that Language Poetry did come to its end just then.

On the other hand, maybe because I was a hundred miles from New York, it became even more important for me to hold tight to scrap of identity. If I wasn't a Language poet, what was I? A New York poet, that didn't sound particularly, or, rather, sufficiently self-aggrandizing.

And if wasn't for Alan and James, what then? They were there from the beginning and twenty years later, as we now moved through the Nineties, they were still there. They stayed friends with me, they kept me connected, kept publishing my work. Alan brought out books of mine, one co-published with Brenda Iijima another with Jack Kimball. And James published books of my poetry through all of these years.

Also, as I get older, I'm more and more conscious, notwithstanding how tardily I note it and likely how still quite limited and incomplete this awareness is, of what a privileged upbringing I had. What my parents could afford to give me, to allow me, albeit often grudgingly. I used to describe myself as unaccountably lucky. Lucky in love, look who I ended up with, and lucky in letters, look at the life of a poet I ended up with. But I stopped saying that a while ago, as it became clearer, perhaps unforgivably belatedly, how much privilege I've benefited from.

And now, as I take this opportunity to recall those years, that first feeling redounds upon me: how lucky was I. When we moved to the country, turning forty. By 2001, in my fifties. I wasn't teaching. I didn't have any of those advantages that the poets my age with real presence in our world typically leveraged to keep themselves in circulation. And yet.

17.   By Leaps and Bounds

More and more of my day was spent on sales and marketing. Finding customers, negotiating with them, holding their hands once we signed them. We also started getting bigger clients who started giving us bigger contracts. We went from small catalog companies to big catalog companies. Then we went from big catalog companies, as well as credit card companies, to big retailers, like Home Depot and big banks, like Chase and Bank of America, and publishers too, like Time Inc.

What was I doing? Who did I think I was? I was a poet. Not a businessman, not a start-up guy. But I got caught up. I admit it. On the other hand, there never seemed to be a choice. I'd started this business out of desperation. I had to do something. And now I had to plug away at it. What else could I do? Fortunately, it was flourishing. Nevertheless, despite the blandishments, modest as they were, that this amount of success served up, I never was quite able to shake the feeling that this wasn't me. How much longer could I keep fooling them all?

Shortly after moving to that small commercial building, we signed a client that would change everything for our business. LDDS was a minor long-distance telephone company in Mississippi. It was owned by a guy named Bernie Ebbers. In a few years the company would be known as WorldCom and he would become quite famous, and then rather infamous.

Bernie wanted our services but he wasn't interested in us placing calls pretending to be his customers. What he wanted was for us to listen in on the actual calls between his operators and his customers. His new 'switch' — the computer system that routed their inbound and outbound calls — would enable us to connect remotely, from our office, and silently listen to those conversations, which we could then rate and score, just like the other calls we evaluated. This was great. This was so much easier than calling and acting like bona fide callers. Even better, I realized, and it was a momentous revelation, almost all of our clients and potential clients, were getting switches just like LDDS. All we had to do was listen in. And, oh yeah, make sure that what we were doing was legal in the state where the call was placed or received. Vast new vistas of growth seemed to open up, just like that, like the curtains and flies on some big stage, rising one after another, each revealing a grander, deeper landscape.

No one offered this service before us. It quickly became our largest source of revenue. But it wasn't the only new line of business we developed. We started doing customer surveying, and, as email became a more common way for companies to interact with their customers, we started evaluating that channel as well. Our roster of clients kept growing too. Staples, the office supply company, signed up at this time. I drove over to their Framingham office and met the management team. They were in the ground floor of a nondescript building in an office park off the Mass Pike. That didn't last long. Within a few years it became impossible to find a parking spot on their sprawling campus.

I was flying a lot then too, meeting prospective clients. Michigan, Ohio, South Dakota. I had the patter down pat. The thing was, it wasn't all that hard to get new business. The customers were arriving on their own. After a year or so in that new space, we started running out of room again.

18.   Our Very Own Witness Protection Program

When we got to the country, we realized we weren't alone. There was a good number of other young families, just like us. We were part of a wave, in a way it presaged a similar wave, much larger no doubt, that flowed out of New York thirty years later, when Covid struck. We recognized each other at the pancake breakfasts at the firehouse, at fundraisers for the ambulance squad. Back then, the New York Times remarked that new technology was enabling people, they meant us, to work far from the city. Of course, the newfangled technology that the Times was referring to back then was the fax machine.

After a few years though, I started to feel like a native. I too came to mock the pretentious weekenders trying to jump the check-out line at the local supermarket. But I was wrong. The fact is, we would never become locals. That takes three or four generations around here. But I did learn some things. I learned what a roof rake was, and why you need one to rake the snow off your roof when it piles too high, so it won't form ice dams in your gutters and wreak all manner of havoc upon your happy home. I use mine every winter.

Some of the other people we'd see at the firehouse were people who doing work on our house. It needed a lot of work. Robin had also become a gardener, so there was work going on outside as well as inside. It got to the point where I was convinced that every single guy in town who had his business's name painted on the side of his pickup truck was waving to me as I went to the post office. It felt like I wasn't just helping to pay for his truck, but for his kid's college education too.

So many of our friends were transplants that I developed a theory. The US Marshals Service, which is in charge of the Federal witness protection program, doesn't actually seed the people they've given new identities here and there, scattered around the country, I announced at a party. Look at us all. Do we really know each other's real name? Where we really come from? Our true identities? The government has gone ahead and just planted all of us here, in this one corner of Connecticut. They're saving so much taxpayer money this way.

Memorial Day parades were a big deal too, especially after the first Gulf War. Everyone would stand on Main Street and applaud the elderly vets as they went by, followed by the fire department, then the boy scouts and the school band and the town band, this town boasted its own band, and the day care center with the teachers and the parents and the kids in strollers. And then we'd all fall in behind and make our way to the town cemetery where names of war dead were read out and a school kid would recite the Gettysburg Address.

We still go every year, even though it has been decades since either of our kids marched in the band or with the hockey team. For us, the small-town appeal has never worn off. Admittedly, it doesn't have the same impact on everybody. One year we brought along some houseguests from New York. They were the only ones in sight wearing black. I saw the look in their eyes as the bands passed by. While I was thinking how Norman Rockwell this all was, I could tell they were saying to themselves: George Lincoln Rockwell.

19.   Sooner Rather than Later

When the business ran out of space again, we moved the business again. This time, one town over, to Falls Village. Lovely, sleepy Falls Village, where we found ourselves, by default, the biggest business in the town center. This had been the town's supermarket. We put up some walls. Now we had private offices and a lunch room and I leased Macintosh iMacs for everyone, in all those different candy colors. They'd just hit the market. Since I fancied us a start-up, a tech start-up even, I bought us a ping pong table and we ordered in pizza every Friday.

We also had a server and several laser printers. And when we moved in, we ordered so many phone lines that the telephone company had to run a new fiber optic cable to this town from their nearest central station, a good ten miles away. I'd heard that song before. We also had a DSL line installed. It made us feel so cutting edge. This ex-supermarket still had a walk-in freezer with a big wooden door. It made for a good conversation piece for visitors. We stored old files in there. It was also useful for private meetings.

At first, we only had eight workstations out in the open area, but every few months, it seemed, we had to order a few more. Eventually we had to commit the ping pong table to the cooler, we needed the space for more desks. Not much later we took over the storefront next door, a former beauty parlor. That became our break room and the old break room became a conference room.

Now we were signing up more telecom companies like Sprint, and cable companies, like HBO, and PC companies, like Gateway. Then we signed another telecom that wanted so much service that we had engage a call center company, just the sort of outfit whose service we evaluated ourselves, and subcontract a good amount of our work to them. I flew down to their headquarters in Atlanta and spent a couple of weeks training their people, some who worked there and some in other locations they had around the country.

By now The Tele-Monitor Co., Inc. had been in business for more than six years. There were several people who had been with the company for some time, with specialized roles in operations and technology. When it came to sales and marketing, though, that work still fell to me. And that was fine, until one day when I realized it wasn't.

We'd just lost a deal. It was a big bank. I had gone to call on them, and taken someone with me. We took the meeting in one of their regional offices, in Springfield, Massachusetts as I recall. We were ushered into a conference room and I made our presentation, the same sort of presentation I did all the time, this one tailored for a financial services client. It had been easy to craft it since we already had so many banks on our roster, several of whom I provided as references. As we walked out of that meeting I was confident that we'd won the business. They looked ready. Prospects like this were always ready. They always signed.

But not this time. When I got the word a few days later I wasn't just disappointed, I was surprised. So, I called my contact at the bank. He told me that while he and his team were impressed by our presentation, another company had come in and really wowed them. It was a division of a large company, which had recently been acquired by an even huger corporation by the name of Aon. "When they came in, they had, like five people, Michael. And you had one guy with you. And they had some really, really good PowerPoint."

Then we lost another deal to this company. I knew we had a fight on our hands. Up until this point we never had any competition, no real competition. The only other shops I ever knew about who did anything like what we did were even smaller, and seemed really unsophisticated, compared to us. But these people were different. This was a big business, and the people who they had running this unit, I learned as I started digging, were not just really professional, they were all industrial psychologists. How was I going to compete with them?

20.   In the Drug Store

Then our daughter got sick. It was bad. There were a lot of doctors and a lot of tests and then there was surgery. It all went down one summer, in the space of a month.

Partway through I had to go to town and hand in a prescription. The pharmacist knew me and my wife and my daughter and my son. And his sister, who ran the store with him, knew us also. She'd arranged for me to get one those prized cubby holes, set against the wall, off to the side, away from the main floor, where my Times waited for me every morning.

As soon as he read the prescription, he came from behind the counter with a grave look on his face. He could tell. Children aren't prescribed this. Something was very wrong. He put his hand on my shoulder.

21.   *Back and Forth*

Eventually, we were driving back and forth to the Children's Hospital in Hartford, day after day. Day after day of tests. Then came the diagnosis. And then came a weekend of dread, her wracking pain from the growth somehow alleviated by steroids. 'It'll shrink it,' said the neurosurgeon, 'And make it easier to take out.'

After a month of screams in the night, now a terrifying silence. No pain, really? Was this just some trick? Served up cruelly, so if it all went bad, and we lost her, we'd be left with a vivid memory of what we'd lost?

And then on Monday morning, the surgery. A success.

I could write an entire book about this. I've filled up pages about those days. But it is truly my daughter's story, for her to tell, if she wishes. These are just my bits and snatches.

The next couple of nights Robin slept in Isabel's hospital room. I drove back and forth with Lucas. He was four then. It was a long drive for him and I am sure he sensed all the terror that was coursing through us. He'd ask how much longer until we got to the hospital and I'd say, 'it's just a little while.' And on the way back he'd ask again, and I'd say 'Well, it's actually two more little-whiles.' And eventually, he understood, and in a way, it seemed to me, he acknowledged what was happening and why we were doing driving back and forth to Hartford, and he'd say, 'Well, it's three little-whiles altogether, right?'

The last morning, I got to the hospital early. So that Isabel wouldn't have too far to walk, I parked as close as I could to the main entrance. The nearest spaces were reserved for doctors, but I parked there anyway. As soon as I got out of the car a security guard appeared, an old guy, no-nonsense. He asked me if I was a doctor. No, I said. I told him why I'd parked there.

'Oh,' he said, 'Well, you just get in your car and move it."

I looked at him.

"You drive up to the entrance," he continued, "Right over there by the front doors where it says No Parking, and you park your car right there. I'll watch it.'

He made me want to cry all over again.

22.   Didn't Belong

Then school started. Everyone was fine. Running around, hockey, horses, everything. It was hard to believe that it was over.

But something came over me. A couple of months later, it was Halloween, we walked down the street, saying hi to our friends who were out that night too, watching our kids run up to the front doors, trick or treating. This was all wrong, I realized. I didn't belong. I had nothing in common with these parents. Who were they? What were their lives like?

And then, few months further along, we found ourselves in Boston, at another hospital. The doctors in Hartford had informed us that, while they were not recommending any radiation, the vote of the Tumor Committee — who even knew there was such a thing — had not been unanimous. So, they advised us to get a second opinion. The examination at Dana Farber was brief, and though encountering the other parents there and seeing some of their children wasn't all that easy, it all went off rather quickly.

Then, when it was over, on our way across town, in the T, I found myself looking around the subway car. There were ten or fifteen other passengers, some old couples, some middle-aged women by themselves, a few kids. I realized that the odds were very good that at least one of these people could be very sick, or their father or their mother or their son or daughter was very sick, or had been, just like ours. Of course, there was no way to know.

It occurred to me right then that, as we stride through this or that city, and we walk past people, right and left, there is a whole world of human suffering we're passing by, unseen, unheard, invisible. Out of every hundred people, how many are sick? Have a sick daughter or husband? This anguish, misery, grief is everywhere. Cliché? I guess. But it struck me with such force that day anyway. It must be here too. We know it is all around, we just pay it no heed.

23.   The Start-up Life

Back in the office, the highs and lows. No one had prepared me for them. Like nothing before or since. There did seem to be something creative, really and truly, about coming up with a new idea, an idea for a business, or a product or service. It seemed to be quite similar to the work of making art, a poem or a picture. Yes, there were always antecedents and influences, and you might beg, borrow or steal, in a way, but you were in fact making something out of nothing. Something that you wished, hoped, dreamed people would like, would want, would spend money on.

And if they did, if they liked what you put out there, then what a terrific high. And for me, for us, for this company, for a time, that high just kept coming. And it wasn't just about the money, although of course the money was important. We needed the money. We were living off this company. There was a family to provide for, a house and a mortgage, and eventually tuition for schools. But we were making money. Not stupid amounts of money but more money than ever before. Though, again, it wasn't only about the money.

When I came up with something new, and people bought it, that was amazing. And then, as people kept buying it, as one company after another would start talking to us, often they'd heard of us already, each company bigger than the last, famous companies, marquee brands, leaders in their categories, signing up, one after the other, I felt a kind of rush each time. It was related to, but in so many ways altogether different than the charge, if that is the right word, that came from, comes from, say, getting published. Was the difference due to the fact that there was real money involved here? Thousands of dollars, sometimes more, which amounted to, at a minimum, a thousand times more worldly value, or appreciation, or approbation, than anything I'd written had ever generated?

Or was it something else?

It was the late 1990s, and the first wave of internet start-ups were grabbing attention. All manner of idiotic businesses were getting funded and, according to people in the know, there was madness in the air.

Every Op Ed page said so. These companies were going to change the world, weren't they? Starting a business, getting funded, this is what heroic young people were meant to do, wasn't it? Though I wasn't all that young any more, was I immune to all this? The thing was, unlike so many of those start-ups, those dog food delivery companies, we had a real business, with real clients.

And, as the company grew these celebrations became shared moments. At the beginning, it had been just me, or me and Robin. But by this time there was a team. And when we had a win, it was something that we shared. And not in a phony, forced way. The fact was that in a small business like that, we all had to work together. The managers and the people who'd been there for some time all relied on each other. And that too distinguished it from any previous sort of celebratory moment. This wasn't like getting something published, where the spotlight, not that the poetry world could ever afford the electric bill for spotlights, was on you. Or me.

Those were the good times. But they weren't all good. From time to time, we would lose a client, or a company would pay late. Then, all of a sudden, I would have to make payroll, or the rent was due, or the quarterly taxes had to be paid, or the insurance or the phone bill couldn't be put off any longer, and there was no money in the checking account.

When there was no money, there was no one else. It was my business, my responsibility. It was all on me. I was alone. Those were terrifying moments unlike anything I'd experienced before. I'd been fired from jobs, other sorts of lousy things had befallen me, like anyone my age. But nothing like this. There was nowhere to run and there was no way out. All those people were depending on me. They worked hard, week in and week out, and they had their own families to support. That's why they showed up every day. How could I face them? What was I going to tell them?

Somehow the money would be found. We didn't have a line of credit back then or any investors, so when these moments, these crises came, I would have to go to our personal savings and lend the company the money. At least I never had to go, hat in hand, to anyone else.

The thing was, even during our heyday, during these good times, when we had Christmas parties in the private room at the fancy restaurant in Lakeville, even then, when we had a permanent Help Wanted ad running in the local papers because we always needed more people, when we were signing up big-logo-clients, household names, hand over fist, when we were putting in new workstations every month or so, though I still bought them from Ikea, my friend Sean White used to say that our office looked like the biggest Ikea showroom he'd ever seen, even then, those rough times came along not infrequently.

A rollercoaster of chiaroscuro. Too much. Heights so bright, dizzying. The lows so dark. Sometimes I asked myself what was I, a poet, a dumb, downtown poet, doing living this life? I hadn't gone to business school. Was this me?

24. It's Not a Wonderful Life

I hated that blasted fountain and its pathetic, putrescent pond. The pond itself wasn't a bad idea, and Robin sited it perfectly, under the ancient apple tree off to the side of the house, right in front of a curve of old stone wall, near the arbor, with room for a bench where you could sit and take it all in. It wasn't really very big, no more than ten feet in diameter. The guy we had dig it did a tip top job, laying in the lining neatly and seating the bluestone nicely around the edge. It was our fault, really. We didn't do our research. We had it dug three feet deep. What did we know? One foot would have been plenty. That would have been the smart play.

We bought a little fountain, a tiny thing with a minute pump, and had the electrician run a line from the basement over to the pond. We found half a dozen koi and in they went. Robin stocked it with a lovely assortment of water plants. The fish seemed to like it there. You'd see them circling around, going after the food we tossed in. The thing was, the fountain needed a base, which I cobbled together out of a couple of piled-up cinder blocks, because the pond was otherwise just too deep for its jet to break the surface. Once I had it all set up, it produced a nice, gentle burble. It was rather soothing, taking one's ease on the bench after dinner, taking it all in.

Then, a few days later, a blue heron showed up. He — why have I always assumed it was a 'he' — hung around for a few days. He was tall, a good three feet high, and elegant. An intelligent expression, long aquiline beak. From the breakfast room we had a good view of the pond. How countrified, how rural, how rustic-elegant is this, we asked ourselves. The kids were taken with him too. Then one morning, two or three days later, he was gone. I went down to the pond. Something was off. I looked closely. The fountain wasn't working. No water was bubbling up. I thought I'd anchored it securely atop the upper cinder block. Perhaps I could have done a better job. Could the heron have knocked it over? Why would he? But something else was wrong. I looked around, I looked into the depths of our new pond. Something was indeed missing. The koi. All of them. That's why that heron had shown up. It had taken him about forty-eight hours. He cleaned us out and then he cleared out.

That was the beginning of my time in the depths, my personal pond-hell. We never bought any more koi. We learned our lesson. But the fountain was still out of order. I put on a bathing suit and went in. It was one thing to hook it all up before the pond was filled, but now I felt like one of those WWII frogmen in the freezing, pitch-black North Atlantic, attaching a limpet mine to the hull of a Nazi battle-cruiser. It was high summer but this water was frigid. I had to feel my way along the pond's floor. The footing was uncertain. Then I had to bend over, nearly putting my face in the water, to reassemble the arrangement of blocks. It wasn't easy. It wasn't pleasant. I slipped and got dunked a few times. My wife and children, drawn up along the pond's edge, proceeded to hear me let loose with a string of expletives the variety and volume of which I'm not sure they, at least my children, had before heard come out of the mouth of anyone.

And this was just the beginning. No matter what I tried, that damn fountain never seemed to go more than a week before toppling over. Eventually Robin took pity on me and bought an old pair of waders at a tag sale. They had a pair of built-in boots, with suspenders that hitched over my shoulders like overalls. We kept them hanging by the back door. The problem was that the boots were so big, at least four sizes bigger than my Size 10s, that I flopped around like a platypus, not infrequently falling on my face while crossing the lawn. Also, they were so old, and had sprung so many leaks, that within a few minutes of venturing into the depths, I was as wet and chilled as if I hadn't been wearing them at all.

This went on forever, for as long as we lived there, a good twenty years. It became a kind of a joke in our family. Regularly, like proverbial clockwork, every few weeks, from spring to fall, I delivered my ritual curses upon the blasted pond, the bane of my existence. I became Jimmy Stewart. I was living in a version of *It's a Wonderful Life,* and my stupid fountain was that ridiculous finial atop the banister's newel post, at the bottom of George Bailey's staircase, the one that keeps coming off in his hand. He never managed to repair it despite the fact that he and Donna Reed and their kids have lived there for years upon years.

25.   *Getting Money*

Who said it to me? Was it Sean? Maybe a lot of people said this. Maybe it was a saying. Maybe it still is. 'Don't worry if you fail. At least you got money. Next time, it'll be that much easier. For your next business.'

We were going out for money. How else were we going to compete with the big guys? At first there were a lot of No's. Only No's. But that was to be expected, that's what I learned. We had a business plan and budgets and projections. I had my pitches: an elevator pitch, a five-minute pitch, a fifteen-minute pitch, a half-hour pitch.

Eventually people started to yes. It took about a year. First, I did the rounds with venture capital guys. Then there were people who looked just like them and talked just like them, but worked for the State of Connecticut. They were the first ones that said yes. And then there were others. We were going to get economic development money from the state. It was a nice piece of change and the terms actually were considerably less onerous than what we would have expected from the VCs.

These people really wanted us to succeed. They moved quickly and they had lots of ideas. As soon as the first of the money arrived, we kicked off a rebranding effort, crafting new messaging, marketing materials and online presence. My friend David Boorstin was very helpful, providing guidance and counsel, although his most pointed piece of advice, the one that has stuck with me longest, had nothing, on the face of it, to do with branding. We were scheduled to meet one Saturday morning at the office in Falls Village. I asked him not to come on over before 11:00 AM, because I needed to clean the bathrooms first.

"You clean the bathrooms?" he said.

"Of course," I said.

"Yourself? Really?" he asked.

It would never occur to me to ask anyone who worked for the company to do such a task and, now that I think about it, perhaps, also, I was taken with the idea of the boss cleaning the bathrooms himself. It was a nice metaphor. I was sending a message to everyone in the company that I didn't think I was better than them, that I was willing to pitch in, do the dirty work, as it were. Wasn't I?

"Don't do that. Stop doing that. Right now. Hire a service." That was David's advice. More than advice, direction. "You should not be doing that, you're the president of the company."

The Connecticut people were sorry that they couldn't give us more money. They came to visit one day and told me about another economic development opportunity in Connecticut, in a special zone, in Waterbury, an old New England factory town, the Brass City, once an industrial powerhouse. Some would say it had seen better days. I had only driven past it on I-84, gone to the mall there a few times; taken in, from a distance, all those empty nineteenth century factories.

This looked like more money, the only catch was that we had to move the company to Waterbury, and also, by the by, promise to create a certain number of jobs within a specified time. That latter condition was a no-brainer. We were hiring every week. And Waterbury was only an hour from home. So why not? In a matter of days, I was touring empty, ready-to-build-out Class A office space in Waterbury. Waterbury had not just been a big manufacturing center, but a banking hub as well. In fact, the building we moved into a short time later was on Bank Street. Building after building, lovely stone-faced offices, empty, empty, empty. So many choices.

The biggest we were shown faced the town green, where, I was repeatedly informed, JFK had held his Election Eve rally in 1960, the night before he beat Nixon. Someone showed me a photograph. The big, long park jammed solid with people.

Each floor was packed with office furniture. It looked like a vast used office furniture mart. Tufted leather chesterfields missing a button here and there, stodgy colonial revival mahogany credenzas. Off into the dim distance, as far as the eye could see, desk after impressive cherry desk. And every piece of furniture had a label on it. Each of these breakfronts and conference tables, one and all examples of that conservative, confidence-building style, 'You can trust us,' they said, had belonged to one bank or another. That's what the labels said. Banks whose names were vaguely familiar. They certainly weren't around anymore, though some not all that long gone.

As the banking industry had consolidated and shrank in New England, all of those take-overs and mergers had come down, one after another, to this, 'We don't need those buildings, those offices, that furniture... we don't need those people.'

That's why there were all of these empty buildings in this once-proud city, many in great shape, ready for a new life. But when it came to the people, all of the people who had worked in those banks for years, tellers, vice presidents, people who'd built their careers in those buildings, lived their workaday lives here, what sign was left of them aside from these dusty rows of swivel chairs and occasional chairs, row upon row, floor upon floor?

26.   I Could Never Imagine

Yes, he was into music. He still is. We got Lucas a guitar when he was little. And then lessons — he was really good. And, at school, he was in band, of course. Trumpet. For a while, when Memorial Day came, a decision had to be made: should he march with the hockey program or the band? The time came when he got interested in violin too.

People kept telling us that musical talent often goes hand in hand with high-order math skills, and he was certainly very good at math. Where did he get that from? Certainly not from me or Robin. Isabel was a reader, and turning into a writer. It was clear where that came from. Maybe it was my father. He was no musician but he had been an accountant and an absolute wizard at sums of all sorts. Even in his old age, he was so fast. He could tote up figures in his head faster and more accurately than me, using a calculator.

When he was still in middle school Lucas was sent off to the regional high school for math class. He'd finished with all the courses the school in our town could offer. One year the school's ranking on the state-wide math achievement test for his grade had been driven up substantially, solely due to his score.

But he reminded me of my father in another way. One weekend around this time, he couldn't have been more than six or seven, he and I drove over to the town ball field. I don't recall exactly what was on tap that morning. Maybe some pitch and catch? I do remember that after a while I called a break. As I rested for a spell on the bleachers, he wandered over to the little fenced-in skate board area, located past right field. There were a bunch of boys there. They were much bigger, maybe eleven or twelve years old.

For a while he stood there, leaning against the chain link, watching these boys. I was out of earshot. These kids seemed to be ignoring him. Then one of the boys, the biggest, turned his head and looked at Lucas. Had Lucas said something to him? The kid dismounted and approached him. The two of them seemed to be conversing through the fence. After a minute the other boys came over and stood by. What was going on? Did I need to step in? Was there going to be trouble? If only I could hear what they were saying to each other. It would be, like, five against one. And they were all much bigger than him.

The next thing I knew, Lucas was opening the gate and stepping into the park. The biggest boy slid his board over to Lucas who jumped onboard. The other boys got back on their boards and they all proceeded to go about their business, the biggest leaning back against the fence, the rest gliding back and forth, trying to catch some air off of the little jumps that had recently been installed there.

Did already he know these guys? I never asked but I'm pretty sure he didn't. Before my very eyes he'd just struck up a conversation and made a connection, somehow, and within two minutes he was skating with them. How did he do that? What were they talking about? What social skills did this little boy have? I could never do that, not when I was six.

Then I remembered my father. The grandfather Lucas had only met a few times, when he was an infant and my father had entered his second infancy. I remember my father being tickled pink when given Lucas to hold, though not being quite sure how to manage this little bundle of boyhood.

But when I was little, around the age Lucas was now, I used to watch my father engage in that very same behavior, which I've written about, which my son had just displayed, apparently effortlessly, during the walks he and I would take around our neighborhood. Stopping by a house around the corner, where the father was washing his car, over by Marion Avenue where the lady was watering her lawn, and striking up a conversation with them. Just like that. Just like Lucas.

27. Waterbury Ho!

The time came when I met the governor of Connecticut at a dinner in Waterbury, not long after our business moved there. There were at least two hundred people in the hall. When we were introduced, surprisingly, he knew who I was and what I was doing there.

He was also very well dressed. I have to say that I haven't met a lot of politicians in my time, but they've all been men, and they've all been really, really well turned out. Extraordinary suits, superior coiffures. This dinner was held shortly after 9/11. They were handing out American flag lapel pins to everyone. American flags everywhere. Since then, they haven't really left, have they? There's still a giant American flag inside Grand Central that dates from then. Another that's stretched across the facade of New York Stock Exchange, but back then they really, really were everywhere. Every car had a little flag on a pole attached to the driver's window, and at this dinner, they handed out flag pins to all of us. I really didn't want to put mine on.

I remember having a conversation with Barrett Watten about the US Marines back then. They were, as far as he was concerned, if I'm remembering correctly, based on their record in the Caribbean, in country after country there, no more or less than the foot soldiers of American imperialism. That's all you needed to know about them. On the other hand, I replied, when it comes to thousands of Americans, tens of thousands probably, who had brothers or sons or fathers or grandfathers who fought at Tawara or Saipan or Iwo Jima, who died by the thousands, they might have a different association when you say, 'US Marines.' To his credit I would say, Barrett acknowledged that. Notwithstanding all that, I still felt a little funny pinning that flag to my suit jacket. Maybe it just bugged me because everyone else was doing it.

Both the mayor and the governor were there. That was the last time I saw them in person. Afterwards, on TV, a lot. Within a few years of that dinner, they were both indicted for various depredations and specie of corruption, both found guilty and promptly packed off to the big house. I think it was also around that time that my old boss at Warner Bros., he'd been retired for a good while by now, went to prison too. He did some very bad things, with a girl. She was nowhere near eighteen. He went away for quite a while.

Clowns hauled away in cuffs. As far as those pols were concerned, it all seemed rather jolly to us, at the time. Meanwhile, as far as the business was concerned, we were planning our work and working our plan, as the saying went. We were on budget. We were on plan. We were spending what we said we were going to spend. Volume was holding up fine. With our new sales and marketing guy in charge we had reporting and analytics, just like a real company. The marketing funnel looked fabulous, all kinds of people were finding their way to us. Our new look and our new technology were wowing folks. And the sales pipeline was exceedingly healthy. We, or rather, he was moving prospects along, turning them into opportunities and gently but firmly ushering them along to the close. He was great. It was all very impressive. I was impressed. We had a good story to tell and we were telling it.

28.   That Day in September

On September 11, 2001 I woke early. I was headed for Ohio. My flight left Hartford at 7:30 AM. I was doing lots those trips in those days. I'd leave the house before dawn. It was about an hour and a half to Bradley International, Hartford's airport. I always parked at the same lot. They were starting to get to know me. Ohio, Florida, Michigan, I could do each of those in one day. I'd have a rental car waiting at the destination. I'd get back late but I'd be home that night. This particular trip was to see a potential client who was pretty far along in the funnel, and there were three of us going, each departing from a different airport.

I was changing in Philadelphia. We landed there at 8:30. I remember handing my Times to the flight attendant, I was done with it. She didn't put it in the trash bag, but under her arm. She said thanks. It had been a one-hour flight, almost long enough to read the whole paper. I had plenty of time to make my connecting flight. By the time I got to the next gate all the TVs were showing the first tower and the billowing smoke.

I seem to keep writing about how I spent that day, each time with more detail. It's not like I'm remembering more as time goes on. There's still so much I'm leaving out: what I saw in that hotel lobby, on the television, on the highway, on that first trip back. But it occurs to me now, maybe I won't have to do this again.

At first, those first few minutes, people seemed to be treating it almost like a joke. Some piker in a Piper Cub got too close to the World Trade Center. Hadn't a bomber crashed into the Empire State Building during WWII? That happened during some storm, right? Today, though, it was clear. The weather was beautiful. One of those days in the late summer, the air rinsed and dried, crystal clear, unlimited visibility. Did anyone get hurt that time, back then? Was it 1944? These things happen, right?

Then there were a series of announcements. They came quickly, one after another. First, all flights were delayed an hour; then until the afternoon. Then all flights were cancelled. There was a Marriott at the airport and I had some sort of membership with them, so I started walking in that direction. Then another announcement: everyone had to leave the airport, now.

Somehow, I was able to grab a cab. I had the driver take me to City Center. There was a Marriott there too. By the time I arrived, it couldn't have been much past ten, all the rooms were taken. There were dozens upon dozens of people in the lobby, sitting there, watching the TVs that had been set up. That's where I saw the second tower come down. I was able to reach Robin, so she knew I was alive. And I called the office too, but we couldn't reach one of our guys. He was flying out of Newark. And we already knew that one of the planes that crashed had originated in Newark.

All trains had been stopped. The highways were closed. Hertz wouldn't rent a car to you unless you promised to return it to the same city you'd taken it from. It looked like I'd be bedding down in that lobby but at least I was all in one piece.

I don't want to forget the way I felt that day, the fabric of the world ripped open. The towers. First one plane and then another, and then the plane in Washington, at the Pentagon, and the other one that went down in Pennsylvania. People were dying before our very eyes. Hundreds of them, thousands.

And I'd been in those buildings so many times, in the World Trade Center, in the World Financial Center across the street, in the concourse downstairs. That tatty bar halfway up. And what about our friends? James was working near the Federal Reserve, barely a block away. Our friends Jeremy and Kitty, they lived just a few blocks up Greenwich St. from the Trade Center. What about them?

Then, a man, I could make him out clearly, my age, a suit without a tie, just the way I was dressed today, that's what I couldn't get over, jumping.

Over the years, have I ever talked about this? At first the TV reporters weren't sure what they, what we, were seeing. Were we really seeing this? What could make people resort to this? More figures falling, one after the other. I didn't want to watch, I wanted to turn away. If my kids were there, I surely would have covered their eyes. Did I owe it to someone — if so, who? these people? — to keep watching? Or could I just not turn away from this spectacle? This was footage we never saw again.

Then the first tower came down, then the second, the angry clouds of dust rushing out a hundred miles an hour, up the streets, across downtown. We'd never see that again either.

By late afternoon I'd done so much lying to Hertz that they handed me the keys to what they swore was the last rental car in Philadelphia. The interstates had reopened. I headed north, avoiding the New Jersey Turnpike and the city, ending up on the far side of the Hudson. I cut back east over the Tappan Zee, that bridge I'd been crossing since I was a boy. I knew just where to look south, halfway across. This was where, when I was eighteen, crossing this same bridge, I'd glanced around, looking for those mothballed WWII destroyers. They had been missing too.

You could see all the way to Manhattan from here, twenty miles downriver. It was dusk. I couldn't make out exactly what the skyline was missing, but there was a giant cloud right above New York. Huge, high, the biggest I'd ever seen. The setting sun slanting into it sideways from the west, picking out all sorts of terrible, terrifying, gorgeously hideous colors. Colors I'd never seen in nature: yellow, black, rancid purple and green.

Then, as I drove up through Westchester there was something else, something I've never written about, though I've written about this day many times.

I felt it. It was inside me. That morning, that afternoon, as I staked out a quiet corner in that hotel lobby, making sure to sit near someone with a charger, as I tried, again and again, to find a hotel room, making a personal connection with the front desk people so they'd go out of their way and find me a room at the Wyndham, and then, later, sweet talking myself into that sad sack sedan, and then, finally, plotting a route home, my entire existence reduced to executing these tasks, one after another, so I would survive, so I would see my family again, I realized I'd been running on some sort of adrenalin. And now, driving north in the dark, I realized — I was ashamed even to say it to myself, I am still — but there was no way around it: amidst all that death, just acting, doing, nothing else, no time for anything else, I simply felt alive. How could this be? Alive in a way I'd never felt before.

And I know I didn't have it so bad that day. Nothing compared to so many others. I did get home to my family that night.

A few days later, the first Saturday afterwards, Lower Manhattan still barricaded and closed off, the airlines still grounded, I took Isabel to the barn where she did her riding. I think she had a lesson. As we proceeded along the farm's drive, I heard a godawful noise above us. I stopped the car and looked up. Not much higher than the trees, incredibly close, a jet liner roared by, heading due west. It was so close I thought I could see the rivets in the fuselage. And then it was gone. What was this? Another attack? There weren't supposed to be any planes in the air at all. F-16s patrolling the skies over Manhattan had just caused a panic, the papers reported. What was going on?

There was never anything in the news about this plane. I eventually shared the story to an older friend who I think had some law enforcement connections. This is what he told me: it was the FBI at the controls, retracing the flight of one of the planes that flew into the World Trade Center, the one that originated in Boston. I have no idea if that was so, but it made sense at the time. I nodded and as I nodded the following thought came to me. This means that plane flew right over our house that day. Had it flown so low? Those people could have looked out the window and seen our house, my kids standing at the end of the driveway with my dog, waiting for the school bus.

29. All that Dust

My first trip to the city came a few Saturdays later. It was the first
poetry reading of the season in the series sponsored by James's Segue
Foundation. By 2001 the series was holding forth at Double Happiness
on Mott. I drove down early that day, parked in the garage on Kenmare,
across from my old apartment, then made my way further downtown
on foot. There, in front of the court houses in Foley Square: soldiers in
battle dress. That was a sight you never saw in New York. And police
everywhere. Jarringly strange uniforms. From places like Rhode Island
and Pennsylvania. I made it to City Hall Park and joined the crowd
looking west. Smoke was still rising between the twisted-up fingers of
the Trade Center's steel.

Then I walked over to Greenwich St. and turned south, but you couldn't
get any closer than Chambers. I stood near Jeremy and Kitty's building
and looked downtown from there. They and their kids were safe, but
they'd left their windows open that day. It was such a beautiful day.
Their place was only a few blocks from the towers. Everything in the
apartment, absolutely everything, had been covered by that dust.

I went to the reading, and eventually I headed home. It was night already
as I drove up Elizabeth on my way to Houston. From Houston I'd get
on the West Side Highway and then the Henry Hudson and then the
Saw Mill and then the Taconic. Those parkways again, one after another.
As I headed uptown, passing Spring Street, I noticed something. There
was stuff, powder, dust, something, everywhere. In the gutter, on the
sidewalk, under my wheels. At first, I assumed it was construction
debris, the kind you encounter whenever a building is being demolished
or rehabbed in New York. This being rapidly gentrifying Little Italy, I
automatically looked about for the source of all this, a telltale sidewalk
construction shed, say, but there were none in sight. Then I realized: this
was that dust, the dust that had covered everyone and everything when
the buildings fell. For some reason this one block, of all the New York
streets I'd passed along that day, had not been cleaned.

What's in this dust, I asked myself. Then it came to me, like it did to
everyone: it's the people, all the people who they're never going to find.

339

And I'm driving over it, over them. But I realized, it's not just the people. It's also the buildings, the steel and the glass, and the furniture and the paperwork on the desks. The newspapers at the newsstands in the basement and the flowers being sent up to the Windows on the World, and the wine and champagne they stored there. As my mind raced, and I thought about all the times I'd been in those buildings, it came to me that, when it came to things, there was simply no end to the things that were lost. It was an entire world of things. And then, right before I reached Prince Street, the poem arrived.

A poem made up of things, just listing all the things that were lost, including the people, that was the poem that I was supposed to write. I'm someone who makes work out of language that doesn't belong in poems. I'm someone who's always been writing about New York, that's what I said to myself. This is my job. So, I went home that night, and, actually, I proceeded not to write that poem.

I did continue to make my way through the Times every morning, usually in the office before anyone else arrived, still reading it on paper, eventually getting to the obituaries. When I was ten years old or so, in 1960 or 1961, as he taught me to read the Times, my father encouraged me to read the obits, along with the shipping news and the chess column and the ABCs.

In the weeks after 9/11 there were at least two pages of obituaries every morning, some special ones titled Portraits in Grief, in all twice as many as I'd ever seen before. That went on for months and I kept putting that poem off until the following April, when it was my turn to have a reading in the Segue series down there on Mott Street.

Over the years I've developed a habit. There was never any aforethought about it. It just arose on its own, as it were. Further, it is activity that, I believe, is entirely antithetical to so the practice of many of my contemporaries and, indeed, poets who came before us who I myself revere. This habit, let's call it that, obliges me to go through draft after draft, writing and rewriting my poems until they are done. Often two dozen drafts, at least. I need to mention that my poems, when they start off are mere lists of words, phrases, captured language that I've built up, sometimes over months. Then, through these drafts the poem comes to define itself, words grow into lines, lines become stanzas, stanzas are moved about, expanded, excised. Eventually, it's done.

This poem was different. I didn't want to write it.

Over the years I have had occasion to try to write about why we write. In those essays, I've tried to explore questions like, what is a good reason, the right reason, to write? Is there one? More than one? And, when it comes topics like these, one particular dilemma I've tried to grapple with has always proved particularly thorny: although it gives us such pleasure to write, because this indeed is what we were placed on this earth to do, is that a good enough reason to write? Because it feels so good? I'm not sure I've ever come up with a cogent or compelling answer to that question.

I can say, though, writing this poem threw that question into a new light. That's why I put it off for months, all through the autumn of 2001, and into the winter and well into the spring of 2002. There was so much going on with the business right then, but I thought about the poem all the time. But I didn't do anything about it. Then it was a month before my reading, then three weeks, and then I got to work.

By then I'd figured out the poem would start with a list of airplane parts, followed by the sort of structural steel that had been used to frame the building. Then, other things from the offices and the stores. Things becoming increasingly personal. Eventually, clothes and jewelry. And then, the contents of purses, and wallets. And then, finally, the people themselves. Everything that got turned into that dust. That was Part I. In Part II, I mixed everything up, like it was all mixed up after the buildings came down. First a long list of varied things, and then one name, one of those persons. And then a shorter list and two names. And then a list shorter yet, and three names. Until at the end it was all names.

In the final respect all of those things, while they constituted the world, our world, were still just things. What made this loss so immense, finally what was lost, was the people, those names, those people who got turned into dust. That's the title I gave it, *The Dust*.

But I'd never felt like this. I just wanted to be done with it. I did the work in a few days. I printed it out and corrected it for typos. It was basically one draft. It was funny, while I've written about the question of whether getting pleasure out of writing is a good enough reason to write a poem, of all the poems I've written, this one I absolutely hated writing. What was now going on with the business had completely taken over my life, but at least I was done with this poem.

When I read the first time, at Double Happiness, people cried. I read it a lot in the following year. Some people cried each time.

30.   Daisy and the Driveway

Over the years, as our kids grew up, we came to share our house with two cats and two dogs. Their various tenures overlapped. There was a good amount of time I would set out four bowls of food in the kitchen every morning. The second dog was Ollie, another Newfoundland, a Landseer, black and white. In his old age he spent a lot of time in New York City. By then Robin and I both had jobs there. He became a minor celebrity in Chelsea.

A stunning dog, whenever we walked him along 23rd Street, the Gray Line buses would slow down so that the tourists could take pictures. He was always the rambunctious teenager. But Daisy, truer to her breed, was the nanny, gentle, protective. The cats, when they were kittens, would curl up inside her paws. The kids napped atop her.

In the morning, when they were little, the children went to the end of the driveway to wait for the school bus. Daisy would go with them and lie down on the asphalt. Robin would keep an eye on them from a window. The bus would come, the driver would toot his horn, swing open the door and say hi to the dog. The kids would get on the bus, off they would go, and Daisy would slowly make her way back to the house.

Whenever I saw this, if I was, say, running late that morning, a feeling came over me. I felt it also at the dinner table, all of us sitting there. And other times too, like when I'd find myself at the wheel of an SUV full of boys heading to a Saturday hockey game at the godawful far end of Connecticut at some inhumanly early hour of the morning.

I used to describe this feeling by quoting the Talking Heads: "…This is not my beautiful home. This is not my beautiful wife…"

Frankly, it was not easy to accept this was indeed my life. Having a family, a decent home, those were things I'd come to believe I'd never have. Who was I to have such things? A poet; in so many ways the very definition of a loser.

A continual and continuous disappointment to my parents. Barely able to make a living. What did they say when the other parents, their friends down in Florida, started bragging about their kids? Oh, your son is a lawyer trying cases at the Supreme Court? Oh, your son is a doctor, curing cancer? Our son? A poet. He talked us into letting him go to this ridiculous college in Vermont, the most expensive in the country by the way, so he could learn to be a poet. Impressive, no? Then he found himself a great job, something to do with the Guggenheim Museum. It meant he got to go on unemployment every summer. Isn't that special? So, then he ended up working a movie studio and of course he got fired from that. Foreign Service Test? No, we never mentioned that to him. The Post Office test, that we suggested. And where does he live? On the fifth floor of Old Law tenement in Little Italy. Remember when we called them slums? Don't ask me to climb those stairs a second time. An apartment so small his grandmother, fresh from Ellis Island, would have spat on the floor and gotten back on the boat.

Nothing in my life had really prepared me for such a life. I couldn't help but wonder, was all this really mine? Could someone come and take it all away? And, of course, assuming that it was all real, and really mine, and no one was going to show up on my doorstep brandishing some writ with a gang of moving men behind him — would they be Israelis? — what had I done to deserve any of this?

But then, after a while, as I look back now, that feeling started to fade. Maybe it was all those nights reading E.B. White to my daughter. Maybe it was watching those two tiny children grow up into smart, healthy, happy kids. But eventually, it took a good number of years, I stopped feeling like a character in a David Byrne lyric. I wasn't that guy he sang about with the big house and the beautiful wife, nor was I the one who's gone underground, because he no longer has any time for CGBG or the Mudd Club.

While I remembered CBGB and the Mudd Club very well, thank you very much, and Hurrah too, as well as Danceteria and the Pep, and Max's, along with the Lower Manhattan Ocean Club and One University, and the Holiday Bar and the Red Bar, and the Ukes and Puffy's too, the time came when this life I was now living didn't seem so strange. While I can't say that I ever came to the opinion that I really deserved it, I did come to believe that it was real. And as difficult as going to work always was —

work never got easier, no matter how well the company was doing — this life was something real, and good.

Could I have lived my life differently? I didn't not want to be a poet, that's for sure. But when I looked back at my life from that vantage, at the beginning of the 2000s, I could see a lot of decisions that I'd made that perhaps I could have made differently, knowing what I knew now. Who doesn't have similar thoughts?

Was everything that was getting thrown at me, that I was putting up with in the office every day — and in the middle of the night, because waking up in the middle of the night now seemed to be a job requirement — was that the price I had to pay for all this, this life, this wife, this family?

Maybe I could have led my life differently, made different decisions, and still had all this. Maybe I should have gotten an MFA and hopped on the tenure track at some college or university. Why not me? Maybe there were other options I had never considered. There had to be. But I had made certain choices. Willingly? Perhaps. Wittingly? That was another question. And now I had to live with them. And yes, this was the price I had to pay to have these things that meant everything to me. Not the cars or the houses but the family. And the fact was, things were looking up.

31. *Sitting on the Beach*

The business was, as the VCs liked to say, moving to a new level. It wasn't a lifestyle business anymore. That was an insult they threw at you if they decided your business, if you, didn't have enough ambition. Now we had a way forward. We were going to have what they called a cash event in twelve quarters, maybe eight. A cash event meant you were going to go public or sell the company. And then, well, maybe I'd start that bakery that I'd been talking about. Baguettes and boules. A wood-fired oven. Or that car company. I really liked that idea. It would require vastly more capital than we'd raised this time, but, everyone said, once the funders say yes to you, the next time you come around, especially if you did what you said you were going to do the first time, they'll part with their cash much more willingly. And that next time, there'll be more money. Or maybe I'd just hang out and write poems. The VCs had a name for that too: sitting on the beach.

Some of my friends and I used to make fun of poets who didn't have jobs. They wrote too much, we used to say. You could always tell, we told ourselves. They have too much time on their hands. When I started writing essays about how poets live their lives, this was a topic that I touched on right away. But that wouldn't be a problem for me. I had spent my life having barely enough time to write. Late into the night, after everyone had gone to bed, that's when I wrote. And then, after the kids were grown and gone, early in the morning, from five to six, because I couldn't stay up late anymore.

Then, years later, twenty years further along, when I did come to have a place of my own where I could write, where finally, after years and years, I could finally unbox all of my books, some of those same poet friends made fun of me, but for a different reason. Why? Because my desk, the table Steve built for me, was so neat and clean. No papers on it. Ever. When I'm typing, the laptop is there and when I'm done, it's put away. If I'm working on a draft that I've printed out, when I'm done, I put it away. How can you be so neat, they asked. What kind of obsessive-compulsive are you?

This was my answer: for years, for decades, I didn't have a place to write. Like you, or you or you. I wrote on the kitchen table, which was this table. And when I was done, I had to take everything away because we were going to have breakfast there in the morning. That's why I'm this neat.

So, back to those days when my kids were little and it looked like we had a sane, safe, secure life, I was finally able to say: I've paid my dues, haven't I? I was paying them still, life still wasn't easy, still full of things that kept me up at night, but maybe, hopefully, possibly, sooner or later, I'd be able to sit on a beach, even if that just meant sitting at this table, and spreading my papers out.

32.   *Why are All Halts Grinding Halts?*

At first, we weren't worried. We'd been in business for a good ten years now, with solid growth year over year, every year. We were a hot start up. Pioneers. We'd invented an entire category. That's how we styled ourselves. And we'd received several votes of confidence in the form of several sizable investments, some of which, as it turned out, I ended up having to personally guarantee. But they were big nonetheless. And, now we had an extraordinarily expert and motivated management team, focused on moving us forward. This was just a quiet time of year, right? Summers were always slow.

Then September came, and 9/11. By the end of that Tuesday, we'd managed to make contact with everyone who was supposed to be on a plane flying out to Ohio, and everyone turned out to be safe. When we got back in touch with that prospect, however, for one reason or another they didn't need us to fly out there anymore. We never did sign them.

Jim, the sales and marketing guy, and I would look over the funnel and pipeline reports. They were still very healthy. Fat, full of ripe prospects. He'd embedded into these analyses a range of estimates regarding the size of the contracts we could expect to sign with these companies. It was clear that we were going to knock things out of the park. We were on track to substantially out-perform all the goals and metrics we'd committed to. The thing was, we were a little behind. A good number of the opportunities who Jim had placed right at the last stage, that step just before signing, hadn't yet moved ahead. There was a bit of a bulge there.

This made complete sense. Look at what was happening in the world. We were going to war. The world was turned upside down. No wonder these companies wanted to pause for a few days and catch their breath before moving ahead, before making new commitments.

But then, days turned into weeks. Christmas came and went. Now it was a few months. Those juicy opportunities who were sitting on their nicely-drafted-up service agreements, all ready to be counter-signed and Fed Exed back to us, so we could kick off their programs lickety split, they weren't returning our calls anymore. Just as worryingly, the marketing funnel was not filling up with new prospects.

Business had slowed down before, but not like this. Things were different this time. Whenever this had happened before, I'd be studying my personal checking account, trying to figure out how to make next week's payroll. This time we had a nice big cushion, all that money we'd been funded with — or, at least, what was left, which wasn't nothing, it was still a decent pile of cash — but now we were spending it down. Of course, it wasn't meant for payroll or rent or the phone bill, but we had to keep the lights on, didn't we? We had no choice. At least we had this cash, God bless us. And we'd make it up very soon, of course we would, and we would be in better shape than ever, as soon as business picked up again. We were raring to go.

The thing was, things didn't pick up. Things were flat. Same old clients. No one new. Now the meetings I called every few days included the comptroller. In addition to the funnel and pipeline reports we looked at the balance sheet. Forget the P and L, I didn't want to look at that. The question was, how much cash did we have on hand? Then we started studying the aging reports. When it came to the receivables, who owed us money? Most of them were companies who we knew would pay us, we'd been doing business with them for years, they were dependable. We had great relations with them, the only question was 'how soon?' The aging report which got more attention was the Payables. Who did we have to pay this week? Who could we put off for another week?

And then it got worse. The country went into a recession. Now, twenty years later, no one seems to remember, but in the wake of 9/11, we were blessed with a nice little recession. The huge financial meltdown that came seven years later, 2008's financial crisis, that's the one we recall, but there was one after the attacks too. That's when Americans were urged to go shopping. That was how we were going to beat the terrorists.

Then, in the spring of 2002, we started losing long-term clients. At first it wasn't all that worrisome. Some attrition was normal. The thing was there weren't new customers taking their place.

Now and then, actually, more like every day, it occurred to me that if only we hadn't moved to Waterbury, if only I hadn't gone out and gotten all that money, if only I hadn't hired all these people and loaded us down with all that new hardware and software, we could have easily ridden this out. But now we had such a big nut, we had so many fixed costs, so much overhead.

33.   Here Comes the Sheriff

It was a beautiful Saturday morning. We'd cooked up something special for breakfast, waffles maybe. Everyone was downstairs, in our robes and pajamas, discussing what was in store for today. Ollie drowsed in the corner, keeping a weather eye open for any scraps that might fall to the floor. Then there was a knock on the mud room door. Sharp. And again.

When I opened it there was a guy standing there, a manilla envelope in his hand. Older than me, trim, white hair, dressed in chinos, neatly pressed, heavily shined black oxfords, an ironed polo shirt with some sort of small shield embroidered over the breast. I thought I saw a bulge in the cuff of his khakis. I remembered a NYPD detective I'd had lunch with, years ago, a good fifteen years earlier, when I was still doing the mystery shopping in the bars and restaurants. He was an old friend of my father-in-law. While we were having our coffee, he reached down and showed me where he kept his pistol. In a holster at his ankle. This guy asked me if I was Michael Gottlieb.

Robin called out from the breakfast room, "Who's there?" I didn't answer. Behind him, in the driveway, parked in the circle, was a dark Ford Victoria with an official-looking whip antenna. By the time I looked back at him and nodded, Robin and my children were there, behind me in the doorway.

I saw him look over my shoulder, with a slightly different expression on his face. Somewhat less assured perhaps, scanning. Scoping for a threat maybe. Then, presumably satisfied that none of us were armed, he looked back to me.

He was a sheriff and he informed me, as he pushed the envelope towards my chest, in a way that seemed altogether practiced, a gesture that caused me to instinctively raise my hands, into which he thrust it, that I was being served, and I was being sued.

Right there in front of my wife and children. Served. He nodded to me as he turned briskly away, his expression changing into something else, close to a sympathetic look. As if he understood: lousy things were happening, and it was lousy that he had to do that to me with my wife and little kids around, but at least I hadn't made any trouble for him. I'd taken it like a man.

The thing was, maybe I wasn't all that surprised. A guy had finally shown up on my doorstep, after all these years. Everyone crowded around as I opened the envelope.

34.   *There Was No Alternative*

I had no fall back. This had to work. I'd started this business ten years earlier because I hadn't been able to figure out anything else to do. And I still couldn't. All of those people depended on me. Not the clients — the hell with them, so many of them had scurried away like, like... but the employees, all of those people who had been with me so long, who'd stood with me through good times and not so good, and now I had failed them. And then there was my family. They hadn't asked for this. I had been doing all this for them, hadn't I? And what was I going to do, how was I going to take care of them?

There were no answers. A waking nightmare. It had started forming, like a tropical low off the Azores, the previous year, not long after we'd moved to Waterbury. The vague disquiet grew, week after week, month after month, gaining definition, scale, scope, towering over me now. Every waking minute, half of the night. Waking in the middle of the night, every night. Every so-called worst-case scenario became true and then spawned others, worse, spinning off like twisters careening across some featureless landscape. And it just went on, month after month, for several years. There was no way out. Every time things looked like they couldn't get worse, they did. Over and over again.

Robin was there of course. My kids were still too young to hear the details. There were a few friends who knew what was going on, but what could anyone do? Growing up, I'd always felt like an only child, I thought I was altogether familiar with loneliness, what with a basically friendless youth, and those first solitary years in New York, but this was different. There were so many low points. It's hard to stack-rank them.

Was everyone gone by now or was there just a skeleton crew? I know all of the senior people, that management team that I'd assembled one by one, had been given their last checks. Did we go out for a final drink? There was no money for that. There was nothing to reminisce about. It was all too raw.

35. The Quiet After the Storm

The last day, there was nothing left. It was 2003. I'd held on for almost two years.

All of the people were gone. All of the equipment, gone. I spent the last week cleaning up. I piled up the garbage in one of the offices and then I vacuumed the space. I started taking the garbage home, filling up the station wagon, several times.

I stood in what had been my office, looking out the window at a quiet Bank Street. Downtown Waterbury had always been quiet. This quiet today seemed different, and familiar. Why?

Then it came to me. I had felt this quietness before. It was the quiet, peculiar, oddly peaceful, of failure. When there's nothing else to do. I remembered it from Warner Bros., when we were done packing up the Contract Department. That was the last time I'd felt this, twenty years earlier. My boss, Sidney, had been forced to retire and my job was done too. They had never kept their copies of the contracts in order at the studio. They wanted ours. So that was my last project before they laid me off. And when everything was done, I walked through the empty windowless file room and then sat in my empty office. All of the bound indexes and the looseleaf binders I'd assiduously kept updated were gone. There was nothing left to do.

Then I remembered, there was another time I felt this.

Yet years earlier, when I was working for Learning to Read Through the Arts. Maybe it was the last year I was there. I would soon leave for Warner's. There had been some sort of falling-out with the Guggenheim. Every year the program mounted an exhibition of the kids work, paintings, drawing, sculpture. Usually, it was at the Guggenheim itself. Not this year. This year we were installing the show on the second floor of an empty office building in Times Square. We were in what had recently been known as the Allied Chemical Tower, originally the home of the New York Times itself. It was the building from which the ball is still dropped in Times Square on New Year's Eve. The director of our

354

program had some connection to the real estate developer who now owned this building. It was kind of a wreck inside. The triangular floors were so cramped it was hard to see how a newspaper had ever been produced here. Desolate now, reeking of failure. It took two or three days to hang the show every year. When we took breaks, we'd sit on the sills of the big windows that faced uptown. I'd watch the traffic come down Broadway, down Seventh Avenue.

The traffic was unending. If New York City was the capital of the world, that being a truth obvious and unarguable as far as I was concerned, then this, this very intersection — notwithstanding that this was the late 1970s and this was Times Square at its most tawdry, as drab and dangerous as it ever got — had to be itself the beating heart of the city.

Everything was going on out there. All of the hustle, commerce, action. In here? A sad show of kids art. Who was going to come to it if it wasn't at the Guggenheim? Why were we even bothering? Was this the end-stage for the program itself? It might have been.

You could see all the way up Seventh Avenue to Central Park. A glimpse of its canopy of green, always shocking amidst all this gray and grime. As I studied the traffic endlessly flowing downtown towards us, I noticed trucks, every two or three minutes, one after the other. Big flatbed tractor-trailers. Each of them bearing a single bolted-down, Brobdingnagian spool of newsprint. Just one reel per trailer. They came downtown and turned west onto 43rd Street. They were all headed to The New York Times. There was no end to these trucks.

Out there the world was going on. The Times was getting ready to print its first edition. Did they have already those other printing plants, in Queens and New Jersey? I'm not sure. When I got up in the morning, the edition I read, like everyone else, was the Late Edition. That wouldn't get set and printed for hours yet. Or was it Wednesday, and were they already printing the Book Review and the Magazine and the Arts and Leisure? Getting ready for the weekend, getting those advance copies to their advertisers, like my father in his day. The world was going on, moving on, pell-mell, heedless, someone was making news and The Times was covering it, and here I was stuck in this godforsaken, silent, abandoned office building. This place stank of failure. How was I ever going to get out of here?

Decades later, I looked out of a window, in a similarly desolate office, thinking the same thoughts. The failure was different this time. It wasn't just in the air. It was inside me. I'd brought it forth. And while, back then, the way out, the way forward, was difficult to discern, this time there seemed none at all.

36.　Aftermath

After the end, what's next? I went home with the last load of trash and woke up the next morning with no work, no office to go to. But the employees had been paid, on time, and their insurance was paid up to the end, and all the taxes were paid. I did get sued though. There were a couple of suits. But the new lawyer, the wondrous Patrick, negotiated deals.

Also, we couldn't have gotten by during those days without the help of family. I often wondered how people who don't have that kind of help survive. My brother-in-law helped us a lot, my brother and sister-in-law too. I started looking for a job. I was done with the entrepreneurial life. No more start-ups for me.

37.   It Took Two Years

I filled out application after application, but only for large companies. That seemed a safe way to go. I interviewed at a few places. IBM brought me down to New York for meetings, but nothing came of it. Eventually, my luck turned.

It was a software company that I didn't know much about, except they were German. And SAP was a big company. All I needed to know. It turned out that they were looking for someone with just like my kind of expertise with call centers. It was hard to believe.

As part of the interview process, I came down to their New York office. The guy I was interviewing with gave me the street address. Morton Street, all the way west, he said.

'It's in the West Village. Will you be driving in or taking the subway? If you take the subway —'

I told him that it so happened that I knew the right subway stop. I didn't mention that I once lived on Morton Street. In what seemed like no time at all I received an offer. And so, in the middle of 2005, two years after my old life ended, a new one began.

38.   This Thing Is Called a BlackBerry

At the end of the first week, the guy who I was reporting to asked me to come downstairs.

By that Friday I'd realized that people at this company were not offended if you asked them for their org charts, nor if you had to ask them twice to pronounce their last names. I'd also figured how they liked their PowerPoints. I didn't have an office, only a workstation. No one did, save the very most senior people. Since I was the newest kid on the block, the most recent hire, I'd been assigned the least desirable desk of all, on the upper floor of this open plan, fashionably appointed office in a recently renovated loft building, in the back, near the doors leading to the rest rooms. I didn't care.

He told me that they needed me to go to Germany the following week, to the corporate headquarters. And then, the week after, to Belgium.

'You know, what I think you should do is spend the weekend in Brussels. You ever been to Brussels?' Then he asked me if I'd gotten my BlackBerry yet.

So before I knew it, I was on the afternoon Lufthansa flight, JFK to Frankfurt, trying to teach myself how to use this newfangled BlackBerry. The flight attendants all greeted me in German, as they would on every flight I boarded for years, assuming from my last name that I was one of them. That first visit to the company's campus outside of Heidelberg was a whirlwind, meeting my new colleagues, young, dizzyingly competent, modishly attired Germans all.

That Friday, one of them drove me to Mannheim and put me on the high-speed train for Brussels. I arrived around dinner time. Saturday morning, I got up early and wandered through town. I ended up at the Grand Place, the Grot Markt, in the center of the city. I sat myself at a table at the sole café open that early, on the southwest side of the vast square. It had the makings of a lovely day. Taking the opportunity to unlimber my pathetic French, I ordered a croissant and coffee, and then a chocolate brioche. I watched the city wake up. Impossibly small delivery vans trundled here and there across the great expanse of paving. Later, packs of minute cars

359

pulled up to the old town hall on the far side, and brides and grooms and their parties, one after another, dashed inside. I planned my itinerary for the day. There was a gallery I wanted to check out, a couple of museums.

It was still too early for anyone back home to be up, but I started writing emails to Robin and Isabel and Lucas. Breezy, brief, observational, humorous, at least I thought so. They'd see them when they woke up in four or five hours, over breakfast, and maybe laugh.

But as I wrote these emails, and I thought of the three of them in their beds, still asleep, a new feeling stole over me. Something new to consider. I was overtaken. It possessed me. Eventually the waiter came over and asked quietly, in English, if I was okay. I was weeping.

Here I was, on top of the world, armed with my fancy BlackBerry, sipping my café au lait in one of the world's great cities, now launched into a good job in a fast-growing company. And I was making money, more than I'd ever paid myself when I had my own business. Everything was going to be okay.

Now that I think about it, I really never used to cry. Not like that, never. Really. That wasn't me. It wasn't that I was so stoic. I guess, regardless of how bad things were, it just never occurred to me to cry. Maybe as a kid. Surely as I child I cried, after a rock fight. But when I got older? Not really. Not until I had a family. And then, it's not like I ever made a decision about it. I just cried. I guess this is me after all.

That morning, sitting in that café, all this, this new life, seemed real. It wasn't that it seemed unreal. But could it be snatched away from me at any minute? No, it wasn't that. I knew I was making a decent impression. Things were going to work out at this new job. It was just the contrast. That was it.

When things were bad, they were so bad, things were so dark. It seemed like it had been really dark not that long ago. There had been no hope. No way out. Absolutely no way out. And now, all that was done? In the past? My family was okay? I was okay? Really? What I should have said to the waiter: moi, je suis George Bailey.

39.   Just Before the High Line Opened

Now that I had a job in New York City I needed a place in New York City. The office was a good hundred miles from my home. Too far to commute. But it had to be cheap. When I showed her listings for spare bedrooms on Craigslist, Robin scoffed at me, "You're too old to share an apartment with a bunch of slackers on the Lower East Side." Eventually we found a place in Chelsea, on the top floor of an old brownstone.

It was a seedy studio with laminate floors and tired appliances but the rent was doable, on what used to be called the Seminary block, on Twentieth Street between Ninth Avenue and Tenth. Most of the Seminary's nineteenth century campus has long since been sold off for condominiums. There's a hotel there now too. While the church was still trying to make a go of it, it would often show up in exterior shots in TV shows like Law and Order. They must have been trying to make money anyway they could. Before that, back in the Seventies, their greensward was open to the public. You could pass through the lobby of the Ninth Avenue building, incongruously mid-century, stroll along the walks of their keep and loll about on their neatly shorn lawns.

The day I moved in, Robin and I brought down some odds and ends from the house to furnish the place. It looked like a graduate student's apartment. After I finished unpacking, I looked out the window. Here I was, back in Chelsea, three decades later, a couple of blocks away from my first apartment. Across the street, two young couples were playing doubles on the Seminary's tennis court. This was 2005. There's an apartment house there now.

A few months later, sitting by the window while reading a Wallace Stevens biography, I came across, among its illustrations, a postcard he sent to his wife-to-be back in Pennsylvania, soon after he arrived in New York after law school. It was some sort of photo postcard. One side bore his somewhat affectionate note to her. On the other, a snap he'd apparently shot, from the sidewalk in front of his apartment. What he saw every morning as he left his building. It appeared to be a view of the same buildings in the Seminary that I could see from my apartment, from the same spot along West 20th Street. What were the odds of that?

I didn't like being away from my wife and kids. I would leave the office at the end of the day on Thursday, head to Grand Central, spend the long weekend with them, working from home on Friday, then take the train back on Sunday evening. On the other hand, I was getting a lot of writing done. There wasn't a lot else to do of an evening. But, it was true, I was back. Back in the city I'd left fifteen years earlier, but never stopped missing. As much as I missed my family, and never stopped missing them, and never stopped feeling somewhat guilty about it, I was pretty thrilled to be back.

I would show up in the office before eight, an old habit. It proved helpful now with all those early conference calls with people in Europe. It was a pleasant walk down Greenwich or Washington. Tenth Avenue was still all parking lots and warehouses, no fancy condos yet. But you could tell what was coming. There were already galleries everywhere.

A few months later the first segment of the High Line opened. It started at Twentieth Street, a few steps from my apartment. At its southern end it terminated, as it does still, at Gansevoort. That's how I'd walk to work. At 7:30 in the morning the Highline would be entirely empty. I would be gloriously alone, save for the occasional groundskeeper tending to her seedlings. Not much later though, the next stretch was opened, reaching 23rd Street. Everything changed then. The first day the new segment opened, the walkway was infested with early morning runners. Why hadn't they been around before?

After work, I'd stop at Chelsea Market to pick up dinner on my way home. Back then, almost twenty years ago, most of the shoppers seemed to be locals, only a few tourists here and there. The Italian specialty store was run by a balding, middle-aged guy, he might have been Florentine, maybe not, who was a big Ferrari fan. SAP was a sponsor of their F1 arch-rival, McLaren. I'd don one of their caps whenever I went in, just to get his goat. He'd nod to me gravely across the counter. Then we'd proceed to merrily malign the manhood of the lead driver of each other's team as he fastidiously sliced me a quarter-pound of soppressata.

The first book of mine that came out after I returned to New York was *The Likes of Us*, published by Michael Scharf. We'd have dinner on Second

Avenue or somewhere in the West Village, and plan the book. Michael, in his gentle way, made the process a pleasure. With his dry humor and deadpan delivery, you could easily miss all the haymakers he was delivering, some directed at himself, others to mutual friends, others, yes, at you. A few years later, when he got married and moved to India, his absence made a bit of a hole in the poetry world in New York that, for me, never quite got filled.

I was particularly struck by how much the city had changed, and came to write about this at some length. Streets that had been empty and deserted and, yes, dangerous when I'd first arrived in New York were thronged with people now, young people of course. Where had all they come from?

One evening I was walking along Ninth Street or maybe it was Eleventh, it was an eastbound street for sure, on a block east of Fifth. I must have been coming back from a reading at the Poetry Project. There, sitting on the north side of the street was a Bentley. A Bentley, parked for the night on the streets of New York. I stopped and gaped. I think it was a Continental, dark-blue. Now, I was no fan of Bentleys, at least none built after 1960, and I was extremely unlikely to be a fan of anyone who owned a late-model Bentley, for reasons that I think should be obvious. But what struck me, what seemed amazing, what on its face was such an unmistakable augury — no, not an augury, since this was not about the future, this was about the here-and-now, a resolute demonstration, that's what it was — was that someone, *this guy*, somehow I knew it was a guy, felt so comfortable in this city, so safe in this neighborhood at least, that he'd left his shiny, spotless coupe, the one for which he'd forked over several hundred thousand dollars, right out there on the street, all night, all by itself, in this city. That was stunning, that's how much this city had changed.

40.   This is What We Call an Attaboy

There were tedious parts of the day. There were difficult people at work, and yes, some bullies too. And fittingly, I guess, due to its market position in so many industries and geographies and segments, which came to inform the way the company thought of itself, which naturally had an impact on its recruiting, you could detect a consanguinity among the people who peopled its hallways. There were not many folks there who weren't what back then were called Type A's. That made things interesting. On the other hand, there was free lunch every day, and an expensive espresso machine that made decent cappuccino.

In those first few weeks, just being around so many people after being home for a couple of years took some getting used to. There were about two hundred people in the New York office, not that many compared to the several thousand at the campus in Palo Alto, or the thousands upon thousands in Germany, but still. I was meeting a lot of people all at once, and, naturally, even though I was introduced properly, it took me awhile to put names to all of the faces.

The guy I worked for back then had a charming habit of stopping at a florist in Grand Central on Monday mornings, on his way in from Fairfield County. He'd pick up a bouquet which he would have his admin plunk down on the desk of someone who he'd decided had done something special the week before. He was well known for this, though as of the third or fourth week I was there, I had yet to be apprised of this particular, piquant morale-booster.

One of those Monday mornings, while I was, as usual, on a call, a woman came by and placed a vase of flowers on my desk. She smiled at me and walked away. What? What was this? Why was this woman giving me flowers?

The previous week among my swirl of meetings I'd sat in the common area on the third floor with some people from the advertising and branding teams, also located in the New York office, and discussed how we could work together. One of them was a woman a bit younger than me, dark-haired, quite pleasant. Though it was just a get-acquainted session, we all agreed that it was a productive meeting. It had been a good meeting, but not that good.

I looked at these flowers and said to myself, 'This is not going to end well.'

I got up, picked up the vase, and walked over to her desk on the other side of the floor. She looked up quizzically as I approached. 'Hi,' I said, 'This isn't easy for me to say. I appreciate this. These flowers are lovely. But I can't really accept them. I think you're very nice. But I need to say that I am a happily married man and I don't think I should be accepting flowers from women.'

And, with that, I put them down on her desk. She still hadn't said anything. She just looked at me. I turned around and went back to my desk. About half an hour later a dark-haired woman, a bit younger than me, approached my desk. This time I wasn't on a call. She was very nice about it. She told me that the woman from the branding team to whom I'd returned the flowers didn't in fact have a crush on me. I might be good looking and all that, but I'd gotten it all wrong. The branding person hadn't given me the flowers, this woman had. She worked for my manager, and course I'd been introduced to her. And, of course, I had confused these two women, and these flowers were not the token of a woman's affection but just a somewhat unusual sign of appreciation from my boss.

I learned that this kind of little gesture of encouragement and approbation was known as an 'attaboy,' a term which, I wondered, might have an entirely different meaning if addressed to a person of color, like a black guy for example. I also came, eventually, to sufficiently overcome my embarrassment that I not only became friendly with that woman whose intentions I had so wildly misjudged, but also, as I am doing now, came to feel comfortable enough, although frankly it took a few years, to tell this story.

41.   *Seeing the Future, Someone's*

After a year or so I started doing different things at this company. I joined the office of the chief marketing officer and there, and then on similar teams, I was set to work on the kind of questions which I learned only the largest companies can afford to dedicate one person to sit around and think about. After a year or two I'd go work on something else. At first, these were not infrequently topics I didn't know much, or anything, about. That didn't seem to concern anyone besides me. I got used to working with people who knew a lot more than me about a lot of things.

They were young, everyone was younger than me, and smart, so smart. And they were working in different countries, all around the world, new groups every year or so. While typically our work would be entirely remote, as it was then called, we'd often speak every day. I got a kick out of this, working with these folks, learning from them, hearing eventually about their lives and their hopes and dreams. From time to time, I'd go see them, flying to some place I'd never been before, like Barcelona or Dublin or Sao Paulo or Singapore. We'd all shut ourselves up in a conference room for a few days, then go out for dinner, then maybe to a bar.

They were so different than the poets I knew. Maybe that's obvious: the worldviews, the skill sets. But they were also different than the business people I'd come into contact with over the years. Some of those had been mere clock punchers, others more rarin' to go, like the VCs I'd encountered along the way. It was hard to put my finger on it. Was it possible that these new colleagues were all just, at heart, more optimistic?

One of my first trips took me to Shanghai. I spent several days at the company's just-opened facility, in a new office park, way out of town, far from the Bund.

My last night there, it was a Friday, the managers who ran the office announced that they were going to treat me to dinner. A banquet, at a mall, in the middle of the city. The most indelible moment of that trip however came before we got there, before dinner, before all the rounds of mao tai, just as we leaving the office.

A gaggle of co-workers were standing about on the sidewalk, waiting for the mini-buses to take us all to the subway station. Actually, the subway was elevated out there. Then the vans arrived. Everyone piled in. It was so crowded that people were sitting on people's laps. They made me sit up front, next to the driver, in a seat of my own. As we trundled off, I turned round to take in the scene.

All of these young people were gabbing away, in Mandarin of course. I didn't understand a word, but it was clear what they were talking about. There was laughing, some stage whispers and gibes, a few good-natured jeers. It was Friday, they had to be talking about the upcoming weekend, what they had planned. And they were talking about the week they had, this or that difficult customer. Happy, relaxed, a little tired.

And suddenly I felt that I had a glimpse into their world. It was a world where things were getting better. They had good jobs with good prospects. They were making good money. Times were good and getting better, and times were going to continue to get better. That's the future they saw themselves in. This realization was so powerful. Over the years, working at this job, getting to know this person and that, visiting one office after another, I felt it often. It was in the air.

Of course, I didn't feel part of that world, the one they lived in. I knew that things didn't always get better. But it wasn't just that. I was also a good thirty years older than them. I didn't have as much future in front of me as they did. And, of course, this was years ago, in a China, in a world, that's changed utterly since. I often wonder how those kids are doing now.

42. *Paying Attention*

When Drew Gardner and I met for dinner, it was often at an Israeli hummus place on St. Mark's, on Wednesday evenings, before heading over to the Project for a reading. Later, after I moved to the Upper West Side, we tended to get together at one of those slightly tricked out burger places on Broadway, near Columbia, or sometimes further uptown, in Harlem, closer to his neighborhood. It was always a pleasure to listen to his sardonic but spot-on synopses of what was going on, what was really going on, in our part of the poetry world.

All those years, when I was away from New York, I assumed I'd been doing a decent job at keeping up. But I came to realize after a number of these dinners, with Drew and other younger poets, the folks I found myself spending most of my free time with, that this world had decidedly changed since I'd moved away, years ago.

From time to time, Drew would tilt his head and squint slightly, summoning up a simulacrum of weary disillusion. As if he was having trouble accepting the reality, despite all of the conversations he was obliged to have with me, these frank exchange of views as they say in the world of diplomacy, dinner after dinner, month after month, that anyone my age could remain so irredeemably, breathtakingly oblivious. Then he would proceed to parse out who, among my generation of poets who were still out and about, as well as among the Flarf poets, could and couldn't be trusted. And who, when it came to the Conceptualist poets, could or should still be considered a friend. Of course, all of that was meant in jest. Or, most of it. Or some of it.

There seemed to be more internecine warfare than I remembered from the old days. But maybe not. I had known some these younger poets for some time. But before I left the city they had been in their twenties and thirties and starting out. Now they were in their forties and things were getting serious.

What struck me most, I suppose, was how these poets no longer thought of themselves as second or third generation Language poets, if they ever did, but now identified as Flarf poets or Conceptualists. I thought that was fantastic. Nor was I discountenanced by the way they looked at poets like me as an older generation that they might or might not be somewhat indebted to, but, clearly and decisively, had moved on from. That seemed fine and dandy, altogether apropos. And, the fact that many of them often seemed sparring, or at war with each other, that seemed all good as well. That's what poets, writers, artists should be doing. Of course, they should. Shouldn't they?

But what also struck me, what I guess I wasn't prepared for, was how much bigger this poetry world was than I had remembered, when I had been starting out, when there had only been five or six of 'us.' Five or six of us who I counted, who were in New York, who were all doing the same thing, more or less. Now, there were dozens, scores who I needed to count as 'like us,' more or less.

And I wasn't that surprised to hear from him about all that — as they say in British football — argy bargy. Not just sharp elbows but sharp teeth too. In the same way, I guess I wasn't surprised to hear from, say, Liz Fodaski, another young wonderful writer who I got to know back then, about other vicissitudes of life in the poetry world. There is, was, always had been, that concept of 'doing your time,' as it was put. That is, organizing readings or putting out magazines, helping out with a small press, all of those unpaid, of course, putting-in-the-hours that are expected, especially of younger poets, because of the nature of the poetry-world-economy that were, that are, expected. And, the fact was, not enough credit for those good deeds, as it were, seemed to be redounding back upon those who had put in all that time and effort. I heard that from other young poets too, like Deirdre Kovacs. Were women getting the raw end of this deal more than the men? I wondered.

As we would make our way west along St. Mark's Place, heading back to Second Avenue, Drew, in his unerringly accurate way, would continue what I came to think of as his color commentary. He wasn't the play-by-play guy. He did the color. In many ways, it was anthropology. In his endeavor to be complete, though this was not a completist sort of thing, when it came to this new and perhaps improved version of the poetry world that he was peopling for me, he deigned never to leave unnoted his fellow denizens' most entertaining fallacies and their fumblings of late, accompanied by a pithy analysis of the corresponding underlying political dynamic and relevant psycho-social disorders at play. So much of this behavior was in fact quite similar to that which was still embodied and enacted by my old friends, and me too, I would make a point of averring, a reassuring irony we found occasion to remark upon not infrequently. In our shared opinion, chief among those manifestations was, of course, that particular poetry world strain of widespread, far-reaching, persistent, in fact hoary and unreconstructed, unbridled narcissism.

Also, from time to time, Drew would reveal what I always knew was there, beneath his brutally frank commentary and often-acidulous analysis of our world: an underlying decency. No, more than decency. Empathy.

We were crossing Second Avenue. We were probably late for the reading. The Don't Walk sign was already flashing and I saw him glance uptown to check the traffic. Were we going to get flattened by a M15 bus? He was half a step ahead of me. He half turned, making — but then stifling — a kind of chivvying gesture. I told him not to worry, I was going to get to the curb.

"I need to be more careful now," he said. "You've slowed down since you had the surgery." I stared at him. By then it had been at least two years since my diagnosis, and yes, there had been surgery, but he'd never mentioned this before. I hadn't noticed any change in my gait, but he had. And without comment, for a couple of years now, he'd slowed his pace to accommodate me. As I looked at him, I wondered, if our places had been reversed would I have been so solicitous, wordlessly, as now it was clear, he'd been all this time?

43.   *You're so Hard on Yourself*

I was now also occasionally getting together for dinner with Rob Fitterman, usually at a restaurant near where he lives, often in the East Village. For a while we'd meet at the Bowery Bar and treat ourselves to a cocktail first. And then, when it was time to visit the restroom, I would get to revisit my salad days. In its bathroom were framed photos of scenes and installations at Area, the club which the owners of this restaurant had opened in the Eighties, on Hudson Street, just below Canal. I had signed up Area as a client for the detective agency. I went there a lot. I'm sure I never would have gotten past the ropes if they hadn't put my name, or whatever name I was using for that purpose back then, on the guest list. Robin and I drank for free, took in the dioramas and the famous people.

In the mid-seventies, years before Area was a gleam in anyone's eye, when putting together my first book, a project I've written about in another memoir, I stumbled across the alley behind the club. I took a picture of the aerial bridge that links two buildings back there. Along with other photos of similar structures around Manhattan, it got incorporated into the collages that illustrated that book.

Those dinners with Rob are now years in the past. But just a few months ago, at the same time as I started writing this, I unearthed that original photograph and the original collage itself. They had resided, sealed in a folder all these years, ever since Alan gave me them back to me, after *Local Color/Eidetic Deniers* went to press. A few months ago, they were hung in a show in Great Barrington, Massachusetts. A maelstrom of feelings: memory skipping like a stone over time. Those dinners with Rob almost twenty years ago; evenings at Area forty years ago; taking that picture, almost fifty years ago. And that picture, that collage: holding them in my hand now, freed from their packing, as fresh-looking as when they were new and I was young.

Then I would return to the table and Rob and I continue our conversation.

He'd stroke his beard, maybe pass his hand over his bare pate, cast his eye into the middle distance, screw up one side of his mouth, take another sip of Scotch. It wasn't that he didn't take a lot in this world seriously, in fact he did: his work, his thinking about poetry. His thoughtful analysis of Conceptual poetry and how it represents a step forward from Language poetry which he offered up, impromptu, one evening at BB, stays with me still. But the fact is, he didn't take himself or anyone else that seriously.

It was times like that that would bring back an evening I spent with him and Kim Rosenfield when I first arrived back in New York. They had had me over for dinner in their apartment in Washington Square Village. After I finished them telling my story, what had happened to my business and how that had led to my return to the city, one of them said — was it Rob or Kim, I wish I could remember — 'Wow, you're so hard on yourself.'

That's stuck with me ever since. I thought I'd just delivered a dispassionate recitation of what had gone down. How could I have told it differently?

When it came to hubris, I thought I had a good handle on how much of what had befallen me, my family, my business, was my own damn fault. Some, a lot of it, maybe most, but not all. I had given this a good amount of thought, naturally. I wasn't havering over what had gone wrong, nor spending my days wallowing in what-ifs. That just wasn't me; I don't know why. I don't think it's particularly admirable. I spend plenty of time on equally pointless mental meanderings, just not those.

But when it comes to what went wrong, I couldn't see how any objective analyst could arrive at any other conclusion. I thought I'd just delivered a neutral recitation of facts. How could I have told it differently? By making clearer how market drivers, geo-political crises, business and technological transformation, had conspired to dash my business upon the rocks? Forces beyond my control? I still can't see it any other way: it was mostly my fault. But I respected their point of view. And Kim is a psychologist. She should know. What did they see that I was missing?

44.   No Helmet? Really?

Did I meet Miles first or Tom Raworth? I can't remember. I do remember
meeting Miles Champion up in the country. He was visiting Geoff Young.
As I recall, he came through a few times back then. Once we had him
and a bunch of poets over for dinner. We'd just had some work done on
the house and I showed Miles around, taking him, at one point, into the
renovated bathroom off our recently redone bedroom. Now we had a
separate tub and shower. Weren't we fancy? 'Look at that tile work.'

It's been years and years but my wife still won't forget. 'Do you really
think one of your poet friends cared about our bathroom?' I sure she's
right. I'm also sure that Miles, if he hasn't forgotten all about it, would
be too tactful to hold over me how ridiculous and basely bourgeois had
been my behavior that evening.

When I returned to the city, he and I would meet for dinner now and
then, before he got married and started a family of his own. I never asked
him if the way he read, you could reliably clock him at three thousand
words per minute, the absolute opposite of how I read, was something
which he'd gotten from Raworth, famous for reading similarly. Did we
all assume so? I can't remember. Two lovely fellows, warm and engaging.
And they both read like racing locomotives, at full throttle, smoke
streaming behind. And they were both English. Case closed.

Miles would zoom up to the restaurant on his bicycle and we'd have
dinner. And I would inevitably, invariably, berate him for not wearing a
bike helmet. Who doesn't wear a helmet in New York City? But who was
I to keep bringing that up? I wasn't his mother. Miles was a big boy. He
didn't need me nagging him. Did I keep bringing it up to make a point?
That I was really a lot older, more responsible, more grown up than him?
And, if so, who was I making that point for? Who was supposed to be
getting that message? Him? Me?

45. *No One Had Ever Pulled Noodles for Me Before*

We were sitting in a smartly bare restaurant in the East Village, the light slanting in through the glass garage doors facing the street. Nada always picked the place. Another time, I was served the most fabulous falafel sandwich I ever had in my life. There we were, seated comfortably on a bench in front of Taim, studying the passersby on Seventh Avenue, the bountiful baba ganoush dripping, lubricious, onto my fingers, staining my new dress shirt. And then there was the hot pot, I'd never had hot pot before, at a place on First Avenue. Nada patiently, always patiently, explaining to me what we were eating, and in what order, and why.

I'd first met Nada Gordon at one reading or another, back before I left New York. Was it after that reading that the following ensued? We were all milling around as usual, trying to figure out where to go for dinner. She put her foot down, refusing, absolutely refusing to go to some place or other, Phebe's maybe. Some place that seemed entirely innocuous and inoffensive to me. I mean, Nada had opinions about poetry and poets, just like everyone else did, and does. But what struck me was not the way she felt free to share this or that remarkably strong opinion, which distinguished her not at all from the rest of us, but that so many of her most strongly expressed points of view seemed, strikingly, to have to do with a topic about which, by comparison, I hadn't for a long time been able to summon up any particularly vehement feelings, not after a few years as a vegetarian in my twenties, namely what kind of food she was putting in her body.

When the two of us would now meet for dinner, after I returned to New York, the place she'd pick would always turn out to be great. I felt like I'd known Nada forever. And we would talk, about our lives, our work, what was going well, what was going to hell, the people in our part of the poetry world who were driving us crazy, who were unredeemably lazy but apparently possessed of some preternatural ability to take credit anyway.

I'd long considered myself an adventurous eater. After moving to Little Italy in 1979, I'd take that walk down Mulberry into Chinatown several times a week, venturing to restaurants that none of my friends knew about, say, on East Broadway, a sort of culinary frontier back then. And later, when I came to eat in restaurants for a living as a mystery shopper, I thought I knew my way around the food and beverage world in New York. But that was a long time ago.

Nada was doing something, in a quiet, unassuming but entirely passionate way that I came to see as akin to what was, what is, so compelling and powerful about her poetry: that braiding of multivalent voices — quiet, insistent, lyrical, staccato. I think this was around the time that her book *Scented Rushes* was published. She was reintroducing me to this city which, starting years ago, for years, I had, first with the vainglory of youth, and now, decades later, perhaps quite vainly, that is, in vain, claimed as my own. She took me here and she took me there. I thought knew these streets but now they were so very different. Nada was reintroducing me to this city.

46.   Oh Andrew

Why, now that I was back in New York, did so much, perhaps all, of my social life with other poets take place in restaurants, over dinner? Was it because I wasn't around on weekends? That's when I was home, back in the country with my family. Or, was it because everyone now had to have jobs, not that this was news, it had been like this for thirty years, and couldn't hang out in the afternoon? Was it perhaps because the *work* of literary life, doing the publicity for a reading, getting a book manuscript ready for publication, reviewing submissions for a magazine, had all become digital activities? All of that work was now work which we didn't need to do all together, sitting on each other's sofas?

So, dinners it was. It was an easy walk from the office on Morton Street over to the East Village, if I was meeting someone for dinner before a reading at the Project. On the way, crossing Hudson, I'd spare a glance at the apartment building I'd lived in when I was in my twenties, when I first got published, when I met James and Alan, and he published that first book. That was thirty years ago now. But if I was going to have dinner with Andrew Levy, I didn't need to cross Hudson. I'd just head down to Tribeca.

As the years went by, my dinners with Andrew eventually fell into a pattern. The conversation became predictable. We hardly ever talked about literary matters, virtually no gossip, no analysis of who was up and who was down, what was going on with us. Very little of that. What we eventually ended up talking about to the exclusion of almost anything else was Andrew's family. His mother, in particular.

Andrew hailed from Indiana and still had family there. His mother was old, and living alone and, as the years went by, increasingly frail and then, failing. It was all, clearly, hard on Andrew. He wasn't the only one left to look after her, but it became obvious that the primary responsibility for her was falling to him. And he had a family and a job hundreds of miles away. He often flew out there. He was full of stories, the kind of stories that all overwhelmed adult children have, full of frustration and horror and complicated feelings. It was his responsibility to make sure she had the care she needed. It was up to him to make sure she was safe, that the caregivers he'd hired to come to her house actually showed up. He had to deal with her needs, her outbursts, her crises, and on and on.

Although some of this, much of this, transpired later, later than 2011, essentially the end point for this memoir, it eventually came to make sense to include the rest of this account here, partly because it did all seem to start for Andrew now, but perhaps more so because of how all of this, from start to finish, served to draw me back, inevitably, ineluctably, to my own loss, my own losses. First my father, then my mother. I haven't written about their deaths, until now. What I wrote about was everything else that was going on, with my family, with my business, with me. Everything that was so consuming.

But as I listened to him during those dinners, I came to be overcome with guilt too. I'd long felt I had been as present as much as I should have been, although I too was far away, during my parents' last years. But the weight of all that, all that weight that Andrew was carrying, certainly hadn't fallen solely on me, or either of my brothers. My mother had been responsible for my father as he declined, and my mother's passing was quick and sudden. I didn't feel more guilty than most when it came to what kind of son I had been, even though, around him, I realized I was in the presence of an exemplary son.

Instead, this is what I felt guilty about: I didn't want to be talking about this. I wanted to be talking about poetry stuff, and also, I wanted to be talking about me, things I was doing, things I cared about. But we didn't. We talked about his mother, and what he was going through, and the rest of his family, and I hardly ever said anything, at least that's the way I remember it now.

Then, the time came when I stopped feeling guilty. We would sit and have dinner and he would talk. I would sit back and let him expand, sharing at length whatever it was that he'd been going through since we last met. He talked because he needed to. Maybe he didn't have many others who with whom he could talk like this. Even if he did, what matter? I didn't need to own half of the conversation. We didn't need to spend any specific amount of talk-time however apportioned, talking about me, or my things, or things I cared about. This wasn't a negotiation or a transaction. Look at what he was going through. Instead of resenting him for making me listen to all of these sad stories, some dreary, others dreadful, I should have been grateful, and indeed I believe eventually that's what I did feel. Gratitude, that he chose me to hear him out when it came to all of this. Listening was enough. I just wonder why it took me so long to grasp this.

My only regret is that when his mother did finally die, just a few months ago as I write this, I couldn't be there in New York to have dinner with him. I wasn't able to sit across the table at some joint on Chambers, and take it in, as he painted with all the color that a poet like he has in his palette, all the terrible things that occurred at the end, and maybe some things that were not terrible, because, even though it's not much, that's what I wanted to believe I should have been able to do for him.

47. *Outside the Outsider Art Show*

Something was going on in the office that Friday. An in-person meeting had appeared on my calendar so, instead of heading home, I stayed in town on Thursday night. This was September, four months after I had returned to New York, in 2005. I had no plans, but I'd heard about an opening at a gallery on 24ᵗʰ Street. I grabbed a bite, dropped my bag at the apartment and headed up Tenth.

I remembered well the openings in Soho, those Saturdays, in the 1970s and 80s. Making your way from one gallery to another, from 420 on West Broadway — they had an elevator, so fancy — to stops along Spring, then down to Broome. Seeing the same people again and again, collectors, girls, a friend now and then. But this evening in Chelsea, it was different. I was stunned. There were thousands of people in the street.

Swarms flowing in and out of the galleries. Gangs, claques, clutches of art lovers standing, smoking, chatting, hugging, laughing. And all so well dressed; much better dressed than I'd been back in those days, so much better than I was now. And young. They were so young, one and all. Where did they all come from and how could there be so many of them?

How had the art world gotten so big? While it had recently dawned on me that the poetry world, at least the part I was interested in, had grown substantially, very substantially, over the years, this was something altogether different. This was exponential. Were these all artists, along with their friends, and their friends' friends? Everyone showing up for their pals' openings?

Also, there were so many more galleries now. This wasn't a neighborhood, like Soho in its heyday, what we had here was a district. Like the diamond district or the garment district, or the notions district or the gift district, or, really, perhaps not unlike the financial district. Perforce, since there were so many more galleries here than there ever were in Soho, did that explain why there were so many more people tonight infesting these blocks? Or was there something else going on? Okay, sure, it was clear to all and sundry, even back then, that evening in 2005, how the art world had metastasized globally, and what this new reality had brought forth. How art had been transformed into another treasure asset, like rare wine, antique autos and super-premium watches. Equally inarguable was art's role now to support the asset allocation and risk mitigation strategies of the globalized economy's newly minted very-high-net-worthies. But still, these people on the streets were not those people, were they? These people were young. If these kids had money, it hadn't come from privatized gas consortiums in the former Soviet Union, or real estate empires in Shenzen. Had it?

I'm not sure I ever answered those questions for myself but I kept going to these openings, not terribly often, because I preferred to be with my family on Thursday nights, but now and then. One evening, it was dark already, I exited from one of those big old buildings on 26th Street, where you go up and down in a tiny elevator run by a kindly, forever put-upon but preternaturally patient operator. Was it an Outsider Art show? I think so.

As I headed towards Tenth, on my way back to the apartment, someone tapped me on the shoulder, "Excuse me, sir?"

It was a young guy, in his twenties, on the slight side, with glasses with thick black rims, a somewhat dandified touch to his caparison. Was it the cut of his tweedy blazer? He had a very slight, unlocatable accent. "Did you just come out of that show?"

"Well, yes." I said, "Is something wrong?"

"I was just wondering what you thought of —"

At first, I wasn't sure what was going on. Why was this guy talking to me? What did he want? He wasn't trying to pick me up, was he? No, it didn't seem like that. Then he asked me my name and asked me what I did. I told him my name and, after some prodding, admitted that I was a poet.

That seemed to confirm some hunch on his part.

"But I'm really no one that you need to pay any attention to. I'm not, like, important —" I continued.

That didn't seem to dissuade him. He persisted.

His name was Vladislav Davidzon, he was finishing up a degree at the CUNY Graduate Center and he told me who he was studying with and who he was reading and asked me if I knew this poet or that poet, and it didn't take me very long to realize that he was indeed picking me up, but not with any amorous intent. Instead, for some reason that entirely eluded me that night, and does still, he must have seen something when he caught sight of my mug, or the drape of my jacket — though likely not that, since it surely was of decidedly less choice fabric than his — and he thought I might be someone who it might be interesting to meet, or worthwhile to know.

Somehow by the end of this encounter he had abstracted from me my contact info and a sort of relationship began. We'd have a drink from time to time. Did he think I could do something for him? If so, he surely was disabused of that delusion early on. Vlad was clearly ambitious and eager to make a mark. Where and how I wasn't sure. Someone, unkindly, might say he was on the make, but the fact was that the ambition clearly pumping through his veins was no different than what I knew had coursed through mine, and my friends' when we were that age. I invited him to a book party or two and he met some people in my world. He became friends with Nada.

What I so enjoyed about Vlad, and do still, is his remarkable power, unparalleled really — I don't think I've met anyone who can do this like he — to ventriloquize so smoothly, on the one hand, the most shameless boasting regarding whatever it is that he's done most recently. Sometimes it's what he's just gotten published, sometimes it's the festival or fair he visited last week, sometimes it'll be the international luminary of letters or heavyweight politician he's just lunched with. First comes the breathless but casual reveal, 'this is who I was talking to yesterday,' which inevitably obliges me to register amazement at, and to genuflect before, his frankly amazing ascent to ever higher worldly realms. I mean, I don't know anyone who's done the step-and-repeat at Cannes or who's a bona fide unbuttoned-bosom-buddy with Bernard-Henri Lévy.

And then in the next breath, on the other hand, often in the same grammatical sentence, sometimes within the same compound clause, Vlad will shift over to his other mode. He will get up and stand next to the person who's just made all of those comments, that personage who's shared all of those unbeatable boasts, and then make a telling, cutting, humbling comment about them, about himself: "As if I knew what I was doing there," or "As if I belonged there." That follow-on filler, that bring-us-all-back-down-to-earth qualifier, will invariably made it clear that he understands what he is doing. He had, he still has, a frank understanding of the impact of this kind of talk and is confident enough in himself, in what he is doing and what he has done, that he can drop the mask. It makes him kinda lovable.

I don't see him now so often, and it's not because I'm not in New York. He lives in Paris now, and he's married. And he spends a lot of time in Ukraine, where he reports from, and of course I worry about his safety. But not his sanity. In every email I get from him I still see that knowing, half-smile. And I hear his murmur, 'I know what I'm saying sounds a little over the top, but hey...'

48.   Hummus and Empanadas

It was such a pleasure to spend time with younger poets now that I was back in the city. The conversations I had with them often ended up focusing on their lives, our lives, how they were living their lives, how they reconciled what they understood as their responsibilities to their work as poets, with all of the other responsibilities they — we, we all — have when it comes to making a living in this world, when it comes to those who we love and love us. As we talked, over hummus and empanadas and borscht and soba I came to realize that this was, in fact, not just a topic that had been there, in my poems since I started getting published, but one which very well might require a different kind of attention.

So, eventually, I sat down and wrote an essay about this topic: what kind of jobs do poets have to take so they can do their real job, as a poet. And, who else, or what else, can or should we feel responsibility for, or to? Aside from our work and the people who we love and who love us? What are our responsibilities to the poets who are part of the world, the community, that we are part of? What about the poets who came before us and will come after us? And, of course, what about those who may read what we write? That essay, *Jobs of the Poets*, was the first of a series on these topics.

The same impulse, I believe, led me to start think about doing some memoir work. The seeds for that writing were planted, like so much else, I realized, as I sat down and started in on that, in *New York*, that book Geoff Young had published years earlier.

49. What Katie Saw

Shortly after that first essay and that memoir came out in book form, an anthology of Conceptualist poetry was published. I was tremendously flattered to be included with all those younger poets, Conceptualists real and true, several of them my friends.

There was a party and reading at the Museum of Modern Art to celebrate the book's launch. I arranged to attend with my friend, the great poet Katie Degentesh.

We met at the West Fourth Street station and took an E uptown. As we rode, I shared with her my anxiety about the upcoming event. As I recall, Katie didn't have much of a response.

Of course, there turned out to be a dram of drama. As part of the reception there was a reading in the museum's library. When my turn came to read, Charles Bernstein, seated in the front row, stood up and stalked out of the room.

When the event was over, and we were all leaving, standing there on the 53rd Street sidewalk, preparing to go our separate ways, I thought I saw a certain look in Katie's eye.

I braced myself. I remembered a story she'd told me and Robin. She'd been marching, half-running, across Central Park one day, after work. She was late for something or other. As she rushed along, she came across a family of German tourists arranging themselves for a photo. The wife and kids had commandeered a park bench. The father had planted himself squarely in the middle of the path, blocking pedestrian traffic, fussily directing them to pose just so, oblivious to the inconvenience this was causing all passersby. She was in a hurry so she cut between him and his family, just as he was taking another snap. This elicited a torrent of irate expostulation — all in German — from the parents, and the kids too. These idiotic, rude New Yorkers. What's wrong with them?

Of course, they had no idea that Katie understood exactly what they were saying, not until she turned on her heel and gave it to them with both barrels, in exquisitely accented German: "Excuse me?"

Of course, what she was really saying, to my mind, was: 'You stupid, slobbering, clueless currywursts, get the hell out of my city.' Or sentiments to that effect.

Knowing well that this perfectly composed young woman was entirely capable of turning on a dime, or a pfennig, and unleashing a firestorm of unbridled imprecation, I feared the worst. But she didn't say anything. Katie just gave me a look.

'You sad sack boomer losers,' said the look. It was combination of pity and wonder, with a liberal dash of disgust sprinkled o'er. 'What is the problem with you guys? Your generation? Just get over yourselves already.'

That wounded. A bucket of bile in German would have been easier to bear.

At least that's how I read her expression. Of course, it occurred to me as I watched her head down the street, maybe she hadn't noticed anything and I'd gotten her all wrong. Maybe no one had seen what went down, except me.

50.   Writing that Memoir

Excerpts of that memoir, 'The Empire City,' preceding this one in this book, were first published in a magazine, *Mark(s)*, by Ted Pearson. And the essay, 'Jobs of the Poets,' was first published in *Jacket* magazine by John Tranter. Shortly thereafter, the book in which they were brought together, *Memoir and Essay*, was co-published by Alan Davies and Jack Kimball. Alan was of course the first person to publish my poems, in his magazine. And then he went on to publish my first book and published or co-published several more over the years. I'd known Jack for a while by now. This was the first of two titles of mine he brought out.

I don't think any of us involved publishing that memoir expected that it would have much more impact in our corner of the poetry world than, say, any other book of mine. While it did have three distinct foci: New York in the 70s and 80s, and the early days of the Language Poetry scene in New York, I believed its principal focus was the third: me. Me, coming of age as a poet. I'm wasn't sure then, or now, that this was an entirely wholesome subject. I mean, really, who cares? Or, more to the point, why on earth did I, do I, have the gall to believe that anyone would care enough about my life to read a book about it?

I thought I'd taken pains to write about everyone in the same light, painting everyone in the same sympathetic way. We were all young, or at least a lot younger than we were now. Foolish perhaps, but young, and that explained so much. Explained everything. Didn't it? Not everyone took it that way, despite the fact that these events were already a good thirty years in the past by the time the book appeared.

But when it came to someone who I did write about, I was in the wrong. Very wrong. In the new edition of that memoir, which precedes this one in the book you now hold in your hands, I have seen fit to make a change, in a section that touches on the way I came to read my work at readings. There, I mention Michael Gizzi and his comment to me, after a reading, that I really did read slow. Very slow. And, in originally recounting that story, I described the momentary fit of involuntary pique that seized me upon hearing him say that; the entirely uncharitable way I damned him in my mind, to myself, before realizing a second later that, well, yes, actually he was right. Of course, he was right. Notwithstanding that, it turned out, I was never able to change my ways when it came to giving a reading.

The thing was, while I assumed it was clear to any reader that the curse directed, silently, at Michael — someone who I'd become friends with after moving up to the country, who I had the greatest affection and respect for — that silent imprecation that arced across my consciousness upon hearing his critique, was just an involuntary spasm of spite. I was taken aback as I heard myself muttering it to myself. I mean where did that come from? I knew it had absolutely nothing to do with how I really felt about Michael. No way.

I heard that he'd laughed when the passage was read to him. As indeed, I believed he should have. I thought it would be clear to every reader. But I was wrong. After Michael died, I was informed me that what I had written was disgusting. How could I? No matter how I tried to explain what I'd really meant, no matter how many apologies I offered up, it didn't make a difference. There it was, in print. And, the longer this went on, the more horrible I felt. I could, I can, only imagine the impact of those words. It also seemed to me that, likely enough, all of my protestations at that point came across as after-the-fact special pleading. As so may it seem what I am writing now. But hopefully, now, anyone coming across that story anew cannot read it, in its rewritten form, in any way other than how I really, originally, meant it. I do realize, though, that the damage is done and it is possible that I can't any change any minds at this point.

This reminded me again how important it was to try to be careful, and accurate, and how, even within this corner of the poetry world, even when it comes to these memoirs which I have no illusion will be read by more than a few, damage can be done. What carelessness can do. And how, through what I see now can be described as nothing other than carelessness, I did bring pain when it came to one poet, for which I do apologize.

51.   *Diagnosis*

He didn't like what he saw.

I liked my internist. I trusted him. His office was in the country, in Canaan, one town over. Even though I was in the city most of the time, I remained his patient. We'd been going to him since we moved up there. You need to see the urologist, he said. When was the last time I went to a different doctor? There was the eye doctor. The dentist. Anyone else?

When I went to the urologist, he didn't like my numbers either and in due course it was time for a biopsy. I came to know him well over the years, many years. He knew all about SAP and was also into foreign cars, and appreciated the Formula 1 swag I occasionally was able to lay on him. I found him thoughtful in the way he chose his words, the way he showed his care, leavening it occasionally with humor.

But a few days after that test, well, it was different. He kept dialing, eventually pulling me out of a meeting. I stood there at the edge of the common area at the office on Morton Street. The big open space, trendy tables and chairs, half-peopled that afternoon. The managers and their direct-reports, proceeding through their one-on-ones, studying their screens, poring over print outs; work-buddies gossiping over espresso and Diet Coke; one or two people sitting apart, picking at late lunches. He got right to the point: 'You have cancer.'

One call, that's all it took. As I put the phone back in my pocket, I had the strangest feeling. Suddenly it was clear, something was starting, had already started. As if my life was now accompanied by an audio track, one with an over-excited color commentator at full-rip. This was now some sort of stakes race. He was shouting as the gates clanged open and the thoroughbreds charged out, "And they're off!"

Overnight there were a lot of doctors in my life. A lot of decisions to be made. Despite the fact that I felt fine, and that was typical, it was clear that something had to be done, and soon. And there were too many choices. I ended up opting for surgery, the kind of surgery that made use of the latest, most fashionable robotic technology. The same choice that all of my friends and coworkers, who were faced with the same decision, also ended up making. Why not? This made perfect sense.

I was used to making decisions, wasn't I? Furthermore, I was now an expert in how people made very-high-consideration choices, that is, buying costly software. These were not just bet-your-job decisions. They were, as we joked at work, bet-your-career decisions. If you got one of those software purchases wrong, you'd not just have to find a new job, because you were certainly going to get fired, but you'd have to find a new career, since no one in your industry would ever hire you again. So, I for one knew how to make a decision, didn't I?

A few days after that phone call Robin and I were sitting in the urologist's office. He laid out the facts and the options, and again he didn't pull any punches. He didn't just say that after treatment I wouldn't be able to father more children, not that we planned on any, it was the way he worded it: 'And, you're going to be sterile.'

As we left, he handed me a paperback. I can't find it now though I'm sure I never threw it away. The title was something anodyne like, *What To Expect Now That You Have Prostate Cancer*. That night, as I thumbed through it, I came to a chapter that laid out possible positive aspects to all this. 'This chapter I have to read,' I said to myself. As I recall, it was a short chapter. It said not much more than this experience might prove to be an opportunity to engage in some useful meditations upon mortality, a topic that our fast-paced, youth-obsessed society really doesn't pay enough attention to. I threw the book across the room. 'I'm a poet,' I shouted at the walls. 'Read the job description. *Must be comfortable focusing unremittingly on mortality*. I've been thinking about death since junior high school!'

So, there I was, not that many weeks later, presenting myself at Mount Sinai Medical Center on Fifth Avenue for a day's worth of tests in preparation for my upcoming surgery.

It took, on and off, all day. I had to get undressed and then dressed and then undressed again. I had to wait, and wait more. In the middle of the day, there was a break for a few hours. As I got off the last table, the technician, an older Black guy with a gentle face, handed me back my papers. Surely, they plainly stated why I was there. Softly he said, "Good luck."

I just stared at him. Luck? What? This wasn't supposed to be about luck. Why was he wishing me good luck? This was supposed to be science. All science. No luck involved.

Somewhat discombobulated, I stumbled out onto Fifth Avenue. What to do until the next test? I wasn't hungry. Or maybe, I wasn't supposed to eat anything. I started wandering down the street, then remembered that I was only a few blocks north of the Metropolitan Museum. A perfect place to kill time.

What shows were up that day? I can't remember. I do remember wandering from room to room. Maybe it was when I was leaving, going down the grand staircase, taking in the names carved on the wall, the museum's various benefactors going well back to the 1800s, the philanthropists, the tycoons, the oligarchs of their time, that it struck me. So many of the names I saw here were the very same names that graced the halls and pavilions and the buildings of the hospital where I'd spent all morning.

This is what people with that kind of money did, still do, with their money. Because they are public spirited? Guilty about something or other? Seeking to make a point? Telling us something about themselves, or us? Something about our respective, relative places in this world? Nan Goldin has done great work on this topic, including at that museum. A few years later we bought a print of hers, to support the efforts she leads. It hangs in our living room now. Whenever I look at it, I remember that day at the museum.

Two weeks beforehand I went into Outlook and put a meeting on my manager's calendar. I invited his manager too. Thirty minutes. In the subject line I wrote: Personal. Mike and Paul probably assume I'm quitting, I thought. They were both ex-IBMers, older than me, the only two guys I ever worked for there who were older than me. Kind of smooth but tough and no-nonsense, in a familiar way. Very corporate, American version. God knows how many waves of layoffs, rationalizations, reorganizations they had survived, or, indeed, had themselves engineered.

They both came on the line right on time. They were friends and had worked together for years. They'd probably had a pre-meeting about this call. They heard me out quietly as I told them about my upcoming surgery. My plan was to take a week off afterwards, to recuperate, burning some vacation days for that.

"No. It doesn't work that way," Mike said. "You're not going to use your vacation time for this. This is what disability is for." I had been working since I got out of college, three decades earlier, but never in my life used disability insurance. I had only the vaguest idea of what it was for.

In a few sentences they explained how I'd file for that, and they went on, these two old hard-bitten corporate bosses, whose idea of small talk was to tell me, at length, at often excruciating length, about the previous weekend's eighteen holes, to briefly, sympathetically, discuss what I was going through, because they understood, they had friends who had been through this. They knew, better than me, what was about to ensue. By the time that half hour was concluded I'd learned something else, something that I never expected to be taught by these two guys.

I had been having conversations, and in the months to come would have so many more, with all kinds of people who, upon hearing about what I about to go through, or had gone through, decided that their experience, or their cancer, or the cancer that someone they knew had, was so relevant that they needed to tell me all about it. The thing was, I usually didn't want to hear it. It didn't have anything to do with me. And why were they telling me? Did it make them feel better? Did it make them feel like they knew how I felt?

But Mike and Paul didn't do that. They just made it clear that they knew, and they understood. They were men, and knew other men who'd been through this and it was enough to let me know that. And, by talking to me that way, by the end of that call I understood something important: my wife and kids would be right beside me. My friends and family would be there for me. But they might not, quite naturally, be able to grasp exactly what all this meant, what it was doing to me. They weren't men, men of this age. But these guys were, and they understood. And so, what I understood by the end of that call was this: I wasn't alone after all.

52.   That First Week or So

I spent much of the week after the surgery on a chaise in the back yard. It was fine April weather. I would read a little Proust and then doze. And then I returned to the office and went back to work. Everyone, all of them, the surgeon and his people in New York and my doctors up in the country, kept telling me to be patient. It would take time for everything to get back to normal. Oddly enough, I don't remember being anxious about that when first learning about this particular procedure. In a week or so I would be back to normal, and firing on all cylinders, that's what I thought I heard. Of course, I would. Of course, it didn't work out that way.

After a few weeks, a month or so, it was clear something was wrong. I was leaking, which was normal, which was expected, at first. But it wasn't getting any better. And when I had an accident, it was humiliating. Also, I was sick with something. It seemed like the flu. There was fever. I was coughing all the time.

The surgeon thought I was reacting to the ED drugs they'd prescribed. Everyone gets that medication after the surgery, I was told. It promotes healing. So, they switched me to another pill, but it didn't help. As the months went by it got worse. Every time I coughed, I leaked more. The coughing itself was bad enough. I had to rush out of meetings, or get off calls all the time. I couldn't stop coughing.

Then, eventually, my internist, that country doctor, the one who the year before had started me on this journey, took one look at me, shook his head and drew some blood. As he suspected, it wasn't a question of having a bad reaction to one drug or another, like those fancy doctors in New York assumed, but actually, I had Lyme disease. Actually, a splash of Lyme with shot of Ehrlichiosis for good measure.

I blame Proust. We timed it out. I'd been bit by a tick back in April, when I'd been lounging about in the back yard, reading a page or two of *Within a Budding Grove* between naps.

53.   *What? Where?*

Towards the end of that year, I made my way back to the urologist's office for the first time since I'd gone to the hospital. We reviewed the test results and he repeated what the surgeon had been saying all along: they thought they got it all. There was every reason to be optimistic. As far as the incontinence was concerned, for some guys it just took longer than for others. I was making improvement. I just needed to keep doing those Kegels. When it came to what's called sexual function, I told him how far along I'd come, how much better things were now. Almost all better. I gave him a percentage. "I'm this close..."

In his typical frank way, if frank is the word I'm looking for, he told me that it takes six months. After six months you get back all the function that you're going to get. I just looked at him. We were already past six months. Whenever we talked, and we ended up talking several times that first year, I'd study his face. He had a gentle face.

Some of the news he delivered, appointment after appointment, was only good news. The cancer never came back. But back there at the beginning, those unadorned sentences coming out of his mouth were body blows. As I got to know him, I came to decide that picking the right words was very important to him, I guess this is true for all doctors, for anyone who has to deliver bad news. The words he chose were designed to deliver the news as accurately as possible, period.

As he gave me that news in December, he reached for his prescription pad. There was the next thing to try. There was always a next thing. "This is called Muse," he said. I liked the sound of that. Just what a poet needed. Then he explained.

'Wait,' I said, 'You want me to put... what? ...Where?'

'It comes with an applicator,' he said.

'Are you kidding me? Nothing is supposed to go in there, only out.' I said, 'And nothing solid. That catheter after the operation was a nightmare.'

'Just try,' he said.

This was the moment when it became clear to me that things were not going well. And I was headed somewhere uncertain, unmapped, with no fixed destination and no scheduled arrival.

It was horrible. The medication itself was a little pellet filled with some drug that was supposed to do the same thing that the ED pills were supposed to. The applicator was the worst. And the directions. I tried twice and that was it. 'No way,' I told him.

Of course, by the time I was reporting back to him I was reporting other things as well: I had developed rip-roaring case of tinnitus. That led to appointments with new specialists to confirm that this wasn't a side effect of the ED drugs. Not all that unusual, nor some sort of new cancer. It turned out that I'd just been standing too close to the speakers at that Chambers Brothers concert in high school. Or maybe I'd turned up the volume too high on the headphones in the early days of my business, when there was no one else to transcribe all those phone calls. Long term damage, it turned out. Just coincidence that it was manifesting itself now.

And then, crossing the street one day, 8th Avenue in fact, in front of the Gap that's now gone, the one I never passed without remembering the Woolworth's that used to be there, some idiot on a motorbike crashed right into me. It wasn't as if I was crossing against the light or anything, he just was an idiot. He sped off and some passersby helped me to my feet. He struck me in the knee and it took weeks before I could walk to work again. And that knee was never the same. But the conversation I had with the orthopedist after that little adventure was just one in a series, like an edition of prints, 8 out of 30, one in a series of conversations I was having doctors, new doctors, all sorts of doctors.

Not long after appealing to the Muse for the second and last time I was in the bathroom at work, the fancier bathroom on the second floor with nice tile on the walls where guests were directed, and I felt something, a little bump where, when it was soft, you weren't supposed to notice anything. I had an appointment coming up with the surgeon. A couple of doctors examined me during that visit. The surgeon, who was wearing a spectacularly elegant shirt that day, French cuffs, flowing tie, said, 'No. No, no. This is definitely not Peyronie's.'

Peroni's? What was that? I have Italian beer, down there? How'd that happen?

"But, just in case..." he said.

And now I was off again. New waiting rooms, a new hospital, new appointments, new doctors, new tests, new news. News to hear, digest, accept. And it just went on and on. It was indeed Peyronie's, of course.

I found all this shameful. What was wrong with me? Back in the Sixties, maybe I hadn't taken part in enough encounters of the sort avidly engaged in by the more open-minded among us, ones which would have freed me from the humiliation I felt now. It went on and on. I was repeatedly counseled, there were other things that could be done. There was always more. There were pumps, there was more surgery, there was stuff you could inject. Of course, in between injections you had to keep that stuff in the freezer. 'Wait,' I said. 'Not only do you want me to stick myself with a syringe, right there —' 'Don't worry,' the urologist said, 'I'll show you how to do it the first time' '— but I'm going to shoot myself up with something that's been sitting around all week at zero degrees Fahrenheit?'

I knew, I know, there are a lot of men who do just that, every day, but still. And then I was informed with some excitement that there finally was a treatment for this new disease I had, but it seemed positively medieval. There was a good chance it would turn one's member black.

Finally, I said, I've had enough. This had been going on for years now. How many doctors had I been to? I wasn't the same person I was at the beginning. I wasn't going to die from that cancer, that seemed clear. But I had been disfigured. I understand that's the appropriate term of art.

It could have been worse, of course. It is possible that I could have been left with no sexual function at all, that I could have ended up totally incontinent for good. Incontinent, impotent, such powerful words. When it comes time to diminish, to denigrate a man, what more powerful words? Also, that Italian beer of a disease, didn't progress as far as it could. And of course, the cancer could have got me.

Back at the beginning, one of my first appointments had been up at Columbia Presbyterian with a highly recommended radiologist. He specialized in this. He turned out to a pleasant, open guy. I decided not to go forward with him, but it was a good meeting. He asked good questions. Just before the nurse called me in, sitting in his empty waiting room, I watched as a man entered the suite with his wife. Was he older than me? Hard to tell. What was clear: it had won. The cancer. There wasn't much of him left, skin and bones. He could barely make it across the room. His wife helped him into the chair. They both looked at me, with equanimity it seemed. That was what was in store for me, if I didn't do something, and quick.

That would not be my fate. And I would learn to live with all this. The most important thing was that I was not alone. Mike and Paul had been retired for some time by now. But Robin was there beside me, as she had been from the beginning. Calm, patient, cheerful, loving.

I often had reason to consider, during those days and ever since, how much I depend on her. Simply, everything I have is because of her. Why didn't I end up dead in a ditch years ago? How come I am sitting here in a studio in the country, overlooking a pastoral valley, writing this, not shunned, solitary, embittered, holed up in a godforsaken corner of some city?

Sometimes I find myself idly conjuring an alternative autobiography: there I am, hunkered down in some shabby room in an SRO, and, what do you know, my kids come to visit. They show up once, maybe. They won't be back. They look around. I can see what they're thinking. What's worse? The disorder, or the stink, or the rank desolation staring back at them?

The empties by the door, the water stains on the ceiling. That threadbare throw rug, the sole survivor — the only thing they remember — brought from the last house we'd all shared. Is it that? Is that the most painful for them to behold? Or is it the equally pathetic attempts I'd made to make the place mine? A few books, all I have left, piled in the corner. Maybe one of mine, so I can tell people — yes, I am a poet. Or I was. One last painting, the only one that hadn't been thrown out by the clear-out cleaners, hanging crooked over the broken-down couch. A pair of cinder blocks standing in for its missing legs.

But that's not how things turned out. Oh, I think I'm smart. I think I am tough. I have fortitude and have faced adversity, what I'll call adversity, more than once. And I've been the beneficiary of plenty of privilege. But why am I still here? Why didn't I end up like so many of my friends from the olden days? It's clean living I often say, when asked. Clean living! But I know the real reason.

I know I wouldn't be here today if it wasn't for her. That's how I made it through those years: a sick child, the failing business, all of those doctor appointments and disappointments. One, two, three. As soon as one was done and done, along came another. Sometimes, looking back, it seems like that. One after the other. But now, I think that no matter what comes next, I'll be able to get through that too, because I know she'll be there.

54. Start Living like a Grown Up

One evening my brother stopped by. He'd never visited before. He took in the vinyl flooring and the sad appliances and the wheezing air conditioner and said, point blank, "Why are you living like this?"

What? This place was great. It was comfortable. And fashionable too. In the corner, a set of Arne Jacobsen chairs Robin had found on eBay were drawn up to a Knoll knock-off table that was topped with a burl fruit bowl, a gift from a vendor in South America.

"You're not in graduate school anymore."

"I never went to graduate school."

"Grow up, Michael. Start living like a grown up."

The fact was that Robin wasn't crazy about that apartment either, and so a few months later, I found another studio, this one also in Chelsea, three blocks away. There was a doorman there, and a pool in the basement that I never used once, and it was roomier and yes, more comfortable yet. The walk to the office didn't take much longer, and there was a staircase to the High Line right there.

55.   The Tenth Anniversary

Whose idea was this? Mine? Maybe it was James's idea. Could it have been Stacy Szymaszek's? The tenth anniversary of 9/11 was approaching. Whoever's idea it was originally, James took it upon himself, generously, graciously, to run down the leads and do the leg work. The idea was that the tenth anniversary would be just the right time for some sort of reading or rendition or production based on *The Dust*.

In short order James got the dramatist Fiona Templeton, another Roof Books author, engaged in creating a performance, and he connected with Stacy, the director of the Poetry Project at St. Mark's. I really didn't do much. Mostly what I did was let other people do their thing. I knew Fiona slightly, had seen some of her productions. But I knew and trusted James. After all, was there anyone in this world I knew longer than him? Who had published me more? And Stacy signed right up. This performance would serve as the Project's commemoration of the tenth anniversary of 9/11.

I knew these were the right people. Fiona had a vision. The important thing was to let her realize it. Beforehand, I didn't really know what she had in mind. That night, the night after the 11th, I saw the production for the first time, just like everyone else in the Parish Hall at St. Mark's.

But before it began Stacy gave an introduction I found extraordinarily moving, describing a reading she attended when I read that poem, a reading in the West Village, at a bar, a reading I'd entirely forgotten about, shortly after she moved to New York, and the impact it had on her.

And then Fiona's performance began. Two young women read the poem from either side of the area that served as the stage, in front of the seated attendees. The rest of the cast, dressed as bystanders and firefighters, moved up and down the aisle between us, the seated audience, streaming towards and then away from the destruction and death described in the poem.

Somehow, when it was over, an hour seemed to have passed. How could be? When I read the poem, it never took more than fifteen minutes.

What I didn't realize that evening was, however, that the poem had done something else. Or rather, would, and it was a long time before I learned about this. Years later, when I asked Stacy's successor, Kyle Dacuyan, about the possibility of getting a reading at the Project, to promote a book of mine that James was going to publish, *Mostly Clearing*, he asked me if I might, instead, want to consider the possibility of a new theatrical adaptation, based on this new book. He asked because he'd heard about *The Dust*. That suggestion did lead to a second adaptation staged at the Project in 2019, and now it looks like yet another may get produced.

They are all very different realizations of this poetry. However, I have come to believe that they do have a couple of things in common. First, each of them represented a vision of my work in a way that I could never, ever, have conceived of myself.

Another thing they have in common is that, in each case, I believe these productions succeeded at least in part because I trusted these people. For me this was about trust. I didn't have to be in charge. I didn't have to sign off on all the details. To let go and to trust was not necessarily the easiest thing to do, though it has gotten easier each time. After all, these are my words, this is my work. But I am learning to let go.

56.   *Does that Count for Something?*

I had made my choices. I'd set forth bravely twenty years earlier, boldly leaving the city, starting a family, starting a business. Some of them were good choices. Look at the wife I ended up with, and this family. Look at them now, I said to myself. Some other choices were not so good.

As I look back at these twenty years, part of me says I had been focusing on family and work, making a living. As opposed to whatever I'd been spending my time on before, during the Seventies and the Eighties. That earlier time, that's when I'd really been a poet, right? Now, I was just a middle-aged guy with a family, trying to get by. I wasn't really much of a poet any more. But was that so? Hadn't I done as much writing during these two decades as when I was younger, before I had a family, before I had many, any responsibilities?

Now, I want to say that if the first memoir in this book, *The Colorama*, is about childhood and youth, and becoming a person, and the second memoir, *The Empire City*, is about coming of age as a poet, then this memoir is about that period, from 1990 to around 2011, when I was trying to figure out that *Jobs* thing: how to have a life and be a poet too.

And so, did I have that whole *Jobs* thing figured out? Really? What a role model am I. And as I looked back at what I'd done, what I'd managed to make happen, what had happened to me, what I kept coming back to was how easily all of this could be taken away. Family, fortune, health. How close it all came to disappearing. I'd almost lost one of my children to disease. I did lose my business and that almost wiped me out, in every way. And then, just when things were looking up, then came the cancer.

And how well had I managed things? In those essays I came to write I argued that one should be able to have a life, a partner, a spouse and a family, and be a poet too. And, if that meant taking a straight job, as we used to call it, so be it. So, how well had I done on that front? I want to say that I was a good husband and father, but well before my kids were grown, I had to leave them, every week for most of the week, in order to make a living, because I'd messed things up so much for them, for us. So much for my big talk about how we could do it all, have it all.

But I did keep writing. Maybe that means something. And a lot of people, people with whom I was young, didn't. They couldn't take it or didn't make it. Although the fact that I for one didn't stop doesn't make me better than them. I know that. It's inarguable.

And now? I was still here, that did count for something, I guess. And my family was still intact, healthy and happy. That, naturally, was most important of all. And so I was, I am, grateful for what I have.

Do I think that keeping on with this had any impact? On the world, on readers? I think I'm realistic enough about the effect that poets and poetry have on the world to be free from any illusion that it would make much of a difference to the world, to anyone, if I stopped. I can say, and I do believe, that if there was no poetry at all, well, that would make a world of difference to the world. But that's poetry, not one poet, and an aging one at that. Nor had I, even back then, any illusion that writing this, any of this, would save me from the cloaking oblivion that awaits us all.

The life of the poet, it was now clear, was the overarching subject of my poetry. It had been all along. I had tried to have a life, and a family, and be a poet too, and after these twenty years, written about here, I guess I'd lived enough life to ask the questions posed in the essays I was starting to write.

But back then, in 2011, when this memoir ends, it never occurred to me to say: enough, I'm done. Nor does it now, more than a decade later. And yet, the externalities, as an economist would put it, remain unchanged: how many will read this? Who will care? What difference does it make?

And so, why? Is it because of the real pleasure, the good feeling that, undeniably, there's no way around it, that steals over you when you sit down and write? This is what you're meant to do in this world, even if the world doesn't give a damn. That's surely part of it. And how much might sheer stubbornness contribute? But maybe it comes down to something else. This is just what I do. This is what you do. This is what we do. And we do it because this is what we're supposed to do. This is the life we have chosen.

Index of Names

A

Adams, Pat 231
Allison, Mr. 48-50
Andrews, Bruce 190, 204, 219, 223-224, 269, 272, 285, 405

B

Bailey, George 302, 327, 360
Bavaro, Mark 293
Beckett, Samuel 111
Belitt, Ben 167
Belushi, John 205
Benjamin, Richard 120
Bennett, Mrs. 74
Benny, Jack 25
Berger, Mel 285-286
Bergland, Brita 209
Bernstein, Charles 190, 191, 219-222, 244-247, 384
Billy 82-84
Bloom, Harold 166
Bond, James 39, 107
Boorstin, David 328-329
Brandfass, Betsi 209
Breton, Andre 230
Brodey, Jim 303
Brown, Andreas 169
Brown, Trisha 179, 233
Browne, Michael Dennis 167
Burroughs, William S. 178-179, 181, 195-196
Byrne, David 344

C

Cage, John 179, 183, 234, 239
Carl 41-45
Caro, Anthony 231
Carson Jack 201
Caruso, Enrico 173
Castro, Fidel 39, 179

Flaubert, Gustave 116
Flavin, Dan 232
Fleming, Ian 106
Fodaski, Elizabeth 369
Ford, Ford Madox 116
Frankenthaler, Helen 231
Fredericks, Claude 167
Frost, Robert 166

G

Gabor, Eva 283
Ganick, Peter 288
Gardner, Drew 368-370
Garland, Judy 201
Ginsberg, Allen 111, 195
Gizzi, Michael 203-204, 304, 386-387
Golub, Leon 203
Golub, Peter 263-267
Gordon, Nada 374-375, 381
Gotti, John 216
Gottlieb, Isabel 282, 288, 297, 319 - 322, 360
Gottlieb, Jacob 151-154, 1-19, 23, 25, 26, 32, 37, 50, 58, 71-73, 81, 92-96, 97, 101-
     104, 105, 110, 112, 123, 127, 130, 134, 139, 202
Gottlieb, Lucas 311, 320, 331, 332, 360
Gottlieb, Richard 229
Gottlieb, Robin 183 - 185, 236-239, 281-283, 285, 290, 293, 297, 300, 315, 320,
     324, 326-327, 331, 336, 343, 351, 353, 360, 361, 371, 384, 389, 396, 398
Gottlieb, Ruth 18, 20, 22-24, 26, 32, 34, 37, 50, 55, 61, 63, 68, 71-73, 81, 92-96,
     99, 103, 123, 128, 129, 132, 135, 148, 151-156, 187, 386
Graham, Martha 234
Greenberg, Clement 231
Greenwald, Ted 190, 201, 240, 304

H

Haley, Bill, and the Comets 109
Haring, Keith 238
Helmsley, Leona 260
Hemingway, Ernest 116, 160, 222
Herman's Hermits 119

Lovin' Spoonful, The 119
Ludlum, Charles 263
Luthor, Lex 197

M

Mac Low, Jackson 190
Mantle, Mickey 26, 28, 31
Mao Tse Tung (or Mao Zedong) 175
Marcuse, Herbert 140
Maris, Roger 29
Martin and Rossi 108
Martin, Agnes 230-232, 237
Mason, James 201
Matta-Clark, Gordon 197
Mayer, Bernadette 190
McCartney, Paul 123
McGraw, Ali 120
Mead, Margaret 111
Meckler, Ronnie 291
Mercury astronauts 59
Michelle 119
Mike and Paul 388-391
Miller, Henry 111
Milner, Martin 87
Monty Python 252
Morrison, Jim 119
Morrison, Van 121
Moses, Robert 198-199
Mussolini, Benito 173

N

Nagy, John 61
Nixon, Richard 159, 207, 329
Noguchi, Isamu 70-71
Noland, Kenneth 231

O

Onassis, Jackie 170

P

Q

R

Index of Section Titles

The Colorama

The Empire City

The Life We Have Chosen

ACKNOWLEDGMENTS

Sections of *The Colorama* originally appeared in The Westchester County Times and in *New York*, published by The Figures Press in 1993. Thanks to the editors and Geoff Young.

Sections of *The Empire City* originally appeared in Mark(s) edited by Mark Wallace and, in full, in *Memoir and Essay*, co-published by Other Publications and Faux Books in 2010, published by Alan Davies and Jack Kimball.

Sections of *The Life We Have Chosen*, as well as *The Colorama* and *The Empire City*, originally appeared in Issue 71 of Otoliths, its final issue, in July 2023. Thank you, Mark Young, for your gracious support over the years.

Grateful thanks to all.

About Michael Gottlieb

Michael Gottlieb is a poet and the author of twenty-two books. In addition to numerous collections of poetry, his published work also includes memoirs and essays. His most recent titles are *Collected Essays* (Chax Press, 2023), *Selected Poems* (Chax Press, 2021) *Mostly Clearing* (Roof, 2019) *What We Do: Essays for Poets* (2016, Chax Press) *I Had Every Intention* (2014, Faux Editions), *Dear All* (2013, Roof Books). A first-generation member of the Language Poetry school, he helped edit one of its foundational magazines, Roof.

He was also the publisher of Case/Casement Books (1981-1999) which featured collages and cover artwork which he created. He started the Last Tuesday multi-media performance series at La MaMa in NYC in the 1980s.

His work appears in numerous anthologies. Several of his works have also been adapted for the stage, including excerpts from *Mostly Clearing*, adapted by Genee Coreno in 2019, and 'The Dust,' his authoritative 9/11 poem, adapted by Fiona Templeton and staged to mark the 10th anniversary of the attacks, both produced at The Poetry Project at St. Mark's in New York City.

In November 2023, St. Mark's will host a new dramatization of his work, "I am Angry at a Force I Cannot See: Based on the Poetry of Michael Gottlieb," directed by Chana Porter.

Eileen Myles has written that his work focuses "much like the narrator does in Robert Musil's epic the 'Man Without Qualities,' on the difficult moment in which one faces one's culture and understands... what it is to be a man." Ron Silliman called 'The Dust,' when it first appeared in print in 2003, "the first great poetic work to emerge from the trauma of September 11." His memoir, *Memoir and Essay,* was described by the poet Elizabeth Fodaski as "doing for New York in the 70s what *A Movable Feast* did for Paris in the 20s."

Michael Gottlieb was born in New York City. He graduated from Bennington College where he studied writing and painting. He divides his time between Manhattan and Connecticut.

About chax

Founded in 1984 in Tucson, Arizona, Chax has published more than 250 books in a variety of formats, including hand printed letterpress books and chapbooks, hybrid chapbooks, book arts editions, and trade paperback editions such as the book you are holding. Chax is a nonprofit 501(c)(3) organization which depends on suppport from various government & private funders, and, primarly, from individual donors and readers. In 2021, Chax Press founder and director Charles Alexander was awarded the Lord Nose Award for lifetime achievement in literary publishing.

Recent books include *Selected Poems* and *Collected Essays*, both by Michael Gottlieb; *Farther*, by Susan Thackrey; *The Face of Time*, by An Li, *Broken Glossa*, by Stephen Bett; *Maths*, by Joel Chace; *Collectives of Poets*, by Lisa Periale Martin; *Time, Wisdom, and Koalas*, by David Miller; *Selected Poems 1980-2020*, by Rachel Blau DuPlessis; *Letters*, by Barbara Guest and Stephen Ratcliffe; *Skeleton Keys*, by Steven Fraccaro; *And or The*, by Serge Gavronsky; *Not a Snake*, by Leonard Schwartz and Simon Carr; and *Brilliant Corners*, by Jeanne Heuving.

Our current address is 6181 East 4th Street, Tucson, Arizona 85711-1613. You can email us at *chaxpress@chax.org*.

Your support of our projects as a reader, and as a benefactor, is much appreciated. To make a gift please visit *https://chax.org/support-chax/*.

You may find CHAX at *https://chax.org*

Text & Display: Iowan Old Style

Book Design: Charles Alexander

Printer & Binder: KC Book Manufacturing